LANGUAGE TEACHING

Language Teaching

Linguistic Theory in Practice

Melinda Whong

Edinburgh University Press

KH

© Melinda Whong, 2011

Edinburgh University Press Ltd
22 George Square, Edinburgh

www.euppublishing.com

Typeset in Linotype Sabon
by Iolaire Typesetting, Newtonmore, and
printed and bound in Great Britain by
Berforts Group, Stevenage Herts SG1 2BH

A CIP record for this book is available from the British Library

ISBN 978 0 7486 3634 1 (hardback)
ISBN 978 0 7486 3635 8 (paperback)

3/6/12

CONTENTS

ACKNOWLEDGEMENTS

I would like to thank the students in my classes at the University of Leeds for allowing me to try out on them many of the ideas found in these pages, and to the staff at Edinburgh University Press who have been so good to work with on this project. I am also grateful to friends and colleagues who have supported me during the writing process. Special thanks go to Cecile De Cat and Martha Young-Scholten who have had so much confidence in this project from the start, and thanks to John Burrell for making me put it aside once in a while. Thanks also to Bonnie Schwartz to whom I owe my foundational training. I would also like to thank those who have read portions of the book, provided information which has found its way into the book or inspired me during this project: in particular, Laura Bray, Kook-hee Gil, Randal Holme, Chris Jenks, Julie King, Steve Kirk, Hui-ling Lin, Heather Marsden, Bede McCormack, Diane Nelson, Roumyana Slabakova, Hannah Sowden, Maggie Tallerman, Mike Sharwood Smith and a very helpful anonymous reviewer. Of course, any faults, misrepresentations or omissions are my responsibility alone.

1

INTRODUCTION

Like many of the most difficult questions, the answer to this question may initially seem obvious because language is such a natural part of our lives. But, what is language? If you find you cannot answer this question very well, or if you find you have lots of possible answers to this question then you are one step closer to appreciating the complexity of language. As a language teacher, it is important to be able to explain what language is. Yet language – that which we are trying to teach – is not easily defined.

The first aim of this book is to discuss some of the many possible answers to the question of what is language. The second is to explore what we know about how knowledge of language develops. These ideas will provide a foundation for the ultimate aim of this book: to illustrate how an understanding of concepts in theoretical linguistics can lead to a better understanding of language teaching in the classroom. In this introductory chapter, we will briefly explore these three aims as a preview to the remainder of the book, beginning with the question of what language is.

The Form/Function Divide

Language can be characterised in terms of oppositions, a helpful exercise for teasing apart its complexity. One common opposition among researchers in linguistics is to see language as form versus language as function. Language as form is concerned with the structure of the language itself, while language as function is more interested in the work that a language does to facilitate interaction among people. The two views do not have to be seen as incompatible. In some ways they are, in fact, complementary.[1]

Language as form is the more contemporary way of referring to a view of language that traces its roots to what was called **Structuralism**.

As indicated by the label, a structuralist view of language is one that is concerned with the shape of language; it is a formalist view which sees language as a system of rules and patterns. This approach is concerned with categorising and labelling different aspects of language as a way of understanding the patterns. This can be done from the very small level of individual sound to the larger level of the sentence. Traditionally, this approach to language tries to break language down to its smallest units. As a result of this reductionist approach, much discussion of language from a formalist view is concerned with detailed and sometimes very subtle properties of language.

For example, a structuralist is interested in the individual sounds that are possible in a language. This interest includes, for example, phonetic descriptions, such as the voice/voiceless distinctions between bilabial /b/ and /p/ or velar /g/ and /k/ in English. From the level of sound a structuralist view moves to the level of morpheme to identify the smallest bundle of sounds that have meaning. So, for example, the word *restatement* has three morphemes:

(1)   re-state-ment

The root, *state*, holds the core meaning, while the prefix *re-* is added to give the meaning of 'do again'. Interestingly in English, the addition of suffixes often functions to derive one word form from another; so the verb, *state*, through suffixation becomes a noun, *statement*; prefixes do not have this ability. As noted in our example, the verb itself, *state*, is a morpheme. From a formalist point of view, words themselves are morphemes. The next level up for a formalist is the level of word order, or syntax, which is concerned with how words combine to form different patterns and meanings. This takes us up to the phrase and then sentence level.

A cross-linguistic investigation of languages reveals very clear patterns for word order within and across languages. Joseph Greenberg studied hundreds of languages, looking for cross-linguistic regularities. He established a set of forty-five properties of language that seem to be universal (Greenberg 1963). So, for example, Universal number forty-three says that if the nouns in a language show grammatical gender, then the pronouns will also reflect gender. As an example, Spanish generally uses the suffixes -*o* and -*a* to mark its nouns as masculine or feminine, respectively; it also distinguishes between the feminine pronoun, *ella*, 'she', and the masculine one, *el*, 'he'. Notice that this implication is true in the direction stated. So, for example, a language could have gender expressed on pronouns, but not on nouns – like in English. Most of Greenberg's Universals are implicational in this way.

This attention to universals paved the way for the development from structuralist linguistics to **Generative Linguistics**. Noam Chomsky took this idea of universals one step further to argue that there is a **Universal Grammar (UG)** that is a property of being human. Developing the ideas of the structuralists, UG is seen as a set of patterns or rules. But for Chomsky these rules are a natural, even biological, property of being human – from this set of rules, a person can generate an infinite set of utterances. In both traditional structuralist linguistics and the more current Generative Linguistics there has not been much interest in language beyond the level of the sentence. This is one criticism of the language as form, or formalist approach.

Adding to this criticism, some linguists argue that breaking language down into bits may be an interesting exercise, but fails to address the essence of what language is: a mode for communicating thoughts. Linguists such as Michael Halliday argue that, in order to study meaning, we need to look at the function of language. **Functionalists**, therefore, are not interested in breaking language down into categories for the sake of identifying patterns, but instead ask what work, what function an instance of language performs. At the sentence level, a functionalist is more interested in looking at the role of parts of a sentence. A functionalist, for example, is interested in the connection between the following two options for expressing the same idea in English in terms of how the speaker is thinking about the scene in question:

(2)   a.   The clown chased the monkey.
      b.   The monkey was chased by the clown.

For a functionalist the choice is going to depend on the context because it is the content of the message that is of primary importance, not the form. So a speaker would choose (2a) if wanting to foreground the activity of the clown, but (2b) if the monkey was the main character in the event. Similarly, a functionalist is interested in how words and phrases fit together. Consider the following examples:

(3)   And then her mood changed completely – ever since leaving, she's been over the moon.
(4)   The colleagues she left behind, by contrast, are all feeling a bit down.

Phrases like *and then* and *by contrast* show the relationship between ideas and help to hold them together. This is called textual coherence.

Functionalists are also interested in how the message conveyed in words extends beyond literal meaning. Expressions like *over the moon* and *feeling down* in (3) and (4) illustrate how spatial notions associate with emotion. In fact, there seems to be a cross-linguistic trend to associate the location of 'up' or 'on top' with good, positive feelings while 'down' or 'low' seems to be linked with negativity. Associations such as these, between language and meaning, are the types of linguistic features that interest functionalists.

While formal and functional approaches to language are clearly quite different, they do not have to be seen in opposition. Instead, they have different interests and perspectives in mind. So, one way to answer the question of what is language is to say that language is both a tool for communicating thoughts and emotions – function, and a systematic set of rules and patterns – form.

Mentalist/Internal and Interactionist/External

Another opposition for viewing language is to think of language as the internal mental process of individuals, as opposed to the external interaction that occurs among people. This does not contradict the above form/function divide, and in fact overlaps in some ways. But it is also useful as another way of thinking about language.

The mentalist approach to language is often framed in terms of the seventeenth-century philosopher, Descartes, who made a distinction between *the mind* as the rational awareness unique to humans and *the body* as the physical collection of cells, organs and tissue that is characteristic of all living creatures. We can use this mind–body dualism to distinguish between the **brain**, which refers to the physical mass of neurons encased in the cranium, and the **mind**, which refers to the more philosophical understanding of how mental processes work. Recent developments in brain science can give us glimpses into the physical workings of language in the brain. Computed axial tomography (CAT) and functional magnetic resonance imagining (fMRI) technology have been used to investigate which areas of the brain respond to different types of stimuli. This has added weight to the older observation by early brain researchers – most notably, Paul Broca and Carl Wernicke – who found physical connections between injuries to specific areas in brain's left hemisphere and language impairment. So-called Broca's area in the frontal lobe is associated with the more structural properties of language while Wernicke's area further back is known to be crucial for linguistic meaning.[2] Current technological developments may eventually lead to a more sophisticated matching between linguistic behaviour and neural structure, but, as we will discuss later, there are limitations on our understanding of this link in current research.

The much older tradition of understanding language as a property of the mind is a more abstract exercise that has made use of theoretical models to explain relationships between various aspects of language. There are two strands of linguistics that have developed different ways of understanding how language in the mind works. Generative Linguistics views language as a special kind of knowledge, distinct from other kinds of knowledge. Generativists present a model of language which separates language from other mental functions; the separation also occurs within language itself as different aspects of language are modelled as being distinct. This view is in direct opposition to a **Cognitive Linguistics** model, which sees language as the same type of knowledge as other types of knowledge, and mental processing as one process without special distinctions. We will come back to the distinction between these views in Chapter 4. For now, the two views are relevant in terms of how they differ in their psycholinguistic, or mentalist, characterisation of language knowledge. In terms of the brain, a cognitivist understands language processing to occur throughout the brain using the same mechanisms as other cognitive processes, while a generativist sees language processing as connected with specific mechanisms in the brain dedicated exclusively to language. Perhaps in time developments in brain science will determine which view is more accurate. Until then, we are left having to choose between these two opposing positions.

But how can we determine which position is correct? Mentalist investigations explore language through two basic types of methodology, a philosophical method and a psycholinguistic method. The philosophical method depends on logical arguments regarding the nature of language. Language was a concern even for Plato over two thousand years ago in what has come to be known as **Plato's Problem:** how can people come to possess such a large store of knowledge when only exposed to a limited set of examples? In the same spirit, generativists applied this question specifically to language, noting that all people, whether schooled or not, have the ability to create perfectly formed sentences (in their native language), unlike other complex mental tasks such as mathematics, which have to be 'learned'. A cognitivist, on the other hand, will point out that our use of language is dependent upon our understanding of the world around us and will note that schooling is vital for developing our language skills. This type of argumentation is as old as the field of philosophy itself.

The second methodology, the psycholinguistic method, has developed more recently. On-line processing tasks can give insight into the inner workings of the mind. One example is a task which asks participants to decide whether sentences presented on a computer screen are true or not. While the participant is making their decision based on the truth value of the sentence, the psycholinguist is actually interested in how long it takes the participant to make that decision. Testing has shown, for example, that the response time for grammatical sentences is faster than for ungrammatical sentences. Thus mean response time studies can give a glimpse into the inner workings of the mind.[3] What that glimpse shows, however, is debatable. Generativists have used psycholinguistic methods like this to argue that language knowledge is automatic, operating without our conscious control or awareness. Cognitivists have used it to show that we categorise language based on associations among concepts that come from our personal experience of the world.

Again we return to the question of what language is. For a brain scientist, language equates to electric impulses in the brain. For a psycholinguist it corresponds to behaviour in response to external stimulus. Generative and cognitive psycholinguists interpret the same responses as support for different views on how language is organised in the mind. A different approach altogether is to view language as a product of culture and as a tool for interaction among people. Taking an external or interactionist point of view, language can be seen as an integral part of culture, as a socially constructed set of practices. This sociolinguistic view of language is more interested in how people in society make use of language to signal identity, to negotiate interaction and to exert power, for example. Sociolinguists are more interested in the role of language in human interaction than in the structural properties of language divorced from context.

Other linguists see the properties of language in terms of the way language is used in social contexts. One of the aims of Systemic Functional Linguistics is to view language in terms of how it is used by a group of people in a shared context. For example, a systemic functionalist is interested in how texts can be identified by properties of the text itself; the text of a political speech, for instance, will be different from that of a story told to a group of children, not just in its subject matter, but also in the language used to convey the ideas. For systemic functionalists, the social context of human interaction will critically define the shape that language takes.

Another linguistic approach to language which can also be seen as 'external' is the study of pragmatics. While a sociolinguist's starting point is the level of society or groups, and that of systemic functionalists the level of text, pragmatics takes a particular interaction or utterance as its starting point. Pragmatics is interested in what a speaker/writer means and explores the possible range of meanings an utterance can have depending on the context. A simple *thank you*, for example, will have a completely different meaning and function if uttered in the following situations:

(5) a. on receipt of a gift from a close friend
    b. on receiving bad news from someone you do not know very well
    c. by an umpire in a tennis match at Wimbledon.

So now we can see that language covers a very broad spectrum indeed: from the physical electric impulses in the brain to the way individuals negotiate meaning in society. Because language spans this internal/external spectrum, the field of linguistics has many subfields that overlap with a number of disciplines, from brain science to sociology, and, of direct relevance to us, to education.

Linguistic vs Metalinguistic

The field of education is important for this last opposition that we will explore: the difference between linguistic and metalinguistic knowledge. **Linguistic knowledge** refers to the knowledge of language that we possess, whether we are explicitly aware of it or not. It is the knowledge that develops without explicit instruction from a very young age to allow us to communicate our intentions and thoughts. **Metalinguistic knowledge**, on the other hand, is knowledge that an individual has about the knowledge of language. In other words, it is explicit awareness of linguistic knowledge. It is also awareness of aspects of language that are part of the culture of a language group.

One type of metalinguistic knowledge closely associated with the language classroom is the set of grammar rules that we can explicitly teach and learn. These can be either descriptive or prescriptive rules. Linguists hold fast to the belief that their task is to describe the grammatical properties of a language in terms of what the speakers of that language actually produce. Their aim is to capture language in terms of the actual habits of its speakers without imposing any preconceived notions of what the language should be like. This type of metalinguistic knowledge is known as **descriptive grammar** because it captures the patterns and structures of the language that people actually use. From a descriptive grammar point of view, it is better to think in terms of the patterns that language users follow instead of the more value-laden notion of grammar rules, which suggest a list of what one should and should not do.

A descriptive grammar contrasts with a **prescriptive grammar**, which is what is often found in textbooks used to teach a language. A prescriptive grammar dictates what rules of language should be adhered to, regardless of what the speakers of the language may actually do in natural language production, whether part of so-called standard speech or a dialect. The well-known example of prescriptivism is the admonition that no word should intervene between a verb and the particle *to* in the infinitive form in English. It is unacceptable, in other words, to *ever* insert an adverb within the infinitive construct, even though English speakers do this routinely in speech and writing. The reason for this prescriptive rule is historical; hundreds of years ago, notions of 'proper' English were based on the properties of Latin. In Latin it is impossible to interrupt the verb's infinitive form because the infinitive is signalled through a suffix on the verb itself; for example, nothing can intervene between the infinitive suffix *-ire* and the root *aud-* in the Latin infinitive form *audire*, 'to hear'. The power of tradition is so strong that some prescriptive grammarians still impose this Latinate property on English infinitives. While this is an extreme example, language textbooks often include 'unnatural' prescriptive rules, most of which are associated with the most prestigious 'standard' forms of English.

A second type of metalinguistic knowledge is the knowledge required for **literacy**. In most alphabets in the world's languages today, there is an arbitrary relationship between letters and sounds.[4] There is no reason why two lines crossed to form a 't', for example, should correspond to the /t/ sound in English. Yet the association between sound and letters allows us to record language on paper in a visual, two-dimensional format. This association has to be explicitly learned. It is possible for a person to have a fully formed grammar of a language, with a very large vocabulary, without being able to read or write that language. For this reason, reading and writing are not considered 'natural' properties of language in the sense that they are not abilities that normally developing children naturally acquire, whether they try to or not. Instead, literacy-related aspects of language such as spelling, punctuation, writing and reading must be taught and consciously learned. This is the bulk of the hard work of the first few years of schooling. Because of the integral role of reading and writing in education, the 'unnatural' nature of literacy can be hard to accept. Yet it is considered a feature of metalinguistic knowledge, not linguistic knowledge, because of the level of conscious awareness that it requires.[5]

So where does this leave us? So far we have considered a range of ways to think about what language is. We can think of language as lying on a continuum from form to function, or make a distinction between internal mental processes and external social interaction. In doing so, we include a full range of academic fields of inquiry. The primary perspective taken in this textbook is an internal, mentalist, so therefore psycholinguistic perspective. The reason for this is not because of any belief that the psycholinguistic view is somehow better or more important. Instead, it is because most of the literature on language teaching that currently exists assumes a more external, interactionist view of language.

Also important to language teachers is an understanding of pedagogical issues in general; fortunately, there are many texts on general issues of pedagogy. This book, by contrast, is interested in thinking about language teaching from the point of view of the more formal properties of language itself, in hopes that teachers can be more confident about their subject knowledge and thus make more principled decisions when they teach. An expert teacher has their work cut out for them. In addition to general principles of pedagogy, they need to understand the complexity of language. Additionally, they need to be familiar with the process of language development.

HOW DOES LANGUAGE DEVELOP?

Whether generativist, cognitivist or functionalist, linguists agree that language develops, but are not in agreement on the question of *how* language develops. By using the phrase *language development* I am signalling the approach that I am taking in this discussion. Language teaching and learning implies an interaction between a teacher and students in a classroom. It is an activity that occurs in a particular culture and society, and in a particular institution. Language development, by contrast, is something that happens within an internal mental system. Thus, by using the term *language development* I am taking an internal perspective that emphasises mental processes.

Nature vs Nurture?

The question of language development is often presented as one of nature vs nurture. But this opposition is somewhat of a straw man argument. It is as unreasonable to say that the development of language is completely a matter of internal biological processes (nature), as it is to say that language development only involves external linguistic input (nurture). It is uncontroversial to say that both are necessary. The debate arises when deciding on the balance between the two and how the two interact. This nature/nurture opposition can be seen as similar to the external/internal opposition we discussed above, but for language development instead of language itself. Before thinking about second language development, we will take a quick look at the native first language context to ask how it is that a newborn child comes to possess a fully developed language within a matter of a few years.

This question of language development was one of the central motivators behind the Chomskyan language revolution of the 1950s. The mystery that inspired Chomsky was the problem of how young children can develop a language system that enables them to create an infinite number of sentences when they are only exposed to a limited number of (often fragmentary) examples of language. For Chomsky, the answer is that there must be some innate predisposition for language already in the brain from birth. **Nativism** sees language as an ability given by nature that exists at birth. But of course, whether a child ends up speaking Turkish or Portuguese depends on the language that the child is exposed to in infancy. Thus, even in the Chomskyan nativist model, nurture in the form of language input plays a key role. Thus it is more reasonable to talk about the nature AND nurture debate than the nature vs nurture debate.

Most people, however, will agree that native first language development and adult second language development seem to be very different. So is there any use in discussing native first language development in a book about second or foreign language teaching? The answer is more obviously yes if you are a language teacher in a primary school working with young children. So what if your teaching exclusively involves adults? Even so, a general understanding of native acquisition is still relevant. Despite the intuition that the two are different, the distinction between native language development and second language development (child or adult) has not been proven to be entirely clear despite decades of research. Indeed, it may be that you know someone (or may yourself be someone) whose second language proficiency is seemingly native-like, yet with first exposure to the language as an adult or late teenager. Arguably, if, as a teacher, you want to make the best decisions about how (and what) to teach, knowledge of all types of language development is important.

Native First Language Development and Adult Second Language Development

Perhaps the most striking thing about native language development is that all children manage to develop a complete grammatical system so that they can speak the language that they are exposed to fluently – that is, of course, unless there is some pathological reason for interference in the development process. Immediately you might find yourself contrasting this with many of your own experiences within the second language context. This intuitive difference is at the heart of what Bley-Vroman (1990) calls the **Fundamental Difference Hypothesis**: in first language development native fluency is always achieved, while in second language development native-like fluency seems exceptional. But the fact that native-like fluency can and does happen makes for an interesting problem.

A second important point about native language acquisition is that regardless of the type and amount of language that a child is exposed to (unless entirely deprived of input), the child will develop language, and will go through the same general set of stages that all children go through. That children have a one-word stage that precedes a two-word stage may not seem remarkable. Children will also develop a large set of meaningful content words like *dog* and *want* before they begin to use grammatical words like *the* or *of*. But less obvious is why children will acquire certain grammatical words before others. As shown in his now famous morpheme order study, Roger Brown found that English-speaking children acquire grammatical morphemes in a specific order. For example, they acquire the present progressive *-ing* before they acquire the plural *-s*, both of which are acquired before the regular past tense *-ed* and the 3rd person singular *-s*.[6] Regular development of this type is now widely accepted as characteristic of native language development.

Also interesting is the regularity of errors that children make – as well as the fact that certain types of error are never made. If you spend time with young English-speaking children, you will notice that they use words like *breaked*, *falled* and *runned*. These 'errors' suggest that the child has acquired the regular rule for making the past tense in

English. It is another stage of development altogether to discover that the past tense -ed rule has exceptions. A perhaps less well-known developmental error that many English-speaking children make is to use the genitive pronoun *my* incorrectly where the nominative *I* form is needed, to say things like *My make a house.*[7]

Contrast these developmental 'errors' with errors that are not made. Children have not been found to make errors with nominative and genitive case in the opposite direction to say things like **Look at I house.* Nor do they put the past tense -ed on words other than verbs to say, for example, **happied*, **noised* or **latered.*[8] In other words, native language development is not random; even the 'incorrect' language produced by children can often be traced to a rule in the child's language system, suggesting some underlying constraints on the development of language.

These kinds of regularities are called on as support for the idea of a Universal Grammar that limits what a language can and cannot do. So, for example, a language will not allow a past tense inflectional marker to be attached to a word that is not a verb. This is absent as a property of English and absent from child language development as well. In other words, UG constrains both what is possible in a language and how language development will proceed. This constraint on language reduces the possible options, making it easier for the child to develop language. Another striking property of native language development is that its core properties do not seem to require explicit teaching. And, in fact, young children seem largely unable to take instruction on board, but instead seem to go through stages of development at their own pace. The now famous exchange between psycholinguist Martin Braine and his daughter, quoted in Pinker (1994: 281), illustrates this point:

Child: Want other one spoon, Daddy.
Father: You mean, you want THE OTHER SPOON.
Child: Yes, I want other one spoon, please, Daddy.
Father: Can you say 'the other spoon'?
Child: Other . . . one . . . spoon.
Father: Say 'other'.
Child: Other.
Father: 'Spoon'.
Child: Spoon.
Father: 'Other . . . spoon'.
Child: Other . . . spoon. Now give me other one spoon?

Have you experienced this kind of response to correction with your classroom learners? Later we will look more closely at error correction in second language teaching. Anecdotally, however, you might be able to relate to the father in the dialogue when you think of some of the errors that your students seem unable to overcome. Your learners' errors may indicate a particular stage in development in which they have reached some kind of plateau where development seems to have come to some temporary halt. It is also possible that a learner reaches a limit on development. It is the nature of second language development that learners often **fossilise**, reaching a point where particular aspects of their grammar stop developing such that the same error persists.

Notice that, both here and above, I have used the word *error*. A useful distinction in the study of language development is the difference between an error and a mistake. Pit Corder (1967, 1971) is attributed with making this distinction clear. A **mistake** is a one-off blunder that anyone is capable of as a slip of the tongue or, perhaps, if suffering from fatigue or if distracted when producing language. An **error**, by contrast, is deviance from the **target language** that re-occurs systematically. The above example of the over-application of past tense *-ed* is considered an error because it is systematic and indicative of a rule. Similarly, the tendency for some second language speakers of English to use the pronouns *he* and *she* interchangeably because of an absence of grammatical gender in their own pronoun system would be considered an error and not a mistake.

Evidence of systematic errors is one of the core properties of second language production that has emerged from second language acquisition studies. This realisation of systematicity led to the coining of the term **Interlanguage** by Selinker (1972) in order to recognise the grammar of the second language speaker as a proper grammar with rules and regular patterns and not a random set of utterances that may or may not resemble the target language in question. In this way, second language development is like first language development; they are both characterised by a degree of systematic development. However, it is important to recognise that it is a *degree* of systematicity. While general trends and stages can be found among groups of language learners, there is a certain amount of individual variability that also exists. While this is true for native first language and second language development, the degree of variability among second language learners is much higher, a point we will discuss again later.

Variability is perhaps not surprising in second language development, especially if one is to take into account the fact that, by definition, a second language learner already possesses a native language. It is only reasonable to assume that the existence of the first language is causing some kind of interference in the development of the second language. So we might expect learners to show variability reflecting their particular native language. This is exactly what early second language researchers who developed the **Contrastive Analysis Hypothesis** thought. Contrastive Analysis is based on the idea that the difficulty and ease of learning a second language depends crucially on the extent of difference and similarity between the first and second languages in question. Though, as we will discuss further in Chapter 3, this hypothesis did not show itself to be entirely valid when put to the test empirically, it has led to other developments in the field. For example, the practice of **Error Analysis** supported the important finding that the interlanguage of second language speakers is systematic, thereby signalling universal properties, whether as a result of the universal nature of language or universals in the process of language development.

The other issue, already touched upon, is the difficult question of age and second language development. Much has been made of the idea that there is a **critical period** for language development. While the idea enjoys much general agreement, there is very little consensus on the specific details. Even establishing a particular age for the beginning and end of the critical period has proven to be very difficult. There is a recognised notion that the end of the critical period corresponds to puberty. Yet many have been quick to point out that a meaningful connection between language and puberty would be very strange indeed. The seminal work of Johnson and Newport (1989) was for a time taken to be evidence that the age of 7 was the cut-off for differences in language development. But this age was quickly challenged by Bialystok and Hakuta (1994) who reanalysed Johnson and Newport's findings to argue that the data indicate 20 to be the crucial age. Others have found that the result may depend on what aspect of language is being tested. Native-like pronunciation, for example, seems to require much earlier language exposure than basic word order. But even so, no specific age has been established for any particular aspect of language.

There has been much discussion of this idea of a critical period for language development and many questions still remain to be answered.[9] One generalisation that emerges from the research is that younger is better. However, even this claim needs qualification since in instructed settings it seems to be true in terms of what ultimately can be achieved, rather than the amount of language development that is achieved when young. It is also clear that the tendency for language development to be more successful with youth is just that: a tendency. There does not appear to be any single cut-off point. All studies show a distributed range that spans from child to teenage to adult age ranges in a gradual way. We will return to this discussion of critical period in Chapter 3.

Language development, then, is a process that occurs within the cognitive system of the learner, whether as a first and native language, or a second or foreign language. We have not mentioned the situation in which a young child develops two languages simultaneously. For our purposes, **bilingualism** will be considered qualitatively the same as native **monolingualism**, the only difference being that two language systems are developing concurrently. In contrast to bilingualism, the main interest in this text is second language development, which refers to the development of an additional language after (at least) one other language is already a fully developed system. The question of child second language acquisition will be only briefly explored in this text, though there is a growing body of work showing this to be an area deserving of recognition in its own right.[10] It is time now, however, to turn briefly to more practical questions of relevance to the language teacher.

What are the Implications for Language Learning and Teaching?

So far, this chapter has been concerned with ideas that may seem quite abstract. Though I cannot imagine any language teacher thinking that a discussion about language and language development is irrelevant to language teaching, I can imagine a teacher wondering what the connections are exactly between theory of language and the language classroom. It is the main aim of this textbook to articulate these connections. A flip through the table of contents will show that the text initially concentrates on theory, gradually moving to issues of classroom practice as the book progresses. But rather than make you wait until midway through the book, let us briefly preview how we might put theory into practice in terms of the ideas about language and language development that we have encountered so far.

We have seen that language can be characterised by certain oppositions. Hopefully, you will agree that there is no single 'correct' view of language. But instead, by approaching language from different angles, we can get a better sense of what it is, in all of its complexity. We can then be more intentional about what aspects of language we are trying to teach at any given time in the classroom. Let us begin with language as form. What implications might this have for you as a teacher? Taking a structuralist point of view, you might view language as a body of knowledge to be passed on to your students. This would take the form of rules, paradigms and organised patterns. But surely this is an outdated view of language, you might say. Perhaps, but if you think of the linguistic/metalinguistic opposition, you might decide that there is some value in trying to characterise the language into neat sets of forms with clear and simple rules in order to develop your students' metalinguistic knowledge, which they can tap into for more accurate language production.

Another form-based view of language is the generative view in which language is natural, biological. Thinking of our discussion of nature/nurture, though it may be controversial how much 'nature' is relevant in second language development, keep in mind that even first language development is said to depend on external input (nurture). A form-based generative view might encourage us to expose our learners to some rich, natural input instead of just presenting learners with simplified texts, as is often the practice, especially of textbook writers. We might also be careful not to engage too much in **teacher-talk** in which we over-simplify, or **foreigner-talk** in which we speak in a non-target way. While we may think that this will aid in comprehension in the moment, it certainly does not model the kind of language we hope our learners to achieve in time.

Instead of a form-based view of language, we can take a view of language as function. With functionalism in mind, we would present language in terms of meaning, rather than grammatical rules. This may involve establishing contexts for language and devising meaningful tasks for learners which require the active use of language. A functional approach to language teaching may have the same target linguistic aims as a form-based approach, but will teach functional use of language. To take the example from the above discussion, passive and active sentence forms in English could by taught by presenting learners with different scenes that highlight the different actors in the event. Whether the grammatical properties of the two types of sentences are ever explicitly taught may depend on whether this is appropriate in terms of learner needs or needs imposed by a curriculum. The aim of this book is not to endorse any one view of language teaching, but to clarify what the different positions are with regard to language so that you have a principled basis from which to choose what is most appropriate for your learners.

But how can we know whether we should draw on one view of

language over another in our classroom practice? As long as the different views of language exist among theoretical linguists, it is prudent for teachers to take on board all views for which there is robust evidence. Thus, to continue with our active/passive example, a thorough teacher may introduce the active/passive distinction through contrasting differences in context before then explicitly drawing attention to the grammatical differences between the two forms. In order to reinforce the grammatical difference, students may be encouraged to practise by manipulating one form into the other through traditional exercises in order to develop metalinguistic knowledge. You might then have your students situate the contrasting forms by discussing scenarios which naturally call for one form over the other in order to put the new knowledge into use. Alternatively, the grammar could be emphasised first and the meaning difference highlighted second. A third option is to avoid explicit discussion of the grammatical forms altogether and instead to focus exclusively on the functional differences between the active and the passive. What matters is that you recognise the differences between the options, and decide how to teach the passive based on your understanding of language, coupled with the needs of your students.

If you are thinking about students' needs, you may be wondering what we should make of the internal view of language as a mental process. While it is dehumanising to think of our learners merely as brains firing electric impulses in response to external input, it may be worth acknowledging this aspect of language development to some extent. If the brain is functioning by responding to external stimuli, it only makes sense that we would stimulate the brains sitting in our classrooms through plenty of examples and the repetition of examples, but within a meaningful context if we want our students to remain engaged. Hopefully, this will help mental structures to develop.

Considering the cognitive perspective which sees all knowledge (including language) as linked by association, we would do our best to present new language by making explicit links to previous or existing knowledge. In short, a mental, internal view of language will encourage a teacher to allow for and foster mental processing. This view also tells us not only that active learning involves language production on the part of the learner, but also that comprehension is a critical part of language development.

Yet reception is clearly not enough. Our learners must also be able to use language. The external view of language will urge us to focus on the extent to which language is connected to social context. This view will remind us that the type of language we use changes depending on where and with whom we use it. To continue once again with our example of the active/passive, we may discuss with our students a genre of language that makes regular use of the active/passive distinction. If we are teaching students in higher education, for example, we might point out that academic writing has traditionally taken advantage of the passive voice to focus the action of the sentence while de-focusing the actor, especially if the actor is the writer him/herself. This focus on the active/passive in academic writing then allows for a discussion of how academic writing is changing as academics are beginning to accept the post-structuralist view that the writer is an integral part of the research and should therefore be acknowledged as such instead of being 'hidden' from the reader. This kind of socially situated discussion will allow students to participate in the target culture more effectively.

To summarise so far, a good language teacher will keep in mind the full range of what a language is in order to foster the development of all aspects of the language – that is, if native-like fluency is the ultimate aim. It is also possible, however, that the teaching context is one in which native-like fluency is not expected. Sometimes people need to learn a language for a single specific purpose. A worker in a call centre, for example, may need to have a competent grammar, a highly developed specialised vocabulary and an awareness of culturally conditioned telephone manner. Whether working towards complete fluency or specialised skill, however, an ability to isolate and foster particular aspects of language is valuable in teaching.

The flip side of teaching is, of course, learning. One would do well also to keep in mind what we know about language development. Even though the ideas presented so far need more discussion, we can still draw some general implications for classroom teaching. The extent to which UG is relevant to second language learning is controversial. Yet it is uncontroversial that the target language you are trying to teach can be characterised by grammatical principles, which many linguists view as constrained by UG. Thus it is at least valid to view language itself as a natural, rule-governed system, and to trust your intuitions about language as you teach.

One common frustration for teachers is that, no matter the amount of correction, some students continue to make the same errors. Instead of being frustrated, you should first ask yourself whether it is an error or a mistake. A systematic error might be traced to some universal property of language, or it might be a property of the learner's native language. For example, a native speaker of French may consistently place adverbs after the verb in English to say, for example, *I finished quickly my essay* because this is the correct word order in French. Mistakes, by contrast, as a natural part of language production, may not be worth worrying about, especially if you are interested in promoting fluency among your learners. High rates of mistakes, however, may signal that the learning environment is causing undue stress to the learner such that they are not able to perform to their highest potential. If this is the case, you might need to consider making changes to your classroom environment.

When viewing errors as a reflection of a student's underlying interlanguage, it is useful to bear in mind the concept of UG because interlanguage grammars are also 'natural' grammars that are restricted to universal possibilities of language. After identifying an error, you might try to determine whether it has perhaps occurred because the student is in a stage where the language point in question is too advanced for the learner. If so, then it may be best to let the error go unremarked, knowing that this language point is not likely to develop until a later stage in the learner's overall proficiency. Alternatively, it may be that the error persists, even though the learner is certainly proficient enough to develop this aspect of language. This suggests that the learner has fossilised where this particular aspect of language is concerned. In this case, it may be useful to point this out to the student and to work together to develop strategies to compensate for this fossilisation. For example, the learner could be encouraged to edit any written work routinely for the particular error in question. In spoken language, explicit monitoring of production may be possible for very disciplined learners.

Whether the work of UG or not, second language learning holds to a degree of systematicity. It may be useful, therefore, to look for areas in which your students' interlanguage indicates that the underlying system is making use of a non-targetlike rule causing them to make a particular error. If a non-targetlike rule is identified, it may be that in time, with sufficient positive input, the student may overcome the error. If the learner's linguistic system is not able to develop in this way, it might be possible to compensate by making use of their metalinguistic knowledge. While a native speaker does not need explicit awareness of underlying language rules, awareness of a rule may help a non-native speaker to self-correct for more effective native-like fluency. We will return to this discussion later in the book.

Finally, we ask what implication there is for the critical period hypothesis. It may seem that there is little you can do in response to the critical period generalisation that younger is better – unless you are a policy maker in a position of considerable power who is able to make language learning part of the primary school curriculum. However, keeping this younger-is-better tendency in mind will help you to modify your expectations since young learners do not develop language ability as quickly as older learners. This is probably to do with higher levels of cognitive ability which develop with age. This also provides guidance on questions of type of input. If you are working with younger learners, you may want to provide 'natural' authentic input in as large amounts as possible. If, on the other hand, you are teaching at the university level, you may want to make more use of explicit rule-based instruction to take advantage of the adult ability to enhance production by making use of metalinguistic knowledge.

The implications drawn from our discussion so far have been summarised in Table 1.1.

Language	Implication
Form (Structuralist)	Teach language as a set of rules
Form (Generativist)	Nurture natural language development with rich input
Function	Give attention to meaning
Internal/mental	Emphasise processing and comprehension
External	Teach cultural norms and expectations
Linguistic	Provide rich authentic input
Metalinguistic	Clarify language rules explicitly

Language development	Implication
Nature	Attend to the quality of input
Nurture	Provide a sufficient quantity of input
Fossilisation	Develop strategies for compensation
Systematic errors	Identify underlying causes
Language mistakes	Consider the classroom environment
Stages of learning	Do not expect abilities far beyond current proficiency
Age	Provide appropriate types of input

Table 1.1   Implications for language teaching

OVERVIEW OF THE BOOK

In this chapter we have considered the range of what might be included under the broad category of 'language'. At the most basic level, language form includes the properties phonology, syntax and morphology. The function of language, however, requires thought and memories as well as physical motor control to receive and produce speech, along with an awareness of the context in which language is needed for interaction. In the remainder of this book we will explore these ideas in more detail and then show that an understanding of language and language development can help us to make decisions about teaching. Before we do this, however, we will discuss the field of language teaching from a historical perspective in Chapter 2, in order to trace the relationship between language teaching and understandings about language.

Chapter 3 explores the biological view of language in much more detail, discussing seminal research and presenting a set of generally agreed generalisations that have come out of research in second language acquisition from this perspective. In Chapter 4 we survey a range of views about language which compensate for major omissions in the biological approach, including the importance of language as a tool for communication. We return to our set of generalisations from second language research in Chapter 5 to begin discussing implications for language teaching. In Chapter 6 we turn to the classroom, exploring a range of approaches and methods for language teaching. This sets the scene for an actual lesson plan, which is presented in Chapter 7. The lesson is deconstructed in order to illustrate how it reflects theoretical understanding of the complex nature of language, and facets of language development. The final chapter of this book further explores issues of language development by adapting the lesson from Chapter 7 to different contexts. In this way, Chapter 8 brings together some loose ends, and allows for a summary of the importance of theory in practice.

FOR DISCUSSION

1. What did you think about language before you read this chapter? Which of your existing views were supported and reinforced by this chapter and which have been challenged? From the point of language teaching, do you find some of the views more appropriate and relevant than others?

2. Can you think of more examples of prescriptive grammar rules which would contradict a descriptive account of what English speakers actually do? Which type of grammar should be taught? Discuss the extent to which teaching a prescriptive vs descriptive grammar is appropriate in different teaching contexts.

3. Based on your personal understanding and experience, compare and contrast native first language acquisition and adult second language development. Are they entirely different and unrelated? Or are there any commonalities?

4. Recall a language teacher from your past experience. What view(s) of language did they seem to hold? Think about what kinds of activities you did in class. Did they focus on the structure/form of language? Or the meaning/function? Was the teacher more concerned with mastering language rules? Or did he/she prioritise the culture associated with the language?

5. Make a list of all the different aspects of language that have been discussed in this chapter. For each one, consider the extent to which you feel as if you had to be explicitly taught and consciously learned it in your native language. Then go through the list again and consider each aspect in terms of whether it needs to be explicitly taught in a second or foreign language classroom.

6. Find a language lesson. (If you do not have access to language textbooks, try finding a language lesson on the Internet.) Consider the lesson in terms of the oppositions about language that we have discussed in this chapter. Where do you see evidence for each view? Do you see evidence for any other ways to think about language that we have not mentioned in this chapter?

NOTES

1. For an extensive discussion of the formalist versus functionalist perspectives, see Newmeyer (1998).

2. For a general overview of the brain, see Carter (1998/2000). For an overview of the brain and language, see Ingram (2007).

3. For a classic and accessible introduction to psycholinguistics, see Aitchison (1998). For more recent volumes written at a more technical level, see Steinberg and Sciarini (2006) or Traxler and Gernsbacher (2006).

4. Note that originally most alphabets had some connection to the sounds or meanings that they represent. See Coulmas (1989) or the edited volume by Daniels and Bright (1996) for extensive discussion.

5. For a detailed discussion of literacy, see Holme (2004).

6. To read the original study, see Brown (1973). This well-known study is described in most textbooks about first language acquisition. See, for example, Ingram (1989). For a good collection of core readings in first language acquisition, see Lust and Foley (2004).

7. Nina, age 2;0, as reported by Vainikka (1993/94).

8. The asterisk is used by linguists to show grammatical unacceptability.

9. For overviews of the issue, see Birdsong (1999), and Harley and Wang (1997).

10. See Haznedar and Gavruseva (2008) for a recent collection of research in child second language acquisition.

2

HISTORICAL OVERVIEW – LANGUAGE AND LANGUAGE TEACHING

ᕓ

INTRODUCTION

Language teaching is not, by any means, a new endeavour. In this chapter we will take a brief look at the history of language teaching in the European context. The theme of this historical review is that teaching reflects the underlying beliefs of time and place, from beliefs about education to beliefs about language itself. As our brief review of history before the twentieth century will show us, many of today's questions and problems are very old indeed. There is evidence, for example, that educationalists of fifteenth-century Renaissance Italy argued for the importance of teaching language function in addition to language form.[1] Looking at the more recent past, our discussion of the 1900s will focus on the development of the academic disciplines that inform language teaching today. A look to the past reminds us that many of the challenges facing language teachers have not changed. What has changed, however, is the way in which the challenges are understood.

LANGUAGE TEACHING: SHIFTS IN UNDERLYING AIMS AND BELIEFS

In thinking about language teaching in the past, it is important to keep in mind the fact that systems for education were very different from today. For instance, the specialisation of academic subjects into the range of disciplines that we have today is itself a relatively recent phenomenon. Language teaching for much of European history would have been seen as a part of philosophy, which was itself subsumed under theology.[2] This is not an unnatural place for language if one considers the legacy that can be traced back to Ancient Greece and Rome to view language as a system of logic and rhetoric. As part of this legacy, the languages that were deemed a necessary part of formal education in the European Middle Ages were the classical languages.

Knowledge of Latin was needed in order to study the classics of Ancient Rome. Latin was also the language used not only for recording knowledge of the past, but also for developing knowledge in theology, medicine and law. The prestige of Latin was also maintained by the role it played in the political powerhouse of that time, the Church.

Because Latin was not a native language in most of Medieval Europe, it would have needed to be explicitly taught and learned. In fact, there was a connection between changes in the use of Latin and the way it was taught. Before the 1500s, Latin was the language not only of legal documents, but also of educated people in the lands which correspond to modern-day England, as it was in much of Europe. Though it was not a native language, it was used for formal communication. Thus the teaching of Latin included an emphasis on the ability to use Latin; in other words, there was a functional approach to teaching Latin.

As the role of Latin in society changed, however, this functional approach to teaching it also changed. When Latin was no longer spoken, the practice of teaching Latin was limited to teaching the rules of the language. Even in the distant past, then, there was a link between the teaching of language and the needs associated with that language. Today, when describing past teaching practices, we often assign the single unchanging label 'traditional', and traditional teaching methods are often equated with learning grammar rules and committing grammatical paradigms to rote memory. Yet it is erroneous to label all of language teaching historically as the same. While grammar instruction may characterise language teaching practices in the more recent past of, say, the nineteenth century, it was not like this throughout the Middle Ages.

Grammar teaching itself has also seen variability. The question of whether to teach grammar **inductively**, encouraging learners to work out rules themselves, or **deductively**, by presenting the rules for practice, also has a long history. There was a shift in the Middle Ages from an inductive approach to a deductive one. With the Renaissance, however, the emphasis on discovery and exploration saw a move back to an inductive approach to grammar again. In short, the past should be recognised as undergoing constant fluctuation and change, with historical changes leading to changes in language teaching. The growth of nation states, with its beginnings in the 1300s, highlighted linguistic differences and identity. With the rise of a French-speaking political powerhouse in Europe, for example, came the use of French among English-speaking ruling classes. The legacy of this French and Latinate influence is still seen in modern-day English, especially at the lexical level.

The growth of a merchant class, improved modes of travel and increased contact between peoples also led to different needs with regard to languages. Thus, while Latin and French may still have held value among the clergy and the ruling classes, the need for communication between members of the middle classes within Europe was on the rise. And in time, education became more and more open to members of society outside the privileged classes. With these changes came a shift away from Latin as the language of power, and with the interest in culture during the Renaissance came an interest in local languages, or **vernaculars**. As a result, while Latin was still taught in Great Britain, for example, it was increasingly done through the vernacular of English.

Another factor affecting education has been innovation in technology. The development of the printing press impacted education, as it extended the domain of literacy to a much larger proportion of the population. Along with this increase in printed documents in general, the use of Latin was becoming restricted to writing only. In time, the vernacular replaced Latin in official documents, a trend which occurred across the whole of Western Europe. English did not replace Latin as the official language for legal documents in Britain until the mid-1600s. But tradition dies hard; for centuries after its use became obsolete, knowledge of Latin was still held in high esteem.

The legacy of Latin also played a crucial role in the development of linguistics in terms of understanding of how language works. Until the 1500s, Latin and Ancient Greek were the only languages whose structure was explicitly known, analysed and written down in terms of their grammatical rules, at least in Western Europe. In the Arab world, linguistic study included both these Classical languages and Arabic and other Asian languages. Yet in Europe, even when scholarly interest began to recognise vernaculars, Latin was the benchmark from which other languages were analysed and studied. So strong was this influence that remnants of the Latin legacy still exist in English today, the famous example being the prescriptive rule not to 'split' an infinitive in English, which we discussed in Chapter 1. This rule illustrates the role of Latin in traditional grammarians' notions of ideal forms of language.

The shift from use of prestigious language to the vernacular is the context in which the approach to language teaching known as **Grammar Translation** developed. As Latin was not a language for interaction, teachers did not use Latin as the medium of instruction, using instead the native vernacular to explain how Latin works. This use of the vernacular meant that Latin was taught in terms of its grammatical rules and the aim limited to the ability to read Latin. From this came the practice of translating passages from Latin into the vernacular, with teaching limited to the rules and structural paradigms of the language. Also central to the Grammar Translation method was the idea of transmitting cultural values to be found in the Classical literature being translated. In other words, Latin taught through Grammar Translation was more of an object of study than a tool for communication. In time Latin itself became limited to a system of grammatical rules – a far cry from the communicative and political tool it once was.

As the need to teach other European languages as foreign languages developed, it is only natural that teachers looked to existing language teaching practices, applying them to the teaching of other languages. Thus Grammar Translation was adopted as the way to teach the living languages of Europe, including English.[3] It is perhaps not surprising that this method achieved only limited success. After all, teaching a language by translating literature and memorising structural rules is not likely to result in fluent speakers or users of language. And by this time, grammar teaching had returned to a deductive, rule-based approach. Addressing the limitations of Grammar Translation in the late 1800s was the so-called **Reform Movement**. In France, educationalists such as Gouin and Marcel proposed breaking language into the four skills and focusing on everyday language. In looking for a more effective approach, reformers looked to developments in linguistics and psychology to establish a link between language teaching and these newly emerging academic fields. English reformer Henry Sweet, in his 1899 book, *The Practical Study of Languages*, also identified language points to be taught and presented them in terms of the four skills, sequencing them from simple to complex. As we will explore in the next section, the idea of breaking down the language into constituent parts can be traced to the practice of the early linguists, while sequencing can be attributed to ideas of knowledge development emerging from psychology.

Another influence on the Reform Movement was the observation that children learn their native language quite early and easily. Noting that infants acquire their native language in a seemingly effortless fashion, applied linguists of the Reform Movement devised a radical departure from existing methods, advocating the **Direct Method**, in which instruction in the language classroom was limited exclusively to the target language. Students were asked to restrict themselves to the target language only, developing the language word by word. With this came a return to inductive approaches to grammar learning as students were expected to work out the patterns and rules underlying language based on the real examples of language to which they were exposed. The most famous example of the Direct Method is the Berlitz

School, which still exists today. It succeeded as a private language school because its clientele tended to be highly motivated adults with a specific need to become fluent quickly. This method, however, was wholly unsuccessful in state schools with large classes of children who were not likely to see the need for multilingualism and therefore viewed language as just one more subject to be learned.

In looking at the history of language teaching in Europe, one theme that emerges is the long history of some core questions which still plague the field of language teaching. Another is the relationship between development of thought in academia and movements affecting practice in the language classroom. In the next section we explore the scholastic foundations of language teaching with the development of linguistics, psychology and the more recent fields of first and second language acquisition.

MODERN FOUNDATIONS FOR LANGUAGE TEACHING

Scholars in Western Europe and North America in the late 1800s became increasingly interested in the properties of language. The legacy of the Classical languages, especially in Europe, fostered the view of Latin as the most logical, and therefore superior, language and linguists tended to use the structural properties of Latin as the norm for studying other languages, imposing the rules of Latin on to other languages. Because of differences between languages, the resulting rules were, unsurprisingly, quite unnatural. None the less, language lessons at this time largely involved learning rules like these, rules which make up a prescriptive grammar.

Another change in the study of language in the eighteenth and early nineteenth centuries came as a result of British Imperialism. Contact with Asian cultures led to a great interest in Asian languages, especially as the British discovered a wealth of knowledge and scholarship about Sanskrit in Asian linguistic traditions. This led to great efforts to trace the relationships between languages, looking to identify family resemblances among so-called Indo-European languages.

Thus there was shift in thinking away from the view of Latin as the sole benchmark for other languages to an interest in a wider range of Classical languages, which also led to an interest in studying languages in their own right. From this came a new aim of describing language as it is actually used. This commitment to a descriptive grammar is what set the structuralists apart from earlier linguists. Ferdinand de Saussure, the 'father' of structuralism, is noted for making the distinction between **langue**, a language, and **parole**, how language is used. The basic premise of structuralism is that there are regular patterns within any language and across all languages, an idea which was foundational for the modern idea of universal properties in language. Because their focus was on describing language as it is used, the structuralists were mainly interested in spoken language.

There were some differences between the structuralism developed in the US by Bloomfield and that developed in Europe by Jakobson of the Prague School.[4] The European structuralists were continuing a line of inquiry handed down from Classics, and building on the work of Asian linguists as they tried to trace the histories of the world's known languages, looking at similarities and differences at the level of linguistic structure. They are perhaps best known for their contributions to the study of phonology with the fundamental observation of phonemes as sets of distinctive features such as voiced/voiceless, for example.

The North American effort was influenced by anthropologists like Franz Boas who were interested in the languages of the indigenous peoples of North America. This approach was also based on a structuralist interest in language systems which reduced language to smaller linguistic units, but with less of a legacy from the Classical languages of Latin and Greek than linguists in Europe. Leonard Bloomfield was the most influential figure in the development of structuralism in America with his scientific approach to linguistic analysis. Despite difference between European and American linguists, their approach was largely the same: to create inventories of linguistic units, both sounds and morphemes, with a broader aim of classifying languages into families.

A significant development at this time was the establishment of the International Phonetic Association, whose early achievement was devising the International Phonetic Alphabet, the IPA, in 1886. This system for characterising all possible sounds in any language is typical of the structuralist approach in two ways. It recognises sounds as universal properties – any language could potentially make use of any of the sounds. And it organises the sounds according to their structural properties. The consonants, for example, are organised in terms of the way they are produced, known as manner of articulation, and physical position during production, or place of articulation.

The structuralists laid the foundations for other developments in linguistics. Linguistic typology saw the work of Joseph Greenberg and his forty-five Universals based on a study of thirty languages. Like the example in the last chapter, many of his universals have survived the test of time. To give another example, Greenberg observed that if objects come before verbs in a particular language, that language is also likely to have post-positions instead of prepositions. Take, for example, Korean, an SOV language in which verbs follow their objects. In Korean a prepositional phrase like *in the house* is expressed as a post-positional phrase, *jip-eh*, with *jip* meaning 'house', and *-eh* meaning 'in'. Greenberg's work can be seen as step towards the idea of universal principles in language.

Taking a more decisive step in the direction of universals was the most influential linguist of modern times, Noam Chomsky. Chomsky's notion of Universal Grammar developed out of this idea that all languages abide by a single set of properties unique to humans. Of course, there is variation from language to language, but that variation is itself constrained to a principled range of linguistic possibility. The fundamental difference between Chomsky and the structuralists was his interest not just in describing linguistic forms, but also in the linguistic operations inherent to language. These operations were originally known as **transformations**. For example, in order to form a yes/no question in English, there is a transformation from the declarative to the interrogative form. This involves an inversion of the subject and auxiliary verb; a sentence such as *John is going to London*, for example, becomes *Is John going to London?* Every language was understood to have a set of principles that controlled transformations. These linguistic principles are said to be generative because they allow for the infinite creation of structures. It is for this reason that Chomsky's approach came to be known as **Transformational Generative Grammar**.

The basic principle constraining transformations is that they depend on structure. **Structure dependency** is a key principle in formal linguistics. Consider the above yes/no question transformation for illustration. If you had to come up with a rule that captures the relationship between the declarative and interrogative forms, you might say that it is a simple matter of moving the first verb to the front of the sentence. Try turning a more complex example into a yes/no question, however, and you will find that this 'logical' rule no longer works:

(1)   a.   John, my friend who **was** an artist for many years, **is** going to London.
      b.   *****Was** John, my friend who an artist for many years, **is** going to London?
      c.   **Is** John, my friend who **was** an artist for many years, going to London?

The transformation depends on structure, not on a linear rule; it requires the main clause auxiliary verb to move to the front of the sentence, not the first verb. This reliance on structure is known as the principle of structure preservation because, even though there has been a transformation, the structure of the sentence has been preserved, with the rules involved in the transformation respecting the structure of the sentence. This is remarkable when you realise that more 'logical' linear language rules not only are not correct in English, but they are also unattested in the world's language, while structure-dependent rules can be found in all languages. In short, natural languages have structure, and constraints or 'rules' operate on structures which are not as straightforward as a linear analysis would be.

Central to Chomsky's understanding of language is the fact that children acquire a complete and complex linguistic system in a relatively short amount of time and at a very young age – in fact, at an age when other cognitive processes have yet to develop. While Chomsky's ideas about language may have been a natural development out of the structural tradition in linguistics, his claims about language acquisition directly contradicted understood ideas of the day. Accepted ideas about language acquisition were a product of another academic discipline that developed in the early 1900s: psychology. Psychology is concerned with the internal, mental development of individuals. The development of language is only one of many aspects of development of interest to a psychologist, and furthermore was seen as akin to the development of other kinds of cognitive ability and knowledge. In 1957 the prominent psychologist, B. F. Skinner, published a book called *Verbal Behavior*, in which he argued that children learn language through imitation and habit formation. The stimulus–response view of learning in general, known as **Behaviourism**, was argued to characterise not just general learning, but the learning of native language by young children as well.

The young Chomsky made his mark in the academic world by challenging the well-established psychologist on his views of language development. His basic claim was that language knowledge is different from other kinds of knowledge and, accordingly, develops differently. For Chomsky, Universal Grammar (UG) is the set of linguistic principles that all humans are born with and which enables the young child to acquire any language to which he or she is exposed. In addition to this claim of nativism, Chomsky argued that children are able to generate a range of linguistic structures that they will not have heard. In this way, language acquisition is not merely a matter of imitation, but instead is generative process; an infinite number of utterances are possible because of a limited number of underlying linguistic principles. In other words, the linguistic system of a child will develop beyond the input to which the child is exposed. This argument is called the **poverty of the stimulus**. There is, of course, the need for a stimulus – the mother tongue that surrounds the child. But that stimulus is poor in the sense that the child will be able to produce linguistic forms that it will not have ever heard. We will return to this poverty of stimulus idea in the next chapter.

The difference in views between linguists and psychologists established a fundamental divide that still exists among researchers interested in questions of language and cognition. Even today, the cognitivists see language as knowledge much like other kinds of knowledge – all of which make use of a single set of cognitive mechanisms. The generativists, by contrast, see language as distinct, using a special or privileged set of cognitive mechanisms. These two traditions will be explored in more detail in the next two chapters. But first we will return to the language classroom to look more closely at what was happening there in the first half of the twentieth century.

EARLY APPROACHES TO LANGUAGE TEACHING

As we have already seen, disaffection with Grammar Translation in Europe inspired educational reformers to develop alternative approaches to language teaching. However, efforts by individuals were not widely recognised at the time because there was no effective means of disseminating ideas. This is because of a general absence of features associated with professionalisation within the field of language teaching. Until the late 1800s, there were no professional organisations, conferences or journals to bring language-teaching professionals together. A groundswell for change was more possible once professional organisations like the International Phonetic Association were established and once linguistics and psychology were recognisable as academic fields. With more formal methods for communicating professional practice, the Reform Movement might have been able to move language teaching away from Grammar Translation. Even so, the ideas of these early reformists may have been too radical to take hold in an effective way. Furthermore, the idea that learners should be immersed in the language like native speakers was not supported with an effective method for implementing this idea in teaching. Thus, after taking two steps forward, there was a need to take one step back.

In the first half of the 1900s, three sets of language teaching practices developed in each of the three large English-speaking regions of the world. The Oral Approach that developed in England had much in common with the Situational Approach that developed in the Australian context. We will consider these two approaches before looking at the Audiolingual Approach of North America.[5] Like other early applied linguists, Harold Palmer and A. S. Hornby in England looked to structuralist linguistics and psychological notions of language development to inform their **Oral Approach** to language teaching. Accordingly, language was identified as a system of patterns and structural paradigms which could be sequenced in a graded way. And, as suggested by the label, there was a strong emphasis on the spoken language.

Central to the Oral Approach was the idea that new language points should be presented in context. In this way, it was much like the view of teaching known as the **Situational Approach**, which developed in Australia among applied linguists led by George Pittman. The Situational Approach made use of objects, pictures and other realia to present new language points. There was also much emphasis on the concepts or notions embodied in language, and not just lists of grammar rules. This progressive view of what to teach was not matched with an equally progressive view of how to teach, however. In both of these approaches, language was taught through teacher-directed activities such as drills, substitution exercises, whole-class repetition and dictation.

These practices were similar to those used by the **Audiolingual Approach**, which developed in North America. Overlap between the Oral/Situational Approaches and Audiolingualism can be found in the emphasis on oral skills, with literacy a secondary concern. The difference, however, was the extent to which speaking was seen as dependent on listening. Proponents of Audiolingualism made much of the belief that a learner needs to perceive language accurately before it can be correctly produced. This emphasis on the aural was a direct result of the influence of Behaviourism. The behaviourists viewed language as primarily speech, not writing. Speech was seen as a precondition for writing. This conclusion was based on observations of native language acquisition combined with recognition of the existence of non-literate societies without written traditions.

Language development was understood to occur through mimicry and repetition. Language could be seen as embodying a connection between a stimulus and a response; an apple, for example, would trigger the word *apple*. Language-learning, like other kinds of learning, was seen as a product of stimulus–response and reinforcement. In practice, this meant a large proportion of class time was devoted to intensive drill work. Through repetition, learners would develop a new set of linguistic habits. In the early stages, language production would be limited to imitated forms. Eventually, however, a person would then develop enough structures to analogise from the learned set of structures to similar structures. This would allow for the production of more creative forms to express new meanings.

One reason for the development of Audiolingualism was the political context of the time. The 1900s saw two world wars, with new global powers emerging in the mid-1900s. The development of Audiolingualism came from funding provided by the United States military, which had identified a great need for language specialists to support the efforts of the emerging superpower. The need to develop a multilingual military in a limited amount of time led to programmes of very intensive study. The very structured and authority-bound nature of Audiolingualism was no doubt compatible with a military environment. The degree of success found by these intensive courses drew the attention of the wider language-teaching community.

In sum, the emphasis on intentional, explicit habit formation was in direct contrast to the earlier beliefs of proponents of the Direct Method, in which learners would naturally develop the language around them. For Audiolingualism, learning required repeated drilling of one language pattern at a time. Applied linguist, Charles Fries, contributed to the development of Audiolingualism with his study of the structural similarities and differences between languages. We will look more closely at his idea of Contrastive Analysis in the next section. But first, we conclude this section by summing up the similarities and differences between Audiolingualism and the Oral/Situational Approaches. Though stemming from different academic and historic traditions, they were, in fact, quite similar in practice. They were largely teacher-centred practices without any notion of autonomous or self-directed learning. Teachers relied heavily on drilling, requiring endless repetition of stock linguistic patterns. Dialogues, presented by teachers, were memorised and recited by students. Repetition through drilling allowed for a focus on pronunciation, rhythm and intonation.

Audiolingualism differed from the Oral and Situational Approaches, however, in its theoretical basis. The latter two approaches had the intention of relating language to specific contexts. Thus, structural patterns were identified and taught based on particular social contexts. For example, a lesson might revolve around greetings or requests. In this way, the Oral/Situational Approaches were more functionally inspired, at least in principle. That the implementation of these approaches relied on teacher-centred lessons with repetition and memorisation, however, undermined the intention of presenting language as functional. The Audiolingual Approach also sought to produce learners who could use the language, and saw its reliance on habit formation as a legitimate means to that end. While both approaches gave thought to the choice and sequence of structural patterns for instruction, the Audiolingual Approach based this on the linguistic nature of the patterns, in contrast with the Oral/Situational Approaches' consideration of function. The question of sequencing of structural patterns owed much to developments in the newly developing field of second language acquisition.

SECOND LANGUAGE ACQUISITION AND LANGUAGE TEACHING

With the development of the academic disciplines of psychology and linguistics came the beginnings of subdisciplines. Of most relevance to language teaching has been the development of the field of second language acquisition (SLA). This interdisciplinary field linked research in linguistics and second language development. Since language in the early 1950s was seen as a set of habits, learning a second language was seen as an attempt to change existing language habits to a new set of habits. This process was seen as involving what is known as **language transfer**. Learners transfer their habits from their native language to the second, or target, language.

Taking a habit formation point of view, the logical prediction is that the more different a language is, the more difficult it would be to learn since there would be more habits in need of change. This is, in essence, the basis of Contrastive Analysis. Charles Fries is known for developing this research agenda with the aim of improving language teaching and learning. The agenda was to compare languages in terms of sound system, syntactic system, morphological system and even pragmatic system in order to identify which language habits would need to change in learning the second language. This notion was further developed by Fries's student, Lado, who hypothesised that there is a direct connection between the degree of similarity between native and target languages, and the extent to which learners would acquire them. Lado's Contrastive Analysis Hypothesis proposed that there would be difficulties in language learning where there are differences between the native and target language, and ease where there are similarities between the two languages.[6]

Armed with the knowledge of similarities and differences between native and target languages, then, a teacher could simply focus on teaching the differences. The similarities should prove unproblematic because transfer of native language habits meant there was nothing new to learn (aside from the differing lexical items). Differences, on the other hand, would be problematic, with errors resulting from native language interference. In short, the logical conclusion of the Contrastive Analysis Hypothesis was that language development could be predicted based on knowledge of the languages in question. If true, this finding would have been revolutionary for language teaching. Unfortunately, however, Contrastive Analysis did not prove itself to be quite so straight-forward, especially for areas of syntax and morphology.

Early damage to Contrastive Analysis came from empirical studies showing that learners did not necessarily make the errors predicted by the Contrastive Analysis Hypothesis. One famous example is a study by Zobl (1980) of French learners of English. This study focused on pronouns in object position because of the differences between the two languages. In English, object pronouns follow the verb, while in French they come before the verb. Following the logic of the Contrastive Analysis Hypothesis, French learners of English should, at an early stage at least, produce sentences like *I them know*. But this contrastive analysis error does not actually occur among French learners of English. In addition to errors that learners do not make, research also shows that many errors that learners do make cannot be traced to differences in the corresponding structure in the native language.

There were also problems with the definition of 'ease' and 'difficulty'. While these notions seem intuitively reasonable, it is not entirely clear how one might actually define or measure them. Difficulty is expected where there are language differences, and differences are expected to cause error. But a learner making an error may not perceive the linguistic point as difficult or even be aware of the error. So in what sense is it difficult? The heart of the problem is that the definition of difference is linguistic while the understanding of the notion of difficult is psychological.[7] Like comparing apples and oranges, this mismatch undermines the validity of the hypothesis. While structural properties of language are a product that can be spelled out in terms of typological similarity and difference, feelings of ease and difficulty are part of a process, and as such, do not have objective qualities that can be readily measured.

As a teacher, you may have had experiences that contradict the Contrastive Analysis Hypothesis. For example, most language teaching materials will include lessons on so-called **false friends, cognate** words that can lead to incorrect use by learners. Two languages will often have developed words from the same word root either because of similarity in language family or from borrowing which comes from language contact. While the two words may be traced back to a common meaning etymologically, they can easily develop over time to have different meanings or uses in each language. This can lead to more problems, not fewer, as learners are likely to think they know the meaning of the word because of the similarity and have difficulty modifying it, even though they have been told the difference. For example, upon encountering the Spanish word *simpático*, an English speaker is likely to assume that it means sympathetic, when in fact it means 'nice' or 'pleasant'. The opposite problem is also likely to be familiar to you as a language teacher. A very different or unusual aspect of language can be easy for learners to learn precisely because it is so different. The difference can draw attention and spark the interest needed for explicit learning to occur.

Echoing what many teachers will know from experience, empirical research found that learners do not necessarily have difficulty and ease where they are predicted to, at least in areas of morphology and syntax. In the area of phonological development the Contrastive Analysis Hypothesis model has been found to be empirically sounder. Within the framework of the Contrastive Analysis Hypothesis, phonologists looked to cross-linguistic typologies, the better to understand language development. This led to other developments which were an improvement on some of the original Contrastive Analysis Hypothesis ideas. The Markedness Differential Hypothesis proposed by Eckman (1977) was based on a classification of linguistic phenomena in terms of whether they are marked or unmarked. While the concept of **markedness** has been defined in different ways, in general the term refers to how common or basic a feature is cross-linguistically.[8] A linguistic form is marked if it is unusual, in comparison with a commonplace, or unmarked, form.

The Markedness Differential Hypothesis was based on a typological grouping of phonological features into sets much like the implicational hierarchies we mentioned in Chapter 1. Within a particular hierarchy, a learner is predicted to be able to learn features of a target language that were marked if their native language also included these features. Secondly, because the hierarchy is implicational, a less marked feature within the hierarchy would be readily learned if the marked feature was learned. By appealing to universal factors of cross-linguistic typology, this approach was more principled, and, not coincidentally, has been found to be more valid as a predictor for the development of second language pronunciation.

The shortcomings of the Contrastive Analysis Hypothesis as a general theory of language development do not mean that the native language is irrelevant when learning a second language. Clearly there are transfer effects. But the difficulty is that transfer is not as neat or straightforward as early researchers might have hoped. One reason for this is because the structure of language cannot be characterised as a set of habits, with second language learning a matter of establishing new habits. Another is to do with the fact that language is complex, involving more than just grammatical structures. One line of research which is interested in language beyond the structural level had developed the notion of Conceptual Fluency, which depends on a view of language in which concepts determine the structures of language. In this view, a language is a reflection of the concepts underlying it; thus the way that a culture organises its concepts will determine the forms found in the language. This is most clearly seen in that language's metaphors. Danesi (1995) argues that a Contrastive Analysis approach may be useful for understanding learners' difficulties at the level of conceptual fluency.

Mainstream research on Contrastive Analysis, however, was based on a structural view of language. The main method used in this research was to analyse errors. **Error Analysis,** a research agenda first promoted by Pit Corder, directly challenged the behaviourist basis of Contrastive Analysis, appealing instead to the **Creative Construction Hypothesis,** which tried to apply Chomsky's view of natural, innate language development to second language learning.[9] Arguing that second language development mirrored first, this hypothesis was often called the L2=L1 hypothesis. Yet it is obvious that this is much too strong a claim.

Before leaving the discussion of Contrastive Analysis and Error Analysis it is worth considering it from the point of view of the classroom. An approach based on errors is quite negative and clashes with the progressive trend in education since at least the 1970s to a more humanistic and supportive approach to learning and learners. This difference in approach between SLA researchers and those interested in classroom teaching may have contributed to the split that began at this time between the field of SLA and the practice of language teaching, a division which we will discuss in more detail in the next chapter. But first, let us briefly consider what was happening in the classroom during this time period.

The generally accepted structure of language teaching lessons in the 1970s and 1980s was **PPP: Present, Practise, Produce.** Accordingly, a lesson would begin with the presentation of some language point by the teacher, followed by controlled practice by students, usually in the form of exercises. Once the language point had been learned, the students would be given a less controlled activity which required them to produce the language point more freely. This very structured approach to a lesson was essentially a culmination of structuralist views of language and behaviourist views of language development. Notice that while great changes in linguistics and the understanding of language development were being proposed, language teaching continued to hold fast to older academic traditions. One reason for this could be the lack of agreement in the research paradigms, as we have seen with the abandonment of Contrastive Analysis and Error Analysis.

Despite the abandonment of the approach, useful developments did emerge from the Error Analysis research programme. Errors were analysed in the context of the language the learner was trying to acquire and not just in terms of the properties of the native language. The shift away from the first language as the only explanation for difficulties in second language development gave more prominence to the process of second language development itself. It was with this shift that it became clear that a learner's developing grammar is systematic. Adoption of the term Interlanguage legitimised learner language as an object of study in its own right instead of seeing it as a faulty version of the target language or as a transferred version of the native language. The recognition that a second language learner's grammar is systematic and not a collection of faulty attempts to mimic the target language nor an inappropriate use of native language 'habits' was supported by a growing body of research. This severely challenged the behaviourist view of language in SLA. Drawing from developments in linguistics, language was no longer seen as a set of habits, but instead a dynamic system of abstract rules, and the second language learner was seen to be developing a dynamic system. We will take this idea further in the next chapter and conclude here with the claim that the development of the idea of systematicity in SLA is perhaps the most important legacy of the Contrastive Analysis/Error Analysis era.

CONCLUSION

In this chapter we have discussed the practice of language teaching in terms of developments in the academic understanding of language and language development. In the pursuit of improving language teaching practices, early applied linguists turned to advances in both language and cognitive development. The lack of success in language teaching practices may, with hindsight, be expected, given the lack of agreement that emerged between linguists and psychologists. Moreover, as discussed in Chapter 1, there has been and continues to be little consensus on how we should understand what language is, whether form or function, a property internal to individual minds or external as a feature of society.

Language teaching practices have also varied depending on education theory as well as social context. In the pre-modern period, classical languages like Latin were taught for reasons of academic pursuit rather than for real communication. With the need to teach vernacular languages, the method of teaching initially remained the same. Yet teaching language solely for reading ancient texts is clearly not appropriate if the aim is for actual interaction with speakers of another language. Grammar Translation, well suited for learning a language as an academic subject, was not well suited for learning language as a useful tool in society.

The first half of the twentieth century can be seen as a time of exploration as applied linguists attempted to develop more effective teaching practices based on developments in linguistics and psychology. The second half of the twentieth century has been one of great exploration in linguistics and psychology, but without straightforward recommendations for how we should teach language. If the effect of the first language could be captured in a simple hypothesis like the Contrastive Analysis Hypothesis, then teachers could come to their task armed with knowledge of the native and target languages and teach accordingly. Instead, what emerged was a very general understanding that interlanguage is systematic. What needs to be clarified is how this can help language teachers teach more effectively.

One claim coming out of this chapter is that application of theory and research to real-life practice requires clear, agreed generalisations from researchers. This may be one reason why change can sometimes be slow. This brief historical overview shows that change in language teaching practices has at times been quite slow. While radical attempts to change teaching, like the Reform Movement, did not persist, they did give way to incremental change. We also saw radical change in the field of language study with the ideas of Chomsky. Perhaps these ideas also need time before meaningful change can take place. In the next chapter we will explore developments in Chomskyan linguistics, with the ultimate aim of asking what implications there are for language teaching.

FOR DISCUSSION

1. Are you aware of language teaching traditions in other parts of the world? How do they compare with the history of language teaching in Europe?
2. To what extent are the 'traditional' practices discussed in this chapter still relevant today? Can you think of a current context in which traditional teaching would be considered appropriate?
3. List three similarities and three differences between your native language and any second language you have learned. Based on your experience as a learner, do your examples seem to support the Contrastive Analysis idea of ease and difficulty or go against it?
4. This chapter concluded with the claim that second language development is systematic. What does this mean? Can you think of examples from your own experience or knowledge that support or explain this claim of systematicity?
5. Do you prefer an inductive or deductive approach to grammar teaching? Why? Would your answer differ depending on who your learners are? Does it differ depending on the particular aspect of grammar?
6. To what extent has your language teaching and/or learning been based on a PPP approach? What are the strengths and weaknesses of PPP, in your experience? In what context is PPP an appropriate structure for language teaching?

NOTES

1. Musumeci (1997) documents this long and rich history in a short but carefully researched volume.
2. See Rutherford (1987) for a discussion of the development of language teaching within the context of academia and for a discussion of grammar teaching in particular.
3. For extensive treatment of the history of language teaching in the English context, see Howatt and Widdowson (2004).
4. For a classic collection of historical readings in linguistics, see Sebeok (1966). Many classics, such as Bloomfield (1933), can also still be found on the shelves of major libraries.
5. See Part 1 of Richards and Rodgers (2001) for a more detailed description of these approaches.
6. To read the original proposals, see Fries (1952) and Lado (1957). Many introductory SLA textbooks provide clear discussions of the Contrastive Analysis Hypothesis. See, for example, Gass and Selinker (2008).
7. For discussion of this point, see Long and Sato (1984).
8. See Haspelmath (2006) for a discussion of markedness which outlines the various ways the term has been used and highlights the problems that these differences in definition raise.
9. For Error Analysis, see Corder (1967, 1981). The main proponents of the Creative Construction Hypothesis were Heidi Dulay and Marina Burt. See Dulay and Burt (1975).

3

LANGUAGE AS A BIOLOGICAL PROPERTY

౨

LANGUAGE: A GENERATIVE VIEW

The middle of the twentieth century was witness to the Chomskyan Revolution. Noam Chomsky's view of language has had a lasting impact, giving rise to a new field of linguistics known as Generative Linguistics. From this, the subfields of generative first and second language acquisition have also developed, though Chomsky himself has had limited involvement in these areas. As we will discuss in this chapter, the philosophical foundation of his theory depends quite crucially on native first language acquisition. SLA, by contrast, goes beyond Chomsky's particular theoretical concern. Though Chomsky himself has never extended his work to SLA, and certainly not to the realm of classroom teaching, other researchers have explored these areas from a generative point of view.

Though Chomsky's generative theory has developed over time, its aim has consistently been to move away from an item-by-item view of language and language development to a model which captures language as a system with universal configuration. While this endeavour initially led to a very complex and elaborate set of algorithms and formulae, the current research is devoted to paring back the model to its most simple and universal properties.

The two main tenets of Chomsky's view of language are that language is constrained by universal principles and that these principles are an innate biological property of humans. The principles of language are generative, allowing us both to interpret and to creatively produce an infinite number of sentences. We will discuss these two central points of Generative Linguistics in terms of what they mean for the understanding of what language is and then what this means for language development.

Chomsky's ideas about language can be seen as a natural development out of the work of the structuralists, as it is concerned with identifying cross-linguistic patterns in languages at the level of the sound, the word, and the sentence. As we have seen, one criticism of the Generative Approach is that it treats particular aspects of language, especially syntax and phonology, in isolation, reducing them in an atomistic way without proper regard for meaning. This is a valid criticism, but it does not tend to bother generativists because their main aim is to identify the structural principles underlying language which give rise to meaning, not to explain meaning itself. For generativists, meaning is the product or result of linguistic structures, not what determines structure. In other words, while our thoughts determine what ideas we want to convey, the linguistic structure itself is constrained by linguistic principles that are not altered by the meaning. Instead, we have to choose from the range of structures available in our language in order to convey our thoughts in the way which best suits the intention of our message.

In the 1960s and 1970s specific language structures were associated with 'rules', known as transformations. For example, there was a rule for 'passive formation' which described how a passive sentence, like *The cat was chased by the dog*, was derived or transformed from an active sentence, such as *The dog chased the cat*. The fundamental difference from the structuralists, however, was Chomsky's observation that language patterns are not logical; they do not abide by rules that can be determined by simple comparison of patterns. Instead, as we saw in Chapter 1, rules are structure-dependent. One famous example from Chomsky (1970) is the observation that the two sentences in (1) may look the same, but they have different structural properties:

(1) a. John is eager to please.
     b. John is easy to please.

They both have the shape of subject + copular verb + predicate adjective + infinitival phrase, but you might have noticed that the role John plays in the two sentences is different. John is the one who wants to please in (1a), but the recipient of pleasure in (1b). It would be difficult to explain this difference based on pattern alone; the next set of examples shows that they are clearly different.

(2) a. John is eager to please Mary.
     b. *John is easy to please Mary.

(3) a. *It is eager to please John.
     b. It is easy to please John.

From these examples we can see two basic generative notions. Firstly, all native speakers will agree that John plays a different role in these two sentences, but very few would be able to explain why. In other words, speakers have knowledge of which they are not themselves aware. Secondly, speakers of a language know what is not structurally possible. The sentence in (2b), for example, is not complex – it does not include any difficult vocabulary, nor is it very long. Yet it is clearly not an acceptable sentence. This is an example of what is meant by constraints on language. There must be some rule or principle that causes (2b) to be unacceptable; and this rule clearly exists whether we are explicitly aware of it or not.

Over the years generative theory has undergone a series of changes, with the name of the theory changing accordingly. The discussion of language rules above is typical of the early theory, known as **Standard Theory**, then **Extended Standard Theory** and then **Revised Extended Standard Theory**! Each step in the development was a step away from describing language structures like those in (2) towards explaining them. This development in theory led to a move away from a growing list of rules to a more general idea that all languages abide by a set of universal constraints, known as principles, within a prescribed set of options, known as parameters. The **Principles and Parameters** approach, proposed in the early 1980s, was part of the next major revision in generative theory, known as government and binding.[1] An example of a principle common to all natural languages is that all languages have a grammatical category for verbs with properties that distinguish them from other categories, like nouns, for instance. The ordering of verbs relative to the other elements in a sentence, by contrast, is determined by a parameter. You will no doubt be aware that languages differ in terms of whether the verb comes before or after its object. There is a word order parameter with two possible settings, usually referred to as the **Head Parameter** because the verb is considered a head that dictates certain properties of the object. This kind of parametric option can explain structural differences between languages.

The idea that there are principles and parameters is still fundamental to the most recent version of the theory, known as **Minimalist Theory**.[2] As suggested by the label, Minimalism is concerned with reducing the theory to as simple and unified a set of principles as possible, to include only a few principles that constrain the core elements of syntax and phonology, while cross-linguistic differences are captured in parameters that are associated with non-core linguistic properties, like lexical properties. All of these versions of generative theory, from Standard Theory to Minimalism, differ in terms of the technical mechanics which regulate language, but they are all the same in terms of the fundamental notions that we are considering here. For generativists, knowledge like that illustrated in (1) to (3) above is considered 'core' linguistic knowledge – subtle grammatical properties that operate when speaking and hearing language, but whose properties the speaker does not explicitly understand. Somehow, each speaker develops a rich and complex set of abstract linguistic constraints of which they may never be consciously aware.

A different type of complexity underlying language is illustrated in another early example from Chomsky (1965):

(4)   He decided on the boat.

If you think about the sentence in (4), you will agree that it is ambiguous – it has two possible interpretations. One interpretation is that someone made a decision while on a boat. The other is that a decision was made about a boat (perhaps to purchase it), though the person making the decision could be anywhere. If this second interpretation is not easy to reach, consider sentence (5), which only has the second interpretation:

(5)   While on the train, he decided on the boat.

Ambiguous sentences and ungrammatical sentences are considered important evidence for the idea that core linguistic knowledge is innate. The main argument is that these kinds of properties could not be learned through imitation or repetition, as the Behaviourists originally argued. The simple logic is that, if the source of this knowledge is not other speakers, it must be that that this knowledge is innate. One property that makes us human, then, is that we have a built-in predisposition for language. We are born with linguistic knowledge that guides and constrains our use of language: in other words, Universal Grammar (UG).

UG is a set of universal properties that limit what a language can and cannot do. It is these limitations that make a language a 'natural' language. As computer programmers and researchers in artificial intelligence know, mimicking an existing language is very difficult; designing a new language as intricate as any of the world's natural languages has proven impossible. Yet young humans develop language with relative ease. Unless there is some pathological obstacle, every child develops what Chomsky calls linguistic **competence**. This competence is knowledge of the core structural properties of one's native language, but as knowledge which is outside the explicit conscious control of the language user. This idea of implicit linguistic knowledge is not very controversial. Most linguists of any theoretical background agree that we have knowledge that allows us to operate as language users without explicit understanding of what that knowledge is. The more controversial claim particular to the generative view is that this knowledge is different from other kinds of knowledge. For generativists, this distinct knowledge is **modular**.

Philosopher Jerry Fodor developed the idea of modularity, arguing that modular knowledge is qualitatively different from general knowledge. **General knowledge** is the knowledge you come to strictly through experience. It can be deliberately altered and consciously thought about. Fodor (1983) distinguishes modular knowledge from general knowledge in terms of five properties. Firstly, it is specific to its domain; examples include the five senses plus language. In other words, the language module relies on mechanisms for language, the vision module on mechanisms for sight, the smell module on mechanisms for smell, and so on. Secondly, it is also different because it is very fast. Consider, for example, some piece of general knowledge, such as how many inches there are in a foot. While you will be able to answer '12' very quickly, it is not nearly as instantaneous as your eyes' ability to see the letters on this page, or your linguistic ability to interpret the question. Thirdly, modular knowledge is automatic – the module cannot *not* operate unless it is physically impeded. You will know this if you have ever been trying to read on a train with someone nearby who is talking on a mobile phone. Unless you physically block your ears, it is very difficult not to hear what they are saying. The fourth property of modular knowledge is that it is not explicit metalinguistic knowledge. We saw this above with the ambiguous and ungrammatical sentences. The fifth and final property is that modular knowledge operates independently in such a way that it cannot be altered by general knowledge. To test this, try speaking to someone for five minutes without using the articles, *a(n)* or *the*. You may be able to do it initially if you speak slowly and think carefully about every word, but to maintain it would be very difficult. And, most importantly, you would not be able to alter your language system so that it no longer included articles. It is a property of the (English) system which could not be changed even if you felt strongly that articles were unnecessary and no longer wanted to use them.

Before leaving this discussion of linguistic theory, it is important to make clear that the theory of modularity is a theory about the mind. We explained in Chapter 1 that *mind* refers to how cognitive processes are represented and understood to operate. In this sense, it is a more of a philosophical construct, in contrast with the *brain*, which refers to the physical organ. As we will briefly discuss in Chapter 5, brain studies by neurologists are beginning to investigate whether particular locations in the brain correspond to language function at a more specific level than the well-known Broca's and Wernicke's areas. This is an area of cutting-edge research which follows a long history in the development of science. It was well accepted, for example, that traits pass from the parent to the child, long before the physical mechanisms of genetics were identified. We turn now to child development to discuss the development of language.

NATIVE LANGUAGE DEVELOPMENT

Perhaps the most revolutionary aspects of Chomsky's ideas have been to do with children's acquisition of their first language (FLA). As with the modifications of linguistic theory, a number of technical points within FLA have developed over time, but the basic premise of the generative view of FLA remains the same. Building on the view of language discussed above, the innate predisposition for language means that language development is going to occur with the help of UG. This 'help' was initially conceived of as some kind of **Language Acquisition Device (LAD)**, but it quickly became clear that this kind of terminology was misleading, as it suggested some kind of gear box in the brain with cogs and switches. It is more accurate to say that the mind responds to the input to which it is exposed by developing language within a set of constraints.

The clearest expression of this idea comes from Chomsky's (1981) Principles and Parameters approach. A child is born with a set of universal linguistic principles, along with a complement of unset parameters waiting for linguistic input. Language acquisition is the process of determining parameter settings based on language input. In the last section we discussed parameters as having two options for a single aspect of language. In fact, a single parameter is understood to implicate a cluster of properties which may not readily seem related. For example, if the Head Parameter is set for verbs to precede objects, then automatically, prepositions will also precede their accompanying noun phrases, for example, *in the house*, not **the house in*. This is important because the child only needs to confirm the global setting of a parameter in order to acquire a range of linguistic properties. If, by determining one aspect of the target language, a child can come to know a range of related subproperties of the parameter, this would explain how a child can acquire the complex rules of a language before other cognitive abilities have yet to mature.

In theory, all the formal properties of all languages can be identified as either a principle or a parameter. These properties – that is, UG – are innate, thus explaining how children can develop their native language at such a young age and with relative ease. One generative FLA agenda, therefore, has been to identify how these principles and parameters account for development. In practice, this has not been straightforward. But commitment to the idea of an innate UG that constrains language development through some variant of principles and parameter has not changed.

Within the generative claim of nativism there are some basic arguments that enjoy general agreement despite debate on more technical details. The first is the fact that all normally developing children develop linguistic competence in a specific language. Of course, they may or may not develop literacy skills, or the ability to speak with the skill of a politician, or have a very impressive range of vocabulary; but these aspects of language are outside the core linguistic knowledge of interest to most generativists.

The second point is that there are stages of development in FLA that all children go through in the same order (though often at different rates). Brown's morpheme order study, mentioned in Chapter 1, exemplifies stages of development of grammatical morphemes among English-speaking children. Additionally, stages in FLA show distinct developmental patterns. We also saw examples of this in Chapter 1 with over-extension of the regular past tense suffix -ed rule to irregular verbs like *break* and *did* by young children. But children are not known to over-extend nouns or adjectives to say things like *I happied yesterday*, even though such a sentence would be perfectly under-standable. This shows that when creating language based on rules, a child is sensitive to the grammatical constraints on particular rules. We also saw that children are resistant to change in their grammatical systems until they are ready for the next stage.

The third point basic to the generative view is the observation that child language development goes beyond what a child is exposed to in their environment. The stimulus is said to be poor relative to ultimate development of the child's core competence. We illustrated a poverty of the stimulus phenomenon in the last section. A child does not need to be told that *John is easy to please Mary* is ungrammatical. Nor do they need to be taught that *He made a decision on the boat* has two possible interpretations. These and many other subtle aspects of language develop naturally as long as the child has been exposed to language. This remarkable aspect of development is the main reason why generativists believe that there must be some in-built mechanism in the brain for language acquisition. It is important to note that, though this discussion has been based on examples in English, the theoretical points are valid for any and every language, including sign language.

Much more could be said about child native language acquisition and the development of linguistic theory. But we must leave these discussions of formal linguistics to turn to the linguistic subfield of more direct relevance to language teaching, that of second language acquisition. What does this biological view of language and language development mean for second language acquisition?

SECOND LANGUAGE DEVELOPMENT

The Current Gap between Theoretical and Applied Linguistics

The Chomskyan approach to language has been often criticised as irrelevant to classroom language teaching, with many expressing scepticism about the usefulness of the Generative Approach.[3] A rejection of formal linguistics by many applied linguists would never have been contemplated during the era of pre-Chomskyan structural linguistics. In fact, the term 'applied linguistics' first began to be used in the mid-1900s, when there was considerable activity within language pedagogy to find theoretical grounding for language teaching practices. As noted in Chapter 2, prior to the 1950s, linguistics and the new field of psychology appeared to be able to supply scientific grounding which language teaching seemed to be lacking.[4] But the current situation is quite different. In addition to reluctance on the part of applied linguists, generative SLA has developed without much interest in questions of the language classroom.[5] This contrasts with early attempts to apply generative research to language teaching, which had profound effects on pedagogy, but only in an abstract and general way. For instance, the importance of 'natural' input to language development is now widely accepted, but more specific applications of how or when to supply this input is not.

Unfortunately, since the late 1960s a rift has developed between researchers studying the formal properties of language and those interested in the teaching of language. A talk given by Chomsky at the Northeast Language Teachers' Association in 1966 marked a pivotal point in the distancing of the two. In that talk, Chomsky was widely understood to have said that linguistic theory is irrelevant to the concerns of language teachers. In fact, what he actually said was: 'the implications of these ideas for language teaching are far from clear to me' (Chomsky 1970: 59). The misconstrual of his remark can be seen as a product of early frustration with the research agenda of Generative Linguistics. The Chomskyan 'revolution' did not lead to an equivalent revolution in the language classroom. There were early attempts to introduce generative theory to language teachers,[6] but these proved inappropriate for the language classroom.

The Chomsky-led move away from habit formation to an innate predisposition contributed to the distancing from teaching, since 'natural' language acquisition does not require teaching. Moreover, Generative Linguistics modelled itself on the sciences, focusing on abstract theoretical principles of language. Because their main aim was to define the properties of linguistic competence, the focus was limited to the abstract constraints of language. First language acquisitionists followed this line of inquiry by looking for evidence of universal constraints in the development of native language. It is only natural that generative researchers interested in second language development would follow suit. Since the 1980s, generative SLA researchers have explored whether there is an innate predisposition for SLA. As psycholinguists, their remit has been to investigate the internal, mental processes implicated in second language development.

This research agenda is primarily interested in the properties of language produced by learners, not learning as a product of teaching. Those applied linguists who are interested in teaching tend to base their research on functional, cognitive and/or sociocultural frameworks, in part because these approaches have clearer compatibility with questions of pedagogy. Sadly, academic debate can at times lead to rigid divisions. There is a tendency for each approach to see itself as the only correct approach. When fierce debates do not find any resolution, it is easy for factions to develop. It is easier to work within one's own faction, debating minor points within an agreed general theory, than to continue to engage with others whose basic theory is at odds. In time, this can give rise to disparate subfields with separate conferences and academic journals, resulting in a situation in which academic discussions between the factions are more and more rare. This lack of cooperation within a discipline can leave the impression that the 'experts' themselves do not have the answers, and result in an atmosphere which cannot be said to be welcoming, supportive or helpful for language teachers.

Another hurdle for teachers to overcome is the abstract nature of linguistic formalisms. While the discussions of Generative Linguistics in this book so far have hopefully been clear, you will probably agree that they are relatively complex. In truth, they are carefully selected points presented in a way that avoids the more complex formalisms of the theory.

The most fundamental criticism of generative SLA, however, comes from applied linguists who point out that there has been a lack of concrete findings from generative research that can give guidance for decision-making in the classroom. While it may seem a natural step to apply findings from research on SLA to the teaching of language as they emerge, meaningful application is only possible once there is a clear view of what needs to be applied. Thanks to the commitment of SLA researchers, there is now a large body of findings, with some generally accepted trends beginning to emerge. This means that there are now enough robust findings from a wealth of studies to begin making connections to the language classroom. The aim of this book is to make some of these connections. In the remainder of this chapter we will consider some of the landmark research in SLA in order to explore the implications for language teaching in subsequent chapters. Hopefully, in doing so, we will also take a step towards closing the gap that currently exists between generative linguistic research and language teaching.

Early Findings: Systematic Development

SLA research has a long tradition of looking for parallels between second language development and native first language development. If there are similarities between the two, then this could be support for the claim that there are similar mechanisms at play in both processes. From a generative perspective, any such similarities would be attributed to UG. The research comparing first and second language acquisition in the 1960s and 1970s, however, did not rely heavily on generative theory, but instead looked for general trends in second language development. Because of the interest in comparisons with native child development, much of the early focus was on children, typically between the ages of five and nine in naturalistic settings.

An important example of this kind of research is the morpheme order studies that investigated L2 learners in order to look for parallels between SLA and the findings of Brown (1973), which showed a regular order in the acquisition of English inflectional morphemes by native-speaking children. The first set of studies tested sixty Spanish and fifty-five Chinese children learning English as a second language (Dulay and Burt 1973; Dulay and Burt 1974). The results showed a similar pattern of development between the child L2 learners and Brown's native speaker learners. Curious whether the result had to do with age, Bailey, Madden and Krashen (1974) tested seventy-three adult learners of English and also found a similar developmental pattern. This research led to the conclusion that second language development occurs in stages, and that the stages are much like those in first language development.

Of course, SLA is different from FLA. For one thing, second language learners have a native language to begin with. The role of the native language, or L1 transfer, is another strand of SLA research which has received much attention. In fact, Bailey, Madden and Krashen (1974) were also interested in this second issue. In addition to testing adults, they constructed their test so that forty of the test subjects were speakers from eleven different native language backgrounds, while thirty-three were Spanish speakers. When analysing their results in terms of native language background, they found no meaningful differences in the developmental patterns. Numerous studies have replicated these findings, leading to a general consensus that English morphemes are acquired in stages which are comparable to those in native L1 acquisition, regardless of the age or native language of the learner. The interesting question for researchers is to explain why.

Though there are different explanations for why this regularity occurs,[7] the more general conclusion which shares wide agreement is that second language learning is not a random process of decreasing L1 transfer effects, but instead one of language development that happens in stages that follow general trends, and that these stages are similar for children and adults, regardless of their native language. This conclusion, accepted by the 1980s, was compatible with the general conclusion coming out of the work in Contrastive Analysis and Error Analysis, which argued that L2 development is systematic. The influence of generative theory on this conclusion was to suggest a new understanding of the source of this systematicity. Researchers hypothesised that UG was the constraining mechanism underlying second language development. If this was true, then the better the properties of UG were understood, the more it would be possible to predict and explain L2 development.

This recognition of the systematicity of L2 learners' grammars required some new terminology. A new label was needed because it would be inaccurate to refer to the learner's grammar as the target grammar, or as an incorrect version of the target grammar. An English speaker learning Spanish, for example, does not have a grammar of Spanish. Thus, Larry Selinker (1972) coined the term interlanguage to refer to the grammar of the L2 learner; an English speaker learning Spanish will have a developing Spanish interlanguage. In addition to being systematic, an interlanguage typically reflects both the target language and the native language. It will change from stage to stage, but does so in a principled way; it is not simply an imperfect attempt at the target language. Most remarkably for generative researchers, interlanguages have been shown to have elements which are natural to language, but not a part of the learner's native language nor the target language they are trying to acquire. As will be discussed in the next section, this has been taken as strong evidence for UG.

As the concept of UG has gained support and acceptance, the question of the extent to which second language development is 'natural', depending on biological mechanisms, has arisen. After all, it is quite obvious that first and second language acquisition are different. This question became framed as one of 'access to UG' in non-native language development, particularly for adults. Like some of the early metaphorical language for native language development, the use of the term 'access' suggests some active, explicit or intentional process. For this reason, it is more accurate to use the term **UG-constrained development**. We will explore the question of UG in SLA in the next section.

UG-Constrained Development

If L2 development is constrained by UG, this entails that L2 development can also be aided by principles and parameters. Guided by the knowledge that L2 development seems different from native language development, however, researchers wondered if the difference had something to do with the fact that the L2 learner already has a complete set of parameters which underlie their native language. The question then becomes whether or not a learner can 'reset' their parameters. Another possibility is that there is some maturational timeline which puts limits on the age span during which parameters can be reset. The quest to determine the role of UG thus became understood in terms of parameter resetting.

One of the most thoroughly discussed parameters is the so-called **Null Subject Parameter**, which regulates whether or not a language requires a subject to be expressed in order for a sentence to be grammatical. As shown in (6a), subject-less declarative sentences are ungrammatical in English, a language with a negative null subject parameter setting. An example of a language that has a positive null subject parameter setting is Spanish, shown in (6b).

(6) a. *Speak English.
     b. Habl-o Ingles.
         speak-1sg English
         'I speak English.'

According to linguistic theory, the null subject parameter includes a cluster of properties, including the properties of modal verbs like *must* and *should*. One well-known early study by Hilles (1986) was a case study which followed the language development of a 12-year-old Spanish boy called Jorge, learning English over a period of 10 months. She found that, at first, Jorge produced English sentences without subjects and without modal verbs. At the time when he began to include subjects regularly in his sentences, he also began to use modal verbs correctly. This result was very exciting, as it suggested parameters could be reset, indicating a role for UG in second language development. But unfortunately, other research on the null subject parameter found learners did not acquire all the 'clustered' properties together. As a result, based on the studies conducted thus far, it is still unclear whether L2 learners, particularly adults, can reset parameters.

One possible reason for mixed results found across studies is the unfortunate fact that there has been considerable disagreement by formal linguists over the exact set of properties which are seen to cluster with the null subject parameter. Even more unfortunately, there is considerable debate over the exact linguistic properties associated with any of the parameters that have been proposed in the parameter resetting literature so far. This messy picture has discouraged many, and is one legitimate reason for the warning by some researchers that SLA results should be applied with caution.

More current research in SLA is taking a much finer-grained approach, recognising that language includes a range of aspects from syntax and phonology to lexical and functional properties. This more sophisticated approach is yielding a view in which different domains within language are seen to develop differently. We will consider one example later in this chapter. This continuous refinement of research in formal linguistics may mean that L2 researchers will have to keep refining their research as well. None the less, the results showing some degree of parameter resetting are enough to suggest that it would be unwise to rule out UG altogether.

There is other evidence of UG-constrained L2 development. As mentioned above, there is evidence that the interlanguage of L2 learners sometimes includes elements of language which are found in neither their native language nor the target language. Learners sometimes go through a stage in which they seem to have a setting for a parameter that is one of the options available for natural languages, but which occurs in languages to which they have not been exposed. A study by Clahsen and Hong (1995) of the null subject parameter which investigated Korean learners of German seemed to find just this. In order to make sense of this study, we need to know a few facts about Korean and German, and a bit more about null subjects.

There are, in fact, two types of null subject languages. The first is a language that allows null subjects because the verb form shows enough information about the subject to allow the subject to be omitted. We saw this in example (6) above for Spanish. The verb *hablar*, 'to speak' in Spanish, has the 1st person singular -o ending, allowing us to identify the subject as the 1st person singular, 'I', in Spanish, even though it is omitted.

The second type of null subject language is exemplified by Korean (and Japanese and Chinese). In these languages, verbs do not show the person/number properties of the subject, but it is still possible to leave out a subject – but only if the subject of the sentence is clear from the context. So, for example, if you just explained that your friend, John, was in a car accident, it would be grammatical to say (the equivalent of) *Got hurt.* in Korean because it is clear from the context that it was John who got hurt. So, now we have three options. There are languages that do not allow null subjects, like English. Then there are languages that allow them because of verbal morphology, like Spanish (and Italian and Polish). Thirdly, there are languages that allow null subjects if the discourse context makes the subject so clear that it does not need stating, like Korean.

So what kind of language is German? German verbs show person/ number, like Spanish, but with regard to null subjects, German is like

English; subjects are required in declarative sentences. So, Clahsen and Hong were curious to see what Korean speakers would do with their subjects when learning German. Thirteen of the thirty-three learners tested seemed to know that German requires subjects, while two seemed to be still using the Korean null subject setting. Because the remaining eighteen do not seem to have either setting, Clahsen and Hong conclude that parameters are not reset in L2 development, with their ultimate conclusion being that UG has no role in second language development.

These results have been looked at again by other researchers, however. White (2003b) notes that five of these learners seemed to have the setting not of Korean nor of German, but of a null subject language like Spanish! This is seen in results of Korean speakers who seem to know the verbal agreement properties in German, despite the fact that Korean does not include verbal agreement, but not the null subject properties. She interprets this as evidence that there is some universal guiding principle for L2 development. This would account for results that cannot be explained by the influence of the native language, nor directly from the input from the target language. Of course, this conclusion has been made based on only five learners of English. However, there have been other studies of other parameters that have also shown three sets of results – learners who have developed the target settings, learners who still have their native setting, and then an intriguing set of learners who seem to have a setting that is known to exist in natural languages, but not the setting of either language in question.[8] These kinds of results have been taken as evidence for a role for UG in L2 development.

As you can see, this kind of argumentation is complex, requiring cross-linguistic study and a sophisticated understanding of formal properties of linguistics. Ideally, teachers will be able to study enough linguistics to make sense of this kind of research. Arguably, however, it is the role of applied linguists and teacher trainers to make these kinds of results clear for teachers. At the very least, it is important that you as a teacher are aware of the overall conclusions, regardless of whether you take in the more theoretical details of this kind of research.

There is another line of research investigating the role of UG that has also emerged. As in native FLA, researchers have asked whether learners come to know subtle properties of a language without being explicitly taught. In other words, can we find evidence that learners go beyond the input, as they do in L1 acquisition, to acquire so-called 'poverty of the stimulus' phenomena. The logic is that, if a learner knows something that has not been taught and is not readily apparent in natural input, this knowledge has to have come from somewhere. Of course, the native language is one possible source. So these studies have to take L1 influence into account as well.

The first study of this type was done with English learners of Japanese by Kanno (1997, 1998), who studied a linguistic property known as the Overt Pronoun Constraint, another property associated with null subject languages.[9] This constraint is to do with the interpretation of the word 'who'. Consider the English sentence below:

(7)   **Who**$_{i/j}$ said that **he**$_i$ bought a car?

In English, 'who' has two possible interpretations, either referring to the same person as the person that bought the car, or referring to someone else not mentioned in the sentence. In other words, (7) could involve either one or two people – either the same person bought a car and claimed to buy it, or one person bought it but someone else is telling us about it. We can illustrate this dual interpretation on paper by using subscripts. The little *i* is indexed to the pronoun *he*, as well as to an unspecified referent outside the sentence, shown by the index *j*.

In null subject languages like Spanish and Japanese, the interpretation facts change depending on whether there is an overt subject in the embedded clause or not. In null subject languages, if the embedded clause has an overt pronoun then (the equivalent of) 'who' can only refer to someone outside the sentence. This is shown for Japanese in (8):

(8)   **dare**$_j$-ga   **kare**$_i$-ga   kuruma-o   katta   to   itta   no?
       who$_j$-subj   **he**$_i$-subj   car-obj   bought   that   said   Q
       'Who$_j$ said that he$_i$ bought a car?'

If the embedded clause does not have a subject, (shown as Ø below), then 'who' refers to the same person as the one who bought the car:

(9)   **dare**$_i$-ga   Ø$_i$ kuruma-o   katta   to   itta   no?
       who$_i$-subj   **he**$_i$ car-obj   bought   that   said   Q
       'Who$_i$ said that he$_i$ bought a car?'

You will probably agree that this Overt Pronoun Constraint is quite subtle. Kanno argues that this UG constraint is not one of which native Japanese speakers, not even teachers, are consciously aware.

Importantly, it is not taught in Japanese language classrooms. This qualifies it is as a poverty of the stimulus phenomenon. Kanno tested English learners of Japanese and found that, despite never having been taught the Overt Pronoun Constraint, about 80% of them knew it. Because this constraint is so subtle, it is unlikely that learners would be exposed to many (if any) examples of these limits on interpretation in natural/un-instructed input. Therefore, the notion of poverty of the stimulus seems relevant not just for native L1 acquisition, but (adult) L2 acquisition as well. As learners from a negative null subject language like English acquire a positive null subject language like Japanese, this kind of UG principle becomes part of the learner's interlanguage. This research has inspired other poverty of the stimulus research and is taken as straightforward evidence for UG-constrained development in second language development.[10]

Instructed L2 Development

So if L2 development is constrained by UG, does this mean that there is no place for explicit instruction? Most generative research has avoided questions of classroom instruction. However, this question of UG-constrained development vs explicit language learning was the basis for a study by White (1992), who investigated French learners of English, looking at adverb placement. French and English differ in terms of where adverbs can occur:

(10) Les chats **attrapent** **souvent** les souris.
      Cats   catch   often   mice.
      'Cats   often   catch   mice.'

White studied two classes of 10–12-year-old French-speaking children. One class was explicitly taught the properties of adverb placement in English. The other class was only exposed to lots of examples of English sentences with adverbs in them. The class who was taught explicitly scored higher on a test of adverb placement than the other class, who did not know that adverbs need to go before the verb in English. This experiment would have been clear evidence that teaching is effective except for the unfortunate fact that these same two classes scored equally badly on an adverb placement test a year later.[11]

From this study it seems that explicit teaching alone does not have long-term value, at least for some aspects of language. Knowing that learners do develop proficiency in classrooms, one way to interpret this result would be to say that some aspects of language development depend on biological constraints that are not readily affected by explicit instruction. This may be especially true of particular areas of language. It is generally agreed that it is more difficult for learners to know what is not possible in a language than what is possible. The French children in White's study will initially have a French rule for adverb placement. When they learn English they may in the short term be able to remember not to use the French rule if they are told that it is not correct for English. But the fact that they no longer remembered a year later suggests that their linguistic competence for this aspect of English did not actually develop. What remains an open question is whether this kind of knowledge could ever develop. Unfortunately, research by generative SLA researchers on this and on the effect of explicit instruction remains extremely limited.

Age and Language Development

Generative SLA researchers often argue that the main reason for failure among adult L2 learners is input. L2 learning that takes place in a classroom is very different in nature to learning in the home, both in terms of quality and quantity of input, to say nothing of questions of urgency and need. L2 development in more naturalistic settings is also generally different. Many immigrant learners, for example, continue to live and associate with fellow native speakers even if they need to operate in the target language for work. And there are the two other fundamental differences between L1 and L2 development that we have already mentioned: the question of age and the role of the native language.

The question of age is usually referred to as the Critical Period debate. Like many notions in language development, the Critical Period Hypothesis was originally proposed for native language development.[12] The claim that natural language development is limited to a particular age has seen the most research, however, in second language studies. The Critical Period, as proposed by Lenneberg (1967), is tied to biology with the time frame for language acquisition often linked to maturation. Specific evidence for the start and finish of this time frame, however, is hotly contested. The influential early study by Johnson and Newport (1989) separated L2 speakers who arrived in the US between the ages of 3 and 15 from those who arrived after the age of 17. They found that, on all proficiency measures, those with an earlier age of arrival outperformed those who arrived later.

Like most influential early work, this particular study has been carefully analysed, criticised and subject to many replications. As we mentioned in Chapter 1, the generalisation that younger is better is not straightforward since younger learners are in fact, not better as regards short-term development; more mature learners learn faster, at least initially.[13] Indeed, both how young and how much better are not agreed upon.

Importantly, this does not mean that older people cannot be successful learners. In addition to examples that you may know of personally, there are documented cases of people beginning to learn a language as adults and managing to achieve what seems like a native level of proficiency.[14] For there truly to be a biological Critical Period, it would have to be the case that no adults ever manage a native-like proficiency. Because this is not the case, most researchers now think in terms of a **sensitive period**, instead of a critical period. Learning in the sensitive period makes higher ultimate attainment more possible, but there is no universal cut-off point for language development. Though adults have an advantage in terms of how quickly they can learn language in the short term, in the long term younger learners can catch up and pass the adults if given a sufficient learning environment.[15]

It also seems clear that age affects different aspects of language development differently. Generally speaking, phonology seems consistently more difficult for older language learners than syntax. Certain aspects of syntax, such as verb–object word order or question formation, by contrast, seem not to be affected by age. Yet other aspects, such as the adverb–verb order we discussed above, seem problematic. This finding that age effects vary in terms of aspect of language has led to the conclusion that there are **multiple sensitive periods**. As we will see in the next section, differences in development from one aspect of language to another constitute a conclusion that is clearly emerging from research in second language development.

Differences by Linguistic Domains in Second Language Development

Given the complexity of language, it is not surprising that the process of language development is complex as well. In the discussion so far we have focused on one aspect of language at specific points of development in order to understand the process better. Focusing on one aspect alone, however, cannot reflect the reality of the complex situation. We will try to put some of the pieces of the puzzle together as we discuss one set of well-known case studies which focus on an area of language which does not require sophisticated understanding of formal linguistics: the tendency for non-native speakers of English to leave out inflectional morphemes when they speak.

Lardiere's (1998) study of Patty, a Chinese adult leaner of English, and White's (2003a) study of SD, an adult Turkish learner of English, focused on learners whose English developed naturalistically as adults living and working in an English-speaking environment. These studies provide empirical evidence for a phenomenon well known to English language teachers. Recordings of their speech over many years document that both these learners regularly omit articles, *the* and *a*, as well as plural -*s*, 3rd person singular -*s* on verbs and past tense -*ed*, and they make errors of form with the copular verb *to be*. While they both make these errors, there are differences in amount. Patty makes significantly more errors with **inflectional morphology** than SD. This can be attributed to L1 transfer since the Chinese dialects that Patty speaks have very little verbal morphology, while Turkish is rich in morphology. At the same time, the very similar rates of errors on articles bolster the argument that L1 affects interlanguage development since neither Mandarin nor Turkish has articles.

Though the study of second language development has always recognised the existing native language as a potential factor in development, in the early days of generative SLA there was a tendency to downplay this factor because it was associated with the behaviourist ideas of habit formation. Language 'habits' from the native language were seen as transferring to the second language context. While this understanding of L1 transfer was refuted, the association between the terminology and the concept meant early researchers hesitated to use it. With the passage of time, however, this association has mostly disappeared.

Yet much of the research in L1 transfer still takes on a Contrastive Analysis Hypothesis type way of thinking. Though it was largely refuted, it is hard to shake the Contrastive Analysis intuition that problems will occur where there are differences between two languages and development facilitated where they are the same. And results like Patty's and SD's continue to reinforce this intuition. However, a closer look shows that the finding is more complex than a simplistic Contrastive Analysis view. What is interesting in both of these case studies is that, irrespective of L1 transfer, the lack of accuracy tends to be a result of omission, not one of using the incorrect form, apart from forms of *to be*. In fact, White found that SD uses the wrong verbal morphology only forty-nine times in 1,744 obligatory verbal contexts; that is a rate of just 0.02%. That the lack of accuracy is to do with verbal inflection being left out and not the use of the wrong form is a systematic feature of development that suggests some kind of production error.

Despite the errors relating to inflectional morphology, there is strong evidence for mastery of related underlying rules of syntax. Both Patty and SD are completely accurate with subject and object pronouns, with accuracy rates of 99 to 100%. These findings are significant because both obligatory subjects and pronoun forms are understood to be a part of the same parameter as the one that requires verbal inflection. Thus, the fact that subjects are supplied and pronoun forms are consistently correct when verbal inflection is inconsistent is evidence that underlying rules of syntax are present. The lack of accuracy with inflectional morphemes like verb inflection and articles must have something to do with some aspect of language production and not knowledge of the grammatical constraints. The main conclusion, then, is that some aspects of grammar, such as pronouns and subjects, seem to be easier to acquire and less affected by the learner's L1 than others: namely, articles or verbal inflection. Additionally, the general finding that different aspects of language develop differently is again supported.

Recent developments in technology have allowed us to explore this idea of variable development from a physical point of view. Researchers in the 1990s were overly optimistic that research using new technologies such as event-related potentials (ERP) studies, which measure electrical activity in the brain, and fMRI scans, which measure blood flow as a way of mapping brain functioning, could pinpoint which areas of the brain were associated with which specific aspects of language.[16] It quickly became apparent, however, that even this sophisticated technology was not enough to truly tease apart all of the elements implicated in language. While research cannot exactly pinpoint where different facets of language are stored, it can and does show that the different aspects are processed differently. The clearest result that is emerging is a dissociation between grammatical and semantic processing. Study of second language speakers shows that age has a direct effect on syntactic processing. Those learners who began learning as young children show the same syntactic processes as native speakers, while older learners do not. For semantic processing, closeness to native-like processing seems to depend on proficiency in the language, regardless of age.[17]

Of direct relevance to our discussion of function words and morphology, neuroimaging research seems to suggest that, as with more core grammatical features of language, age seems to be the main factor for determining whether second language speaker processing ability is native-like or not. Yet what is shown by behavioural studies is that, despite differences in processing as revealed by physical studies of the brain, learners do seem to be able to know even very subtle grammatical properties of language. What is emerging from the research, therefore, is a view in which some areas of language, such as functional morphology, seem to cause difficulty in language development.

Yet it is important to distinguish between knowledge as evidenced through research and production ability as perceived in real-life interaction. By knowing which aspects of language will develop 'naturally' and which need explicit attention, there is hope that, with perseverance, even the most intractable aspects of language can be overcome by diligent language learners with the help of highly competent language teachers. Thus, even the most abstract theoretical findings have useful implications for language teaching. We will come back to this point when we discuss the implications of SLA research in Chapter 5.

Returning to our case studies, the research on Patty and SD has also been influential in discussions of fossilisation. Fossilisation may occur because of some biological constraint on language development, through some kind of sensitive period. It may also be a result of insufficient quantity and/or quality of input. Additionally, the influence of the native language may keep the second language from developing. The two case studies discussed here show that L1 transfer can have persistent effects even at end-state levels of proficiency. This somewhat pessimistic view does not sound like good news for the language teacher. Would it be possible for these or any seemingly fossilised learners to overcome this kind of inaccuracy in inflectional morphology?

Fortunately, a recently proposed framework allows us to revaluate this view of inevitable failure. The Modular On-line Growth and Use of Language (MOGUL) proposal of Sharwood Smith and Truscott allows for a different, and pedagogically more encouraging, understanding of what is happening in the case of Patty, SD and the many other very proficient English speakers who none the less can be somewhat inconsistent in supplying inflectional elements in their language production. We will wait to discuss MOGUL until the next chapter because it contains elements that are not strictly limited to a generative view. We will instead conclude this chapter on language as a biological property by asking whether it can account for all that we know about second language development.

CONCLUSION: WHAT A COMPLETE THEORY OF SLA NEEDS TO EXPLAIN

In a very useful book VanPatten and Williams (2007) outline ten phenomena which have been observed in SLA. Their reason for doing this is to challenge the different branches of linguistics to explain what we know about SLA adequately. Those ten observations are:

1. Exposure to input is necessary for SLA.
2. A good deal of SLA happens incidentally.
3. Learners come to know more than what they have been exposed to in the input.
4. Learners' output (speech) often follows predictable paths with predictable stages in the acquisition of a given structure.
5. Second language learning is variable in its outcome.
6. Second language learning is variable across linguistic subsystems.
7. There are limits on the effects of frequency on SLA.
8. There are limits on the effect of a learner's first language on SLA.
9. There are limits on the effects of instruction on SLA.
10. There are limits on the effects of output (learner production) on language acquisition.

(VanPatten and Williams 2007: 9–12)

The rest of VanPatten and Williams's book consists of chapters written by SLA researchers from different linguistic frameworks. The chapter devoted to the generative perspective is written by Lydia White. In that chapter, she explains how the biological view of language addresses Observations 1, 3, 7, 8 and 9.

We have also noted that, despite any innate UG-constrained predisposition for language that may still exist among second language learners, input is crucial for language development (Observation 1). The above discussion of the poverty of the stimulus phenomenon, in which learners come to know more than what they have been exposed to in the input, is evidence for Observation 3. The limits on frequency, Observation 7, are also clear from studies like Kanno's work on the Overt Pronoun Constraint. With very few instances in the input, learners acquired this constraint. If you interpret this same observation in the opposite direction to say that, even with robust frequency, there are limits, then the case studies of Patty and SD also support this observation; despite the very frequent occurrence of inflectional morphology in the input, these learners have not mastered them in their own speech. The limits of the influence of the first language on second language development (Observation 8) have been seen since the early morpheme order studies showing similar orders of acquisition regardless of native language. The null subject parameter studies discussed in this chapter also show this result, as learners from different language backgrounds are able to re-set this parameter. And finally, White's own study of adverb placement clearly shows that the effects of instruction are limited, Observation 9, at least in the long term.

What about the other five observations? The observation that learners' output often follows predictable paths with predictable stages in the acquisition of a given structure (Observation 4) has also been supported by the generative view. We saw this in the early morpheme order studies, and also in the parameter re-setting literature showing that some learners go from their native language parameter to a mid-point in which their interlanguage includes a setting that is neither the native nor the target language setting.[18,19] We have seen that Observation 6, stating that second language learning is variable across linguistic subsystems, is an area that has recently attracted a fair amount of attention in the generative research. While it has long been acknowledged that phonology and syntax seem to develop differently among adult L2 learners, research on the subsystems of syntax vs morphology vs the lexicon is also finding differences in development. Emerging technologies suggest that the differences may reflect qualitative difference between types of linguistic knowledge. The ability for modular linguistic knowledge to develop later in life may differ, for example, when compared to non-modular knowledge. This is currently cutting-edge research with numerous hypotheses being proposed and tested.

The remaining three observations (Observation 2, 5 and 10) are not readily accounted for by the generative view of language. Note that, for two of the three observations, however, it is not necessarily the case that a biological view of language contradicts them; it is more the case that generative linguists have not felt the need to address these points. In saying that a good deal of SLA happens incidentally (Observation 2), VanPatten and Williams are pointing to research that shows that, while engaging in tasks that explicitly highlight some aspect of language, learners can come to know other aspects of language that are not being explicitly highlighted. Because generative research assumes this, there has been little direct study of the process of incidental learning itself. Instead, the focus has been on the properties of the interlanguage that develop from incidental learning. Similarly, generativist researchers have not been interested in the observation that there are limits on the effects of output (learner production) on language acquisition (Observation 10). This question has not been relevant in a view which depends so crucially on a process whereby an internal mental system reacts to external input. Production in this view is simply a product of what the internal system is capable of at any given moment in time.

That second language learning is variable in its outcome (Observation 5) may seem problematic for the biological approach because we are all considered biologically the same in terms of predisposition for language. We can point to differences arising from a difference in L1 transfer from one native language to another, but the variability among learners with the same L1 would not be explained this way. Perhaps answers will emerge from the current research showing that different aspects of language develop differently. Aside from this, generativists explain learner variability by looking more closely at differences in the nature of the input.[20] Taking a broader view, there are other clear limitations to the generative view, including the absence of research on the functional aspects of language use, as well as discussion of the role of social context in language development. These two charges form the foundation of Functional and Sociocultural views of language, respectively. We will briefly explore these and other views of language in the next chapter before considering a recent approach which tries to account for a fuller range of research relevant to language learning and teaching.

FOR DISCUSSION

1. The examples of linguistic ambiguity given in this chapter are based on English. Can you think of examples of language ambiguity in other languages? Try to think of examples in which the ambiguity lies in the structure of the sentence as opposed to word-level ambiguity (in other words, one word that has two meanings).
2. Consider the five properties of modular knowledge. Are they relevant to knowledge of a second language?

3. Some people argue that if, as argued here, there is evidence that SLA is constrained by UG, then second language learners should be able to acquire language just like native language speakers. Explain why this logic is flawed.

4. All of the SLA research presented in this chapter takes a mentalist, or psycholinguistic, point of view. What effect, if any, would non-mentalist factors such as the following have on the claims in this chapter: motivation, aptitude, level of education, gender, cultural background?

5. Consider each of the ten Observations about second language development in terms of your own personal experience. Do you have any personal examples to support them? Do you have any experiences which seem to contradict any of them?

6. Discuss each of the ten Observations in terms of classroom language teaching. What implications can you draw?

NOTES

1. The original version can be found in Chomsky (1981) with an updated version in Chomsky (1986).

2. To read the original proposal for Minimalism, see Chomsky (1995). For an introductory treatment of Minimalism, see Radford (1997). For a more technical treatment, see Adger (2003).

3. For an early example, see Diller (1971). More recent examples include Ellis (1997) and Kramsch (2003).

4. For more discussion, see Lado (1957) and Sharwood Smith (1994).

5. One notable exception has been Patsy Lightbown; see Lightbown (1985, 2000, 2003) and Lightbown and Spada (2006).

6. See, for example, Thomas (1965) or Rutherford (1968).

7. While generativists such as Krashen or Dulay and Burt (1973, 1974) see this as evidence for an in-built syllabus guiding language development, cognitivists such as Goldschneider and DeKeyser (2001) look to the nature of the input itself to explain the regularity.

8. Other work exploring parameter values that are not found in the L1 or the target grammar has focused on the properties of reflexives (Finer 1991; Finer and Broselow 1986; and MacLaughlin 1998) and case checking (Schwartz and Sprouse 1994).

9. See Rothman and Iverson (2007) for research on the Overt Pronoun Constraint in Spanish.

10. Other poverty of the stimulus studies have focused on other subtle areas of semantics. See, for example, the work of Laurent Dekydtspotter and colleagues (Dekydtspotter, Sprouse and Anderson 1997; Dekydtspotter, Sprouse and Thyre 1998; Dekydtspotter, Sprouse, Swanson and Thyre

1999; Dekydtspotter 2001; Dekydtspotter and Hathorn 2005) and Marsden (2005, 2008, 2009).

11. Schwartz and Gubala-Ryzak (1992) reanalyse White's data, arguing that there is evidence that, even in the post-test done immediately after teaching, the learners are applying a linear rule and not showing knowledge of the linguistic constraints on adverb placement.

12. For obvious ethical reasons, it is not possible to design Critical Period studies in native language acquisition. Unfortunate 'natural' situations that have arisen often include serious abuse or neglect which makes it difficult to compare language development to usual native development.

13. For more discussion of the Critical Period Hypothesis and relevant studies, see Hensch (2004) and Singleton and Ryan (2004).

14. For specific studies, see Birdsong (1992); Ioup, Boustagui, El Tigi and Moselle (1994); Bongaerts, Planken and Schils (1995); White and Genesee (1996); and Bongaerts (1999).

15. See note 7 of Chapter 5.

16. See Mueller (2005) for a review of ERP studies.

17. See Chapter 4 of Slabakova (2008) for a discussion of neuroimaging studies and second language development.

18. For a well-known case study showing parameter re-setting in child L2 acquisition, see Haznedar (2001).

19. Many other studies from the late 1970s into the 1990s have supported a view of developmental stages, with researchers offering explanations from a range of theoretical perspectives from generative to cognitive linguistic frameworks. Well-known examples include the very large European Science Foundation (ESF) project of 1982–8 (see Klein and Perdue 1997) and the Zweitspracherwerb, Italienischer, Spanischer und Portugiesischer Arbeiter (ZISA) project (Meisel, Clahsen and Pienemann 1981).

20. See Piske and Young-Scholten (2009) and papers within for a discussion of input.

4

LANGUAGE AS A TOOL FOR COMMUNICATION

૭~

INTRODUCTION

We began this book by pointing out that there are many perspectives on how to characterise language, and we have discussed how language develops. The main thrust of the book, however, has been to present a mentalist view, and the generativist view in particular, both because it is such an influential view in theoretical linguistics and because it is the view that receives the least amount of discussion in terms of the language classroom. One reason for this is the conceptual distance between abstract linguistic theory and the practice of teaching. Hopefully this book is able to narrow this distance somewhat. It is not a coincidence that the most formal view of language has had the least application in the language classroom. As we began to see in Chapter 3, Generative Linguistics relies on highly abstract constructs and formalisms which can be daunting for anyone without thorough training in theoretical linguistics. As may become apparent in this chapter, other approaches have been more accessible. And more importantly, other approaches consider application to the classroom as a natural objective for their research. Generative linguists, on the whole, have not taken this view.

Unfortunately, there are limits on the extent to which we can explore all the different approaches to language in a single book. This chapter presents an overview of the major approaches, categorised here under the broadly defined labels of Functional, Sociocultural and Cognitive Approaches. To some extent, these all stand in opposition to the generative view. Some are opposed to what they see as a strictly rationalist approach whereby language is decomposed into its smallest possible units. This kind of atomistic method invites the criticism of not seeing the forest for the trees. The other difference is deeply philosophical, as these approaches see language and all of the grammatical principles associated with language as the outcome of meaning and thought instead of viewing grammar as its own system independent from meaning.

In other words, these approaches differ from the Generative Approach in terms of the importance they attach to meaning. While generativists view meaning as a by-product of what can be expressed though formal linguistic rules, these approaches see meaning and the making of meaning as the driving force for language. To the extent that all of these approaches have an interest in the way we use and understand language, they could all, broadly speaking, be considered functional. However, the label 'Functional' will be reserved for a more specific view with Cognitive and **Sociocultural** approaches distinct enough to warrant separate labels.

Because they are all interested in the way we use language they can be (and often are) viewed as in fundamental opposition to a generative view, as suggested in our brief discussion of the form–function divide in Chapter 1. The difference is a real one for linguists concerned with fundamental questions of how language is organised. As we have seen, for formalists, the building blocks of language are grammatical constraints like subject–verb agreement. For functionalists, meaningful concepts like time and space form the foundation of language. While for most linguists these are irreconcilable differences, the view taken in this book is that there is no reason why we should not research and understand both form and function/use.

In fact, we can go further to promote a more conciliatory view that does not dwell on opposition, but instead focuses on the extent to which the different approaches are asking different questions. An even more optimistic view is that there is a degree of convergence which is beginning to emerge among the opposing theories. Regardless, the fact that a range of views exists points to the reality that no single approach seems to be able to account for all of the factors relating to language, and its development and use. Because the different approaches have different useful contributions for understanding language development, there is every reason why a good language teacher should be well aware of the range of ideas.

Though Generativism has made great gains in explaining cross-linguistic regularities in language and language acquisition, there are some very large areas that are not included in the Generative Approach. The function of language as a communicative tool is a glaring omission. In this chapter we will discuss how Functionalism is an approach that takes language use as its primary emphasis. Questions about language function inevitably bring us to questions about social context and societal norms. This is what interests researchers taking a Socioculturalist Approach. The final approach to be discussed in this chapter, the Cognitive Approach, is one that has seen much influence from psychology. It is similar to the Generative Approach in its interest in the mental processes underlying language. But as we will see, the understanding of these processes is fundamentally at odds and much more in concert with a Functionalist Approach instead. After exploring each of these three approaches, we will consider a recent proposal that provides a framework that accommodates a wide range of views. We will use this framework to bring all the discussions of language and language development together, providing a unified basis from which to consider specific implications for the language classroom in the remainder of this book.

THE NOTION OF COMPETENCE

In the last chapter we referred to the 'competence' that speakers have of their (native) language. The idea presented there was that all humans develop a perfectly formed grammatical competence – unless there is some kind of pathological problem. The variation among speakers in their ability to use language, by contrast, has been attributed to differences in '**performance**'. Chomsky's now famous claim was: 'We thus make a fundamental distinction between *competence* (the speaker-hearer's knowledge of the language), and *performance,* the actual use of the language in concrete situations' (Chomsky 1965: 4). Chomsky's terms developed the contrast made by Swiss linguist, de Saussure, in the late 1800s between *langue,* which is the system that regulates language, and *parole,* the actual utterances produced by speakers. For generativists, this distinction provides a useful way to limit the scope of their research. For many others, however, this distinction has been seen as not useful, to the point of being absurd. Dell Hymes countered Chomsky's distinction by proposing what he called **communicative competence** to characterise what speakers need to know in order to be communicatively competent in a speech community.[1] This includes the social and cultural knowledge needed to understand and use linguistic forms in context, and in line with cultural norms.

The idea of communicative competence was well received by researchers interested in developing more effective means for teaching language. Canale and Swain (1980) refined Hymes's ideas by proposing four dimensions of communicative competence. Firstly, they acknowledged that **grammatical** or **linguistic competence** is an essential part of being communicatively competent. This type of competence includes the linguistic forms which are traditionally subsumed under the category of 'grammar', including rules of sentence structure, word formation and pronunciation.

The second dimension is **sociolinguistic** or **pragmatic competence**. This competence refers to the ability to use language to achieve communicative goals, drawing on the norms and conventions of the culture in question. This kind of competence depends on a knowledge of culture and the way we use language to participate in social context. For example, if you were invited to someone's home for dinner and asked, prior to the meal, whether you would like to use the bathroom, chances are you would understand that your host was inviting you to wash your hands. This product of cultural experience was not the communicative intent understood by a friend of my father's, a recent immigrant. When he did not return, my father went and discovered him in the bath – he did not want to offend the hosts by refusing their generous offer! In order to understand the propositional content of many of the exchanges that we have every day correctly, we must have a shared cultural knowledge, based on the norms of the culture.

In addition to these competences, Canale and Swain proposed **discourse competence**, which regulates the way in which language, whether spoken or written, is interconnected. Discourse competence in writing is understood in terms of coherence. Words and phrases such as *however, nevertheless* and *therefore,* for example, connect ideas, helping to hold the text together in a more meaningful way. Other more 'grammatical' discourse devices are personal pronouns like *him* or *her*, which are used to refer to a person already mentioned, and demonstrative pronouns like *this* and *that*, which also pick out an aforementioned referent. You can find an example of this latter type of discourse marker in the opening five words of this paragraph (as well as the examples in this very sentence).

In speaking, discourse markers signal a range of functions including interruption, disagreement, change of subject, and so on. Examples of phrases that serve these three functions, respectively, are given in (1):

(1) a. **Sorry, but** could you say that again?
     b. **Maybe so, but** couldn't we X instead?
     c. **So anyway,** what do you know about . . .?

You may have noticed that two of these examples use the word *but* and two use the word *so*. These little words are very hard to define in isolation, but serve a range of functions in discourse, making it difficult to articulate particular 'rules' for specific discourse markers. It is these kinds of linguistic phenomena that have inspired some linguists to insist on the importance of function in language. Systemic Functional Linguistics has developed very sophisticated analyses of how texts, both spoken and written, cohere to convey particular meaning. As we will see in the next section, for functionalists, the meaning of words like *so* and *but* depends on both neighbouring words/phrases and the wider context of discourse in which these words were uttered.

Before moving to our discussion of Functionalism, however, we need to consider the fourth and final competence proposed by Canale and Swain. **Strategic competence** refers to the ability to keep communication going, an important skill for language learners. A knowledge of strategic competence will help a speaker to negotiate language situations when there is a breakdown in communication. This may require requests for clarification on the part of the hearer or a repair by the speaker if it becomes clear that there has been a miscommunication. In discussing strategic competence, Canale and Swain point out that speakers use both verbal and non-verbal strategies. While this may sound like a step away from 'language', if the basis of language is communicative function, then all aspects of communication are relevant, from gesture to context to shared cultural norms.

ACCOUNTING FOR MEANING: A FUNCTIONAL APPROACH

Communicative function lies at the heart of the Functionalist Approach to language. While communicative function may sound like communicative competence, Functionalism actually rejects the notion of competence because it sees no value in any division between 'competence' and 'performance'. For functionalists, the one aspect of language that is explicitly sidelined in the Generative Approach is, in fact, the defining feature of language: meaning. The functional view sees language as a system for expressing meaning, and thus the primary purpose of language is to facilitate interaction and communication. This does not mean that language does not have structure, but the structure of language reflects functional or communicative uses, not some abstract, pre-determined set of grammatical constraints.

The 'father' of functionalism, British-born Michael Halliday,[2] was a student of John Firth, whose ideas about language grew out of the tradition of European linguistics known as the Prague School, a linguistic tradition rooted in literary studies and semiotics. **Semiotics** is the study of the relationship between signs and meaning. A word, for example, is a symbol which has an arbitrary relationship with the thing that it signifies. The interest in meaning through semiotics, and culture through literary studies provided a natural springboard for a functional view of language, in contrast with the more anthropologically oriented interests of early American linguists who focused on the structure of language. Functionalists are not necessarily dismissive of structural forms, but see forms as a realisation of function. Their interest is in exploring the mapping from function to form.

In fact, within what can be broadly labelled 'functionalism' lies a wide range of approaches to the question of grammar and structure.[3] At the one end, there are theories which may seem very much like the structuralist Generative Approach in the sense that they also view grammar as a system. These so-called 'structural-functional' approaches include Functional Grammar (Dik 1978) and Role and Reference Grammar, as originally proposed by Van Valin and Foley (1980). These contrast with other Functional Approaches which pay less attention to grammatical structure, focusing on language at the level of discourse and interaction instead. Because these approaches are less interested in what is traditionally understood as 'grammar', they can be viewed outside of the range of 'formal' theories about language which limit themselves to the more narrow level of the word and phrase. Going to the furthest end of the spectrum, there are functionalists who believe that there is no grammar at all, that instead grammar is a set of patterns that linguists have imposed on language in order to make sense of it. Before looking at the 'Construction Grammar' view, we will briefly explore a more middle-ground view within Functionalism, as exemplified in Halliday's **Systemic Functional Grammar (SFG)**.

Because the purpose of language is communication, for SFG a sentence is not seen so much as a combination of subject, verb and object, but as a vehicle for conveying information. As we saw in Chapter 1, it is the roles that different parts of a sentence play, and the relationship between these roles that are of interest to a functionalist. In a verbal exchange, for example, there will typically be given information that is already known to the speaker and the listener, and new information; the two combine to make the sentence meaningful. Functionalists use the term **theme** to refer to the starting point of a message, and **rheme**, for the idea that the speaker (or writer) moves to in order to develop or add to the theme. As in many languages, in English the theme tends to occur at the beginning of the sentence, while the rheme occurs at the end.

(2)   Our neighbour   has not yet returned our lawnmower.
            THEME   RHEME

By nature, this idea of theme and rheme relies crucially on context, perspective and meaning.

The most notable aspect of Halliday's SFG approach is the analysis of language at the level of **text**. SFG tends to take the text as the starting point from which to work 'down', looking at sentences, phrases and words, as well as 'up', looking at the context in which the text is produced.[4] While a lay person's understanding of the word *text* is usually limited to pieces of writing, for linguists *text* refers to both written and spoken forms of discourse. SFG has provided a framework to analyse texts in their broader contexts. For example, a text depends on the nature of the activity with which the text is associated, or **field**. Consider, for example, a university lecture. The nature of a university lecture is very much defined by the academic conventions of the university. Also important is the relationship between the participants associated with the text. Given the label **tenor,** this would, in our example, refer to the relationship between the lecturer and the students. Additionally, there is the question of **mode**, which is the medium through which the text is communicated. In our example, a lecture is a spoken text of a relatively formal variety.

Within the text, the forms that are chosen by the writer/speaker can reveal the communicative intent of the text as well. One linguistic mechanism in SFG is the notion of **grammatical metaphor**. By using the word metaphor, this term captures the way that grammatical forms can be extended beyond their literal meaning to have a particular function. One well-known example of grammatical metaphor is that of **nominalisation**. Consider the examples in (3):

(3)   a.   **The great migration from Africa** saw early humans reach Europe about 1.8m years ago.[5]
        b.   Early humans migrated from Africa to Europe about 1.8m years ago.

The option of using a nominalised form of an action as the subject of the sentence in (3a) serves a function beyond just acting as a grammatical subject. In (3b), the migration event invites disagreement because it is presented as a claim. In the normalised form presented in (3a), by contrast, the migration event itself is presented as known information suggesting that it is an indisputable fact, with the time of the event offered as new information. By choosing to use the nominalised form, the writer reinforces a particular view of the historical events, a very subtle but effective use of a grammatical form.

A functionalist view of language is interested in the work that language does and the effect that it achieves. Words and phrases are seen in terms of action. The example given in (4) illustrates this point:

(4)   Next?

Even without context, this single word promises action, especially with the added question mark. With context, this simple word is capable of triggering a series of events. Imagine a stony-faced immigration official looking beyond an exasperated traveller to the next person in the queue. The speech act performed by this simple word is to indicate that the communicative event has been concluded and that the traveller should move on to allow the next person to approach the desk. John Searle's **Speech Act Theory** develops the idea that language is functional.[6] The importance of context is clear in this kind of approach to language. Additionally, both spoken utterances and written text are interpreted with reference to the listener/reader's store of cultural understanding. While some of these norms may be similar across cultures, others will vary just as cultures vary. In this way, language is very much seen as social behaviour.

Because language depends on social norms and context, a functionalist analysis of language is often couched in terms of tendencies and not rules. After all, it would be difficult to articulate hard and fast rules when it comes to human behaviour. For many functionalists, an aversion to rules extends to what may be seen as more core properties of language as well. Regularities which have traditionally been captured by grammatical rules are seen by some as well-used patterns that have developed within speech communities.

This notion is at the heart of Construction Grammar.[7] A **construction** is an identifiable linguistic pattern associated with a particular meaning; it is a mapping between form and meaning. This mapping can be as small as a morpheme or a word and as large as a phrase or even a whole sentence. Building on seminal work by Charles Fillmore (1988), Goldberg (2006: 5) gives the following examples of constructions:[8]

(5)   a. Morpheme   e.g. *pre-, -ing*
      b. Word   e.g. *avocado, anaconda, and*
      c. Complex word   e.g. *daredevil, shoo-in*

d. Complex word (partially filled) e.g. [N-s] (for regular plurals)

e. Idiom (filled) e.g. *give the Devil his due*

f. Idiom (partially filled) e.g. *jog <someone's> memory*

g. Covariational conditional The Xer, the Yer
(e.g. *the more you think about it, the less you understand*)

h. Ditransitive Subj V Obj$_1$ Obj$_2$
(e.g. *he baked her a muffin*)

i. Passive Subj aux VP (PP)
(e.g. *the armadillo was hit by a car*)

Constructions like these become conventionalised by speech communities. This means that it is the users of language who determine the set of constructions that belong to the language, and the degree to which each construction is considered an acceptable part of the language. In this way, constructions are a product of language use and not the product of grammar rules. Thus, it is possible to take the next step and claim that grammar itself does not exist.

Support for this view comes from work in **Corpus Linguistics** which shows that much of language use is formulaic, consisting of set phrases that are repeatedly used. The growing body of corpus data shows regular use of **collocations** and **colligations**, words and phrases that tend to co-occur. As shown in the examples below, there are alternative ways of expressing the same concept. Corpus studies, however, show that as language users we tend to use the more formulaic alternatives.

Collocations:

(6) a. weather forecast (compare with: weather prediction)

  b. marked contrast (compare with: large contrast)

  c. up and down (compare with: down and up)

Colligations:

(7) a. to put it another way (compare with: to say it in a different way)

  b. an endless stream of people (compare with: an endless line of people)

  c. incite a riot (compare with: incite a protest)

While a view of language which says that there is no grammar may seem problematic for language teaching, it is well known to both teachers and students that most 'grammar rules' have exceptions. This makes sense if there are not, in fact, any rules, but instead tendencies that emerge from shared use of a language. This view finds support in the observation that members of a linguistic community routinely change the way they use language. The constantly changing slang of young people provides one example, with words like *wicked* or *cool* used to convey a meaning very different from the original.

Shifts in language occur at the more grammatical level as well. And geographical differences can be traced through changes in accents as dialects continuously diverge. One grammatical shift exemplified in (8) shows how it has become fairly common in English to use the third person plural pronoun *they* in a context in which the traditional grammar 'rule' would require a singular form. Notice that the verb also agrees with the plural *their*, and not the main clause subject *everyone*, as expected by traditional grammar:

(8)   . . . and nearly everyone who's bought **their** houses have altered the doors.[9]

Use of the generic *they* is a result of a change in cultural norms; people in English-speaking countries have become uncomfortable with the use of the masculine form to refer to both men and women. The preference for appropriate language has over-ruled the structural requirement for number agreement in (8).

Our discussion of the functionalist view has brought us to a radical point: that there is no grammar. This conclusion, in fact, even goes further than many functionalists would. What is agreed upon, however, is that language is a system for communication which is central for explaining what it means to be human. The functionalist view of language also sees the development of language as dependent on language use. Language development, whether native or non-native, is driven by a need to communicate. A learner develops a repertoire of language through interaction with members of the speech community. This idea of speech community is even more important for the approach discussed in the next section.

ACCOUNTING FOR SOCIAL CONTEXT: A SOCIOCULTURAL APPROACH

There are many researchers who have been critical of the more mentalist approaches to language learning, arguing for the importance

of social context. These include sociocultural theory, cultural historical activity theory, activity theory, conversational analysis and eth-
nomethodology. As it will not be possible to discuss each of these in
turn, this section will bring together some of the main ideas behind
these views. I will use 'Sociocultural' as an umbrella term and will refer
to this as an 'approach' because the ideas here go beyond the specific
claims of sociocultural theory.

Proponents of Sociocultural Approaches to language have been
vocal in their criticism of researchers who reduce language speakers to
their mental processes. In a well-known paper challenging the field of
linguistics, Firth and Wagner argue that meaning is not a brain-to-
brain activity, but rather 'a social and negotiable product of interaction, transcending individual intentions and behaviours' (1997: 763).
For a sociocultural theorist, a learner is much more than their
grammatical competence, and language is much more than input.
Language is a resource for participating in everyday life; it is an
integral part of social processes. Socioculturalists speak of language as
a cultural artefact, both as a product of and contributor to language
socialisation. In short, language is inextricably tied to social context.

Because of its emphasis on the social nature of language, this view
often takes a more political stance, acknowledging the power relations
that exist among members of a community. It sees language users as
both contributing to and affected by language norms. For this reason,
much of the work of language learning is to become competent in the
cultural, social and political norms of particular communicative
contexts. In this way, language is a tool of **mediation**, connecting
the individual and his/her social environment, or to put it another
way, language mediates between the self and the external world,
allowing an individual to translate their thoughts into social action.

But this mediation is a two-way process; language also allows humans
to think and talk about ideas and events. In other words, language also
mediates in the opposite direction – from the external to the internal. This
latter point is one of the more controversial aspects of this approach.
Language is not an abstract system distinct from use or distinct from
cognition. In addition to being a means for communicating with others, it
is seen as a tool for thought. In other words, it is viewed as a means for
mediating cognition, as a tool that allows for mental activity. What
makes this controversial is the idea that this kind of linguistic mediation
is required in order for humans to make sense of the world. Moreover,
language is understood to be a prerequisite for the development of
consciousness. Thus language is not a set of inborn or innate predis-

positions, but instead a socioculturally constructed mediational means both for participation in society, and for basic cognition.

While the best-known contemporary proponent of the sociocultural view is James Lantolf,[10] the original ideas date back to the Russian psychologist, L. S. Vygotsky (1896–1934) and the earlier part of the twentieth century. Vygotsky's ideas were rejuvenated and applied to the second language learning context by applied linguists in the early 1990s. For this reason, the sociocultural view is sometimes also called the 'neo-Vygotskyan' view. Vygotsky was concerned with developments in psychology at that time, and he explored questions of language development primarily among children. In the context of development and learning, Vygotsky argued that learning is socially mediated, requiring interaction. He went on to propose principles for language development, a number of which have been taken up by contemporary researchers interested in language learning and teaching.

Early stages of development depend on so-called **other regulation,** which means looking to someone else who is more skilled. Through supportive interaction, the learner will be able to appropriate knowledge into consciousness. This supportive interaction has come to be known as **scaffolding,** which is the idea of providing assistance and direction for the learner to support their development. While this notion is relevant to learning in general, it has been seen as especially useful in the context of language development.[11] Through scaffolding, a learner has the optimal conditions for development. The range of potential development is known as the **zone of proximal development (ZPD).** Within the ZPD, the learner moves from a dependent to an independent state.

Perhaps one reason why this idea has many supporters is because it is a view that looks forward to what can be achieved, instead of back to what has already been achieved. And it highlights what an individual learner may be able to achieve independently instead of assessing the learner's current abilities (or lack thereof). It also avoids the common practice of measuring the learner against some idealised target. Another reason why this view has been well received is its emphasis on the value of collaborative learning. The accomplishments of the individual are very much dependent on collaboration with others through scaffolding and other regulation.

For this reason, the process of learning is seen as one of **co-constructing** knowledge. As such, learning is by definition a social process, especially in the early stages. One aspect of the learning process seen as crucial by Vygotsky is imitation. From a contemporary perspective, imitation is viewed as somewhat suspect because of more recent developments in our understanding of FLA. However, in the neo-Vygotskyan view, imitation is not seen as a passive, behaviourist phenomenon, but instead as an active process. Much emphasis is put on delayed imitation, as a kind of personal rehearsal. This is known as **private speech**, a type of inner speech directed to oneself to mediate mental behaviour. This private speech is seen as a tool for thought. Mediation through private speech can lead to **self-regulation**, which is a developmental stage beyond other regulation. Self-regulation is an advanced stage which will come through sufficient scaffolding. Another process that can lead to self-regulation is **object regulation**, whereby learners use physical objects to help them to develop their knowledge.

These various processes all contribute, in time, to the more individual stage of self-regulation. Throughout, development relies on **internalisation**, which is the development of psychological functions. This process regulates the relationship between the individual and the social environment, while at the same time the social environment drives internalisation. The whole system is seen as dynamic – language is a process of developing social norms, while at the same time social norms are shaped by the use of language.

One very recent development from this line of thinking has seized on this dynamic notion to propose that language should be seen as a system that is constantly emerging. Diane Larsen-Freeman and Lynn Cameron have applied the idea of **Complexity Theory** to language, viewing language as in a perpetual state of adaptation.[12] As such, complex systems are characterised by a constantly changing interplay between the existing system and the pressure points affecting the system. This can give rise to an appearance of stability, but in fact such a state does not really exist. In this dynamic systems approach, an individual's brain is seen not as a container for language, but as shaped by language. This very new view is quite different to the other approaches we have explored so far.

Another outgrowth from the sociocultural view has been an increased exploration of the social context. Within a **Situated Learning Theory** approach, some researchers focus on language in terms of so-called **communities of practice**, which are identifiable groups with shared aims, norms and functions.[13] As members of society, we typically belong to a number of communities of practice, each with habitual ways of doing things based on a set of symbolic resources. There is a long tradition of viewing learning in formal educational settings as a type of socialisation. The community of practice view acknowledges this function of education and seeks to teach learners explicitly to be able to participate successfully in the communities of practice that are relevant to them. Many also take one further step towards a politicised view to explore the sociopolitical implications of becoming a member of any particular community of practice. This **Critical Theory** approach is interested in the importance of power relations within particular communities.[14] The ultimate aim in a classroom setting, then, is to empower learners to be able to navigate successfully through the complexity of the communities of practice which they are likely to encounter.

In sum, sociocultural views of language are concerned with the ways in which language affects society and society affects language. This has led to research in social context and the interplay between that context and language. Focus on the individual explores how the learner can become an active part of this social network. In doing so, there has been concern with the process of language development, but at the individual level this process is seen as tied up in the social context. Even the most clearly psychological process – that of internalisation – rests on the need for interaction, as self-regulation comes out of collaboration and reliance on others.

As the emphasis in this approach has been primarily on development, one criticism of this approach is that the description of what language is has been limited to the idea that language is a mediating tool. This somewhat abstract view of language may not be helpful for determining the linguistic aims within a language teaching lesson, but it does provide a starting point for asking how language should be taught since it relies crucially on collaboration and interaction with others. Those socioculturalists who are interested in the more structural properties of language tend to align themselves with functionalist characterisations of linguistic structure since language is seen as a tool for making meaning.

Another criticism of the Sociocultural Approach is that there is not enough emphasis on the cognitive processes implicated in language use.[15] Responding to this, the Sociocognitive Approach recognises the role of society in meaning-making while also focusing more on the cognitive side of the equation.[16] The premise is twofold: that the structure of language affects how speakers think and at the same time is limited by the constraints of human processing. An example of processing constraints is the tendency for languages to limit the number of clauses that occur in a single sentence. The idea is that there are limitations in how much complexity a person can process during communication. This brings us to developments in psychology. In the next section we consider the view of language that holds cognition to be central its approach.

ACCOUNTING FOR EXPLICIT, PROCEDURAL LEARNING: A COGNITIVE APPROACH

The Cognitive Approach to language is based on research in psychology showing that the brain is a system of neural connections. This view of mental processing underpins the cognitive understanding of how language is organised in the mind. While both cognitive and generative linguists are interested in the mental processes underlying language, the fundamental difference lies in their understanding of the nature of linguistic knowledge. As we have seen, for generativists, language knowledge is unique, distinct from other kinds of knowledge. Cognitivists, by contrast, view language as the same type of knowledge as other kinds of knowledge. In other words, language makes use of the same types of processes and knowledge stores as other kinds of knowledge do.[17] In this view, language is a system of connections, not an inventory of symbols and abstract rules. For this reason, this approach can also, broadly speaking, be referred to as **Connectionism**. Because language has been seen as just another type of knowledge, there has been less of a tradition for research on properties of language itself within the Cognitive Approach, yet recent work in construction grammar is quickly changing this. We discussed the construction grammar approach in the section on Functionalism. This is one example of how these two approaches overlap.

Yet, the Cognitive Approach has other influences that make it distinctive enough from Functionalism to treat it as its own approach. In particular, there is a rich tradition of research on the computational tools implicated in language use and development. Cognitivism owes much to the seminal work of early psychologists like Jean Piaget, in addition to early linguists like Benjamin Whorf. Evolving ideas from developmental psychology, just as language is seen as part of a larger set of knowledge, language learning is understood to develop like other kinds of learning. It is characterised as explicit and procedural. Through **associative learning** stores of language knowledge build up over time, based on the input and experiences to which the learner is exposed. Additionally, the processes available to human cognition shape the way knowledge is organised.

One crucial process is captured in **Prototype Theory**, a theory that addresses the basic human cognitive ability to classify as a way of making sense of the world. A prototype is a kind of 'best example' or most typical representation of any given category.[18] To take a commonly used example, the prototypical 'bird' is an animal with specific attributes such as wings, feathers and a beak, which lays eggs and builds nests. Yet, categories are not black and white. Instead, there are 'good' and 'less good' examples of any category. Compare a robin with a penguin. The penguin does not fit the prototype of a bird very well as it lacks some of the core attributes of the bird category, but it still qualifies as a member. This blurring at the edges of a category, exemplified by our penguin, has led to the notion of **fuzziness**. The lack of concrete definition for notions such as categories is the type of thing that draws criticism from generative linguists who, historically, have insisted that language does have black and white categories.[19]

Eleanor Rosch was the early pioneer who developed the term prototype in the 1970s. Her original aim was to address the large philosophical question that asks which is more primary, concepts themselves or language? The concept that ideas, or the way that the mind conceptualises, might be affected by the way a person's language characterises the ideas is attributed to the linguist Benjamin Whorf of the early 1900s, who, along with Edward Sapir, proposed ideas which came to be known as the **Sapir–Whorf Hypothesis**. In its most extreme form, this view states that language determines how people think. Less extreme than **linguistic determinism** is **linguistic relativism**, which claims that language affects how people think. Research in Prototype Theory investigates whether there are connections between the way a language labels categories and the way people think about the associated concepts. The seminal work of Rosch has been developed further by other well-known researchers, such as Labov and many others, who used experimental methods from psychology to test the notion of prototypes and categorisation.[20]

For cognitive linguists, categories stored in the mind find labels through words. Thus research on the mental lexicon is fundamental to cognitive research. What this research shows is that there is no one-to-one relationship between concepts, categories and individual words. Instead the picture is much more complex, a complexity exemplified by metaphorical language. Cognitive linguists have identified **lexical metaphors** as a window into how the way we make sense of concepts is reflected in language. The extension of the meaning of a word beyond the literal can give insight into the way the mind makes connections between ideas. In Chapter 1 we mentioned the tendency to associate that which is good with the spatial notion of 'up' or 'above'. So in English, for example, we have expressions like feeling *high*, *upbeat* or *on top of the world*. Similarly, we have negative expressions like *under the weather* and *downtrodden*. I am sure you can think of equivalent examples in the other languages that you know. Metaphors like these are seen as a natural by-product of the natural human tendency to associate the positive or negative with spatial positioning. Examples like these are used to argue that the primary units of language are conceptual, having meaning at the core, and not structural, devoid of meaning. This discussion of lexical metaphor should bring to mind our earlier discussion of grammatical metaphor. Once again we see overlap between cognitive and functionalist approaches to language. Because both take meaning as their starting point for understanding language, this is not surprising.

In addition to the complexities of human cognitive processes, there is a complexity that comes from the fact that we are all unique, with a unique set of experiences shaping our stores of knowledge. Each of us has an individual set of representations or schemas associated with concepts that are shaped by our individual personal experiences. A **schema** is a template or a framework for a concept or idea. Though we are likely to share a prototype for bird, for example, each of us will have a more individualised schema with lesser or greater detail for particular aspects of birds and birdlife, based on our experience with and knowledge of birds. Additionally, schemas will be connected with a range of categories which are associated by meaning networks.

One way to think about learning, then, is as the development of schemas, a process which relies on the human tendency to categorise. As we try to make sense of new information to which we are exposed, we activate all relevant schema, looking for a match. If there is a schema which matches the information, then that schema is confirmed, a process which reinforces or strengthens the existence of the schema. Similarly, if the information does not fit a schema exactly but is a close match, the existing schema may be modified or added to, based on the new information. If there is no match among the store of existing schemas, then a new schema may be created.

This simplified description of schema gives a sense of how associative learning works. Crucial to this view of learning is the importance of **frequency**. A new signal that is only received once is not likely to create a fully formed or prominent schema. Instead, those existing schemas that are regularly activated will become more and more robust, or **entrenched**. Thus, learning depends on quantity and regularity in the input. The mind is able to construct schemas, or knowledge, based on probabilistic reasoning. While this is true for all kinds of knowledge, of interest to us is the development of language knowledge. In response to a visual or auditory linguistic signal – a word, a phrase or a sentence – there is activation of a range of possible linguistic representations. **Cues** such as context, existing knowledge and the immediately preceding linguistic signal help to determine the most probable match. Also important are current **activation levels** for each schema. The activation of a linguistic representation raises what is known as the **resting level** of the schema in question.

This also leads to what known as **priming**. Representations that are activated more frequently have higher resting levels. If a schema has a higher resting level, then it is primed, or more readily activated, and it requires less robust evidence for subsequent activation. If at a lower resting level, a stronger, more robust signal is needed to activate it. Moreover, because schemas are organised in sets of related representations, creating networks based on association, when any single representation is primed, the network of representations associated with it is also primed.

In this way, language development can be seen as the building up of linguistic patterns based on associative learning, and not the development of abstract linguistic rules.[21] In this process of raising and lowering activation levels, there is a crucial role for time. If a representation is not activated, in time the resting level will gradually diminish, while repeated activation will strengthen the schema over time. If, however, activation of a particular representation implicates a slightly altered form–meaning mapping, the stored representation will also alter accordingly. This is learning. Notice that this view of learning means that the system is constantly fluctuating; it is dynamic. Proponents of Complexity Theory, discussed earlier, emphasise how this change means that language is constantly evolving. Some take this view one step further to claim that this constant change implies that language itself is a system that is emergent.[22] While this may go further than some cognitive linguists are comfortable with, it illustrates how similar views of language can be linked with different research traditions.

This discussion of learning has presented the development of schemas as a product of receptive processes, yet schemas also become strengthened with use. Those who emphasise this aspect of the Cognitive Approach refer to it as a **usage-based** approach. Language knowledge strengthens and builds in the learner's memory banks as a result of repeated usage. And learning is **exemplar-driven**, meaning that stores of language knowledge grow based on examples. As implied in our discussion of prototypes, these examples are not stored randomly, but instead made sense of in an orderly fashion, because it is a basic human mental function to categorise, allowing us to make better sense of the world. There is a rich body of research in psychology supporting this human tendency to categorise. Human brains seemed programmed to extract or impose patterns. In this way learners, including language learners, are rational. They are statistical problem-solvers, working out patterns and constructions from the input. As part of the learning process, they apply a probabilistic methodology, determining what is likely based on activation levels of their repertoire of stored representations.

This raises the question of intentionality. Is this statistical problem-solving an explicit, conscious process, or does it happen implicitly? Within the cognitive tradition there is a clear recognition of a distinction between explicit and implicit learning. Yet the distinction is a problematic area for cognitive researchers, as it is difficult to differentiate empirically between the two. Nevertheless, there is an understanding that learners are capable of and variously prone to use both types of learning. Moreover, both types are subject to **proceduralisation** of activation to the point of **automatisation**. In other words, a schema, or set of schemas, can be repeatedly activated to the point where the activation does not require explicit effort or thought. The example that is often given to illustrate proceduralisation is learning to drive a car or ride a bike. Initially, one needs to think about every move, but eventually, the actions become automatic even to the point where one might have difficulty explaining what one does.

Language production, then, involves the stringing together of linguistic structures, choosing from the store of constructions that have developed as a result of repeated activation. From a processing point of view, stringing together constructions is in some ways more cognitively efficient than generating new and original utterances. The important work in psychology has led second language acquisitionists from a range of traditions to realise the importance of processing in language development.[23] Processing approaches recognise the need for a **transition theory** to explain how language development proceeds from one stage to another. Such a theory is needed to complement a **property theory** like that of the generative tradition, which concerns itself with explaining the properties of language. In the next section we will explore a framework that tries to combine both aspects in order to provide a more comprehensive understanding.

To summarise, in the Cognitive Approach, language learning is a matter of establishing form–meaning mappings and working out the probability of their use and distribution. Language 'rules' can be seen as regular, recurring patterns. As for the more radical functionalists, this allows for a view in which rules themselves are not basic to language, but a product of a built-up store of linguistic representations. The human tendency to categorise systematically, in other words, can explain why language appears to abide by rules. From a cognitive point of view, language can be seen as no more than a set of words and patterns, stored by association in complex networks, and reinforced through activation. Yet a view in which there is no grammar is controversial and, for most language teachers, not likely to sit very well. It is possible, instead, to take aspects of each of the views of language represented by the range of linguistic approaches to find compatibility in such a way as to make sense of the full complexity of language. As a step towards finding compatibility, consider the diagram in Figure 4.1, which tries to situate the different linguistic approaches in relation to each other and in terms of the basic internal/mentalist vs external/interactional opposition introduced at the start of this book.

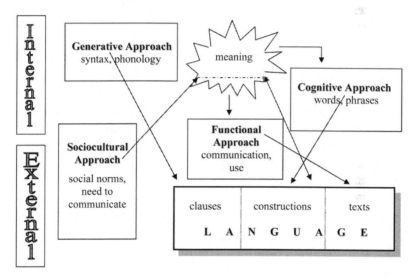

Figure 4.1   Linguistic approaches to language

A consensus-based approach is the one taken in the next section and the rest of this book as we try to make sense of (all) principles of linguistics in the context of language learning and language teaching.

ONE COMPREHENSIVE FRAMEWORK: MOGUL

The work of cognitive linguists has influenced the development of the framework that we will explore in this section. The **Modular On-line**

Growth and Use of Language (MOGUL) framework developed by John Truscott and Mike Sharwood Smith draws from a range of research from differing linguistic approaches to try to make sense of the complex process of language development.[24] It is because of its broad base that we are going to explore it here. As originally proposed, MOGUL is primarily interested in mental, or psychological, processes, taking a generative view of language and a cognitive view of language development. While more 'external' aspects such as society and context are also important we will not explore them in any depth, as the primary approach in this book has been an internal/mentalist one. In this section we will look at how MOGUL approaches the nature of language and language development in order to have one unified theory in which to situate our discussion of language teaching in the rest of this book.

MOGUL develops the idea of the modularity of mind as discussed in the last chapter. It specifies that the language module is limited to 'core' aspects of language such as phonology, syntax and semantics. Since one distinguishing feature of modular knowledge is that it is not available to conscious processing, the processing of core syntax and phonology happens implicitly without our control or even our understanding. Of course, the language module interacts with real-world, or general, knowledge. Unlike modular knowledge, general knowledge is available to conscious processing. As made explicit in MOGUL, language requires both types of knowledge, **modular linguistic knowledge** and (non-linguistic) **general knowledge**. After all, we have to have an understanding of the world in order to make reference to it linguistically. Additionally, however, it is possible to have non-modular general knowledge about language, or metalinguistic knowledge. In MOGUL terms, we will refer to this as non-modular **linguistic general knowledge**.

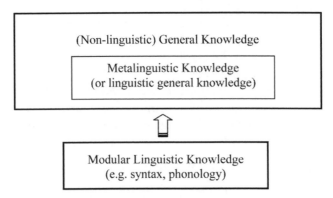

Figure 4.2   MOGUL: Types of knowledge necessary for language

These three types of knowledge are shown schematically in Figure 4.2. To illustrate these types of knowledge, consider what is required in order to make sense of an utterance like (9).

(9)   He knows if you've been naughty or nice.

If you heard this sentence, in order to process it, you would need to know principles of (1) English syntax, such as word order and subject–verb agreement, (2) English phonology, so that the sounds could be segmented into words, and (3) English semantics, in order to understand, for example, that the pronominal subject refers to some entity, not named in the sentence yet known to the speaker. These are all examples of the type of knowledge that is stored in the language module, or modular linguistic knowledge.

Beyond this linguistic knowledge, however, is additional information that speakers from a particular tradition will derive because of cultural knowledge. The use of the phrase *naughty or nice*, combined with the idea of one's behaviour being known, will, for most English-speakers in Western cultures, conjure up some idea of Santa Claus and the delivery of gifts at Christmas. Yet there is nothing inherent to the individual items in the above sentence to give rise to this larger meaning. The knowledge required to come to this larger meaning is stored in the non-modular, or general knowledge, component of the mind. It is mapping between form and meaning like this that would qualify (9) as a construction as well.

While we have explained the more straightforward differences between modular linguistic knowledge and other general knowledge, we have not discussed the third type of knowledge: non-modular linguistic general knowledge. One crucial aspect of the MOGUL framework is that the 'non-modular' component of the mind is also capable of storing knowledge about language. We need to clarify more specifically the definition of linguistic knowledge. To do so, let us take a closer look at the two words, *naughty* and *nice*. The fact that *naughty* and *nice* behave grammatically as predicate adjectives is modular linguistic knowledge, knowledge that will lead every native English speaker to agree that the following sentences are ungrammatical, whether or not they can explain that they are ungrammatical because *naughty* and *nice* cannot be used as verbs or prepositions, respectively.

(10)   a.   *I will naughty/nice my gifts for Christmas.
         b.   *Put the gift naughty/nice the tree.

The meanings associated with *naughty* and *nice*, on the other hand, are non-modular general knowledge. The third type of knowledge – knowledge about language – is linguistic in the sense that it is about language but, because it is explicit knowledge, it is considered non-modular general knowledge. In other words, MOGUL claims that 'linguistic' knowledge exists in both the language module and in extra-modular stores, but despite being 'linguistic', the quality or type of knowledge is different.

Because we are sophisticated users and perhaps teachers of English, we have metalinguistic knowledge that tells us that in (9) *naughty* and *nice* are predicate adjectives. We can know this because we can analyse the properties of these words, working out their distribution patterns to see that they occur in the predicate and modify the pronominal subject. It is this explicit general knowledge that enabled me to create nonsense sentences like those in (10) for illustration. Yet when I use the words *naughty* and *nice* spontaneously, I do not attend to the grammatical or distributional properties of the words. Instead, just like you, I choose these words in terms of their meaning in order to discuss whether Santa Claus will bring presents this year. My modular linguistic knowledge ensures that I abide by correct syntactic structure. My training as a linguist allows me to explain the properties of the sentence, or to talk *about* language; in other words it is linguistic, but explicit, so part of my general knowledge stores.

While there are different types of knowledge, there is only one process in MOGUL by which knowledge develops. Language develops through the on-line use of language. Also known as the **Acquisition by Processing Theory (APT)**, learning occurs through the reinforcement of input, as described in the section above on the Cognitive Approach. When, for example, a new linguistic item occurs in the input, it registers in the learner's mind. If that item is never encountered again, it is not likely to become a permanent part of the knowledge store (linguistic or non-linguistic). With repeated reinforcement, however, that item will in time become a part of stored knowledge. Based on psycholinguistic research, this process of language 'growth' is the same as all kinds of knowledge development, regardless of what type of knowledge it is. Thus, through activation and reinforcement, formal linguistic aspects of input will become part of modular linguistic knowledge while knowledge of meaning and use builds in general knowledge.

You may be wondering what advantage there is for maintaining two types of knowledge, modular and general. From a theoretical point of view, the distinction is needed because of research showing differences between different types of knowledge. In language acquisition, it can help to explain why SLA seems to be fundamentally different from FLA. For native language acquisition, the language module seems to develop quickly and relatively easily. For adults, language learning seems to depend much more on deliberate, conscious learning. This does not mean that the language module is irrelevant for adult language learners, but it does seem that certain aspects of a language are not facilitated in the same way for young native learners as they are for adult second language learners.

The distinction is also useful in terms of language teaching. It is completely feasible for a person to have both modular linguistic knowledge and a sophisticated non-modular understanding of a linguistic principle – as I illustrated above, showing that I have both kinds of knowledge for *naughty* and *nice*. Because language processing can be based on both types of knowledge, this means that there is the possibility that general linguistic knowledge can be used to compensate for modular linguistic knowledge. If a learner is not able to develop modular linguistic knowledge as children do at an early age, they can potentially develop non-modular general linguistic knowledge through hard work and frequent exposure. In other words, there is on-line growth and use of language, whether modular or non-modular. And most encouragingly, there is no reason why non-modular knowledge should not lead to native-like language production – though it may require lots of practice and use.

This last point means that teachers should know which aspects of language can develop as modular knowledge for their learners and which cannot. Then, they should provide the correct type and an ample amount of input for language to develop. It is when thinking about how to provide input that an external view of language becomes useful. Functional and Sociocultural Approaches remind us that learners are more than their mental processes. Any teacher will agree that learners thrive in a supportive atmosphere. Moreover, encouraging learners to achieve their potential, or to work within their Zone of Proximal Development, instead of holding out fluent native speakers as the target is much more pedagogically sound. In addition to a supportive environment, there are culturally based aspects of language that learners need to be taught in order to become competent participants in relevant communities of practice.

A functionalist view is also indispensable for teachers trying to explain language in terms of its use. The functional view also offers an accessible and meaningful way to understand language. There are times in which teaching language by drawing attention to function is more appropriate for explicit instruction than dwelling on structural properties. Moreover, embedding language in context will make it more meaningful. If learners are more engaged because the teaching emphasises the more meaningful aspects of language, this will result in much higher levels of engagement. More language engagement, whether explicit or implicit, means more opportunities for activation and raised resting levels for new knowledge. In other words, there will be language development – both modular and non-modular.

In short, MOGUL is useful for language teaching because it has room for the current range of views in linguistics. Additionally, this framework allows for a complex understanding of what language is, both structurally and functionally; and it acknowledges important findings in psychology that point to how knowledge develops and how it is processed. In other words, it provides a single framework for understanding the complex processes involved in language and language development. We therefore turn to the language classroom, asking what implications we can draw from these theoretical discussions.

FOR DISCUSSION

1. Now that we have considered each of the four basic views of language, discuss the extent to which your own understanding of language prior to reading this book was informed by each of the views.
2. Compare and contrast the four basic views of language, identifying areas in which they are in opposition and areas in which they are compatible.
3. Discuss the extent to which it is important as a language teacher to have a clear view of what language is in the linguistic sense.
4. To what extent does relevance of each view of language depend on the language teaching context? Specifically, are there differences in terms of age or proficiency level? Second vs foreign language teaching? Personal vs academic or professional use?
5. Go through the section on MOGUL and identify explicitly where the different views about language emerge. Are there any major concepts that are not covered in the MOGUL framework?
6. What is your view of language now? Consider your understanding of language in terms of language teaching. What implication could your views have for the way you approach language teaching?

NOTES

1. The influential original discussion can be found in Hymes (1972).
2. Halliday has been very prolific, producing many works in Systemic Functionalism. The first version of his seminal work, *An Introduction to Functional Grammar*, was published in 1985. It has been re-issued, with the third edition, revised by Christian Matthiessen, appearing in 2004. A ten-volume series comprising his collected work has also been published recently, edited by Webster (2007).
3. See Butler (2003) for an extensive discussion of the branches of the various structural-functionalist branches within Functionalism.
4. As Halliday's SFG has mainly focused on the textual level, a branch of SFG has developed advancing the theory at the level of the sentence and below. This branch is now known as Cardiff Grammar because Fawcett, its foremost proponent, has done most of his work with colleagues in Cardiff since the 1980s. See Fawcett (2000). The Hallidayan approach, as a result, is now sometimes referred to as the Sydney approach.
5. This example comes from *The Guardian Weekly*, 23.07.10, in an article entitled 'Britain's human history revised', pp. 30–1.
6. The basic components of Speech Act Theory were proposed by Austin (1962), but then developed by Searle (1969).
7. In addition to Goldberg's approach to Construction Grammar, there is the Radical Construction Grammar approach of Langacker (1987), Lakoff (1987), and Croft (2001).
8. Many cognitive linguists also take a Construction Grammar view of language. In fact, there is a degree of debate as to whether Cognitive Linguistics is a form of Functional Linguistics. See Butler (2003), who includes Cognitive Grammar as a structural-functional approach, while acknowledging that many cognitive linguists prefer to see themselves as distinct from Functionalism.
9. Example found on 28.07.10 using the Compleat Lexical Tutor (http://www.lextutor.ca/), to search the British National Corpus (BNC) Spoken Corpus.
10. For posthumously published work, see Vygotsky (1979, 1986). For more current developments in sociocultural theory and language learning, see the edited volume by Lantolf (2000), as well as Lantolf and Thorne (2006).
11. The term scaffolding was introduced by education psychologist Jerome Bruner. See Wood, Bruner and Ross (1976).
12. For more comprehensive discussion of a Complexity Theory as applied to language and language learning, see Larsen-Freeman and Cameron (2008) and de Bot, Lowie and Vespoor (2007).
13. For early articulation of Situated Learning Theory, see Lave and Wenger (1991), and Wenger (1998) for more on the communities of practice idea.

14. For a collection of papers, see the edited volume by Norton and Toohey (2004), including an introductory chapter with an overview of the development of a Critical Theory approach to language pedagogy.
15. For an enlightening discussion of the sociocultural view as compared to a cognitive view, see Zuengler and Miller (2006).
16. See, for example, Atkinson (2002).
17. For an overview of Cognitive Linguistics, see the introductory texts by Croft and Cruise (2004) or Evans and Green (2006).
18. For early original work, see Rosch (1973, 1975). For an overview of Prototype Theory as applied to language, see Taylor (1995). The idea has seen much development in Cognitive Linguistics, most notably by Lakoff (1987) and Langacker (1987).
19. See, however, Aarts (2007), who argues for what he calls gradience in syntax.
20. See, for example, Labov's famous 1973 study on cup-like objects.
21. For discussion of the Cognitive Approach in FLA, see Tomasello (2003). Nick Ellis is one of the best-known researchers in second language development. See Robinson and Ellis (2008) for a useful overview.
22. There are a number of emergentist approaches to language development. For example Ellis (2003), O'Grady (1999, 2003) and MacWhinney (1999).
23. In addition to MOGUL, there are other processing approaches to second language development. O'Grady (2003) attributes difficulties in second language development to so-called computational complexity such that learners are limited by the current level of their interlanguage. Carroll (2001) looks to instances in which the parser has problems with the input as the time when acquisition occurs. VanPatten's input processing model takes more of a cognitivist view, relying on the learner's need to match language form with meaning, drawing from the forms that the learner currently holds. See VanPatten (2009) and references therein.
24. To read about MOGUL as originally proposed, see Sharwood Smith (2004) and Truscott and Sharwood Smith (2004 a, b).

5

IMPLICATIONS FOR LANGUAGE TEACHING

⟨∂⟩

IMPLICATIONS FOR THE CLASSROOM

So far in this book, we have explored the fields of theoretical linguistics and language acquisition. And we have seen some very different views of language with linguists who view language as an internal mental property of individuals and others who view language as intricately tied up with the norms and habits of particular speech communities external to the individual. But we have also said that these views are not necessarily incompatible; a psycholinguist can analyse the internal processing and production of the same language that the functionalist considers from the point of view of meaning and the sociolinguist analyses in terms of adherence to cultural norms of behaviour.

Within psycholinguistic research, however, there is fundamental opposition, as generativists see language as modular, while cognitivists equate it with other kinds of knowledge. Though this view is irreconcilable, the fortunate point for us is that it does not necessarily matter for language teaching. The common aim in the language classroom is for learners to be able to produce and comprehend language effortlessly and fluently. Moreover, there seem to be areas in which the two views can find consensus, as illustrated by MOGUL, which draws on aspects of both views. Whether language is 'modular' or not, psycholinguists of any perspective agree that there is a difference between automatic linguistic abilities and the more laboured efforts associated with metalinguistic skills. As teachers, we want to move our learners continuously toward the automatic, linguistic end of this performance spectrum, regardless of what the theoretical explanation for the difference is.

Other 'oppositions' can be reconciled if they are seen as opposite ends of a spectrum which, taken together, present a more complete picture of the complexity of language. The 'formalists', for example, are attempting to define the abstract rules underlying language, while the 'functionalists' recognise language as an embodiment of meaning whose core properties are grounded in experience. These are not necessarily contradictory – we can abide by linguistic constraints when we express meaning, drawing on our life experiences. Similarly, the 'mentalists' are busy researching the inner workings of the mind, while the 'interactionists' have focused on language in society. A conscientious teacher will recognise all of these facets of language and work to develop them depending on the particular needs of the students. In this chapter, we will extend the theoretical discussions that we have had so far to the classroom and begin to explore their practical implications. Then, in the remainder of the book, we will turn to more specific approaches and trends in language teaching in attempt to see how a knowledge of underlying theory can inform even the more practical, everyday decisions made in the classroom.

Our application of theory will be structured around the ten observations about second language development presented by VanPatten and Williams (2007), which we outlined in the conclusion of Chapter 3.

OBSERVATION 1: EXPOSURE TO INPUT IS NECESSARY FOR SLA

While the observation that exposure to input is necessary for language development may seem obvious, the implications for language teaching are not so straightforward. There are two main issues to be considered. Firstly, there is the question of quality: namely, what type of input. Secondly, there is the question of quantity.

One way in which we can divide input is to consider implicit and explicit aspects. **Implicit input** can be associated with the natural language of spoken language and 'authentic' written materials. As we saw in Chapter 2, one of the main complaints about Grammar Translation was the lack of exposure to natural, spoken language, a complaint which led to the development of the Direct Method. If we thought that second language learning was the same as native first language development, we might choose to restrict all language spoken in the classroom to the target language, as done in the Direct Method. But attempts have shown that this is not a reasonable choice. One reason for this is input. The nature of classroom learning is fundamentally different; both the amount of input and the reasons for using language are different in a classroom as compared with a family home environment. Given classroom restrictions, teaching also needs to include explicit input.

Explicit input refers to explanations about language, or metalinguistic input. This is sometimes also referred to as **negative evidence** because it includes explanations about what is not correct in the target language, in addition to explanations of the rules of language. While language 'rules' usually refer to grammar rules, such as how to form a passive sentence, there are also rules about language use that can and should be taught. Every language, for example, has mechanisms for expressing politeness. The use of modal verbs such as *might* and *may* or adverbial expressions like *if possible* is a grammatical way to express politeness in English. And beyond grammaticality, a learner needs to know which social contexts expect polite forms as well as the appropriate level of politeness. Explicit rules, then, need to cover language in terms of both form and function.

So should a teacher provide implicit or explicit input? The answer, of course, is both. As illustrated in MOGUL, a learner can develop both implicit linguistic knowledge and explicit metalinguistic knowledge. And both can develop to high levels of automaticity, which will show itself as language fluency. The difficult question is how to know when to provide implicit or explicit input. The answer lies in understanding how different aspects of language develop. We will return to this question when we explore the variability of language development across linguistic subsystems (Observation 6). For now we will say that there are times when learners should be immersed in as much authentic input as possible and times when explicit explanation is necessary.

Whether it is implicit or explicit, learners need to get as much exposure to the target language as possible. The amount of language exposure a learner gets can be affected by so-called **affective factors**, such as motivation, personality, attitude and other emotional factors. Much has been made of the claim that second language speakers do not have the same motivation for learning as native first language speakers. Wanting to succeed on a course in class cannot equate with needing to express yourself to satisfy basic everyday needs. This difference means that teachers need to inspire their students so that they have a healthy and inquisitive attitude towards the target language.

Another aim of language teaching is to facilitate exposure outside the classroom, increasing the amount of input each learner gets, regardless of the differences in ability and motivation among students. While an outgoing, risk-taking learner may feel comfortable participating in on-line chat rooms, for example, even a learner with a shy and reticent personality can find ways to increase the amount of input they are exposed to if properly motivated. Since, as we will see in Observation 2, learners can develop language incidentally when their primary focus is on something other than the explicit learning of language, even the shyest learner will benefit from more 'passive' activities like reading in the target language. In fact, one line of SLA research argues that reading for pleasure can lead to great improvement in language proficiency.[1]

In short, the observation that plentiful exposure to input is necessary for SLA means that teachers should be sure that learners get both implicit and explicit input and that the amount of input is maximal, fostering learners' motivation and interest so as to maximise the amount of exposure.

OBSERVATION 2: A GOOD DEAL OF SLA HAPPENS INCIDENTALLY

This observation builds on the first, addressing the effect of input. A growing body of research suggests that learners come to know particular features of language without explicitly engaging with those features. So, for example, while trying to understand a text in order to answer comprehension questions, a learner can also come to know new vocabulary words or syntactic constraints. Drawing from the range of research, this finding seems to include other aspects of language like word order, derivational morphology and word formation, as well as more extra-grammatical features such as politeness strategies and appropriate register as well. As pointed out by Nick Ellis (2007: 88), 'We "know" far too many linguistic regularities for us to have explicitly learned them.' This observation brings to mind Krashen's distinction whereby implicit development, or **acquisition**, seems to occur alongside explicit development, or **learning**. While Krashen proposed these two types of knowledge as distinct and dissociated from one another,[2] what matters for the language teacher is the comprehension and production abilities of the learner, not theories about the knowledge underlying these abilities.

One implication of incidental learning for the classroom is what has come to be known as Focus on Form. Michael Long has made a useful three-way distinction between Focus on Meaning, Focus on FormS and Focus on Form. A **Focus on Meaning** lesson will limit itself exclusively to the function of language, or strictly communicative teaching, without explicit metalinguistic teaching. **Focus on FormS** captures the other extreme whereby language forms (alone) are explicitly taught in isolation from their use, and drilled without any meaningful context. This often takes the form of grammar exercises. The capital 'S' on Form is used to make a clearer distinction with the more appropriate middle ground, **Focus on Form**.[3]

One rationale for Focus on Form is the observation that much learning happens incidentally. With this in mind, teachers are encouraged to devise a meaningful task that will require the learners to engage genuinely with language. The task should include language which is challenging to the learners' current levels of proficiency, with forms which the learner has not yet mastered. When these forms interfere with the activity of the lesson, the teacher should call explicit attention to them, explaining them clearly. In other words, the teacher should focus on forms, but only in the context of meaningful engagement with language. Thus, Focus on Form is a way of teaching form, but in the context of use or function.

The degree to which the task involves challenging forms, and the extent to which the teacher orchestrates attention to them, is a matter of professional judgement, judgement which should not be random, but instead based on a range of factors, both in terms of theoretical understanding of language/language development and the practical constraints of the classroom environment. Knowing that development occurs through repeated exposure, however, means that a good teacher will be attuned to frequency, supplying sufficient amounts of examples of the forms in question. Additionally, an expert teacher will pay attention to the **salience** of forms in the input. In other words, new forms need to be prominent enough to be picked up on. If new forms do not stand out and learners can understand the input without having to make sense of them, then Focus on Form is less likely to occur.

The discussion of 'forms' generally brings to mind inflectional morphology or specific grammatical structures. Yet there is no reason why Focus on Form should not include a focus on extra-grammatical forms as well. At the level of text, for example, students could be asked to read a short academic essay and a newspaper article on, say, the effect of litter on the environment. This could be done in preparation for a letter which the student is asked to write to their local council about litter in their street. Within this task, the teacher could focus not only on new vocabulary and any complex grammatical points, but also on register, pointing out the features of journalistic writing that differ from those of academic writing and formal letter writing. Focus on Form could likewise be extended to focus on cultural norms for registering complaints in the local setting. In fact, there is no limit to aspects of language and interaction that can, in principle, be explicitly taught by language teachers. In sum, teachers would do well to keep learners engaged in tasks that interest them, knowing that they can and will be learning other features of language in the mean time.

OBSERVATION 3: LEARNERS COME TO KNOW MORE THAN WHAT THEY HAVE BEEN EXPOSED TO IN THE INPUT

It may seem that this observation is quite similar to Observation 2, but there is a difference. Incidental learning means that learners will come to know backgrounded properties of language while they are focusing more explicitly on other properties or activities. Observation 3 refers to an even more implicit phenomenon whereby learners come to know properties of language that they are not even exposed to directly. In other words, there are 'poverty of the stimulus' effects in language development.

In Chapter 3, we explored how poverty of the stimulus is the basis for the nativist conceptualisation of language acquisition and comes from the overwhelming evidence that children come to know more about the ambient language than the subset of language to which they are actually exposed. We then saw that there is evidence for poverty of the stimulus effects among second language learners as well, looking at research on the Overt Pronoun Constraint as an example. This has led to the conclusion that UG-constrained development is relevant in a second language context. Of course, adult second language learners do not seem to benefit from UG-constrained development as thoroughly as first language learners, but the fact that such a phenomenon is possible at all is important and should be a factor for decision-making in the language classroom.

The most general implication of Observation 3 is further support that teachers should not be afraid to include authentic, natural input – in all of its complexity – in their classroom. However, in considering classroom application, the obvious question is how much authentic input should there be? Should teachers only ever use the target language? Should all classroom material be taken only from native sources? In the excitement of the 'Chomskyan revolution', early applied linguists encouraged teachers to take this kind of 'native' approach to their second language teaching. Krashen and Terrell (1983) promoted the so-called **Natural Approach,** in which teachers were to foster language development as much like the native child experience as possible. They were even to allow for a **silent period,** in which their learners were exposed to large quantities of authentic input, but not expected or asked to produce their own language. Advances in the new scientific approach to language revived the idealistic notions which had already failed Direct Method proponents years earlier. Though a completely 'natural' approach may not be appropriate, these ideas have led to the development of **content-based** or **immersion approaches** to language teaching which can be found in a range of settings from primary schools to high-level preparatory academic English programmes. In these courses students are taught academic content in the target language itself as a way of teaching the language.

The fact that second language development is different to first is, of course, obvious to teachers and learners alike. Exploring the reasons may help to determine how to navigate the differences. Age and the learner's existing knowledge of a first language are two obvious reasons for the difference, but another point that is starting to emerge clearly from the research is that different domains of language seem to develop differently. As we mentioned in Chapter 3, there is evidence from new technologies that different aspects of language are processed differently in the brain. Thus it is not surprising that there might be developmental differences as well. While Generative Linguistics has always differentiated between modular and non-modular development, the growing body of SLA research is telling us that a more refined view of language in second language contexts is needed as well.

The research showing equivalence between native and non-native processing on semantic elements of language suggests that learners might respond well to natural, authentic input within the realm of meaning. However, differences in processing syntactic aspects of language suggest that a more explicit approach may be appropriate for the more core grammatical features of language like syntax and phonology. Interestingly, the research showing poverty of the stimulus effects in second language development so far are mostly to do with semantic knowledge. The Overt Pronoun Constraint, for example, is to do with knowing the possible meanings of a pronoun in different grammatical contexts. Other poverty of the stimulus studies also investigate subtle points of interpretation.[4] Again, this suggests that meaning-based aspects of language, including some very subtle aspects of language of which even native speakers are not explicitly aware, can develop naturally without explicit instruction.

This distinction between syntax and semantics also suggests that we should promote active engagement with authentic language, or meaning-based instruction, while also allowing for explicit engagement with language form. In other words, it provides more support for a Focus on Form approach to language teaching. But we can go even further. The MOGUL framework can help us to determine how we should teach the forms on which we decide to focus. If acquisition happens by processing, then students should be given activities that require them to process particular forms actively, remembering the crucial role of frequency, since learning occurs as a result of repeated activation. This tells us that there is a clear place for practice and repetition in language teaching. While this might sound like a return to the more rote practices of drilling, we must resist a strict one-or-the-other mentality. Learners should practise, but in the context of meaningful engagement. If repetitive practice is meaningless, it is no longer requiring active processing, and learning is compromised.

In sum, there is a degree of modular development that seems to be possible for adult second language learners. Because learners seem to come to know more than what they were exposed to, teachers should readily expose learners to natural language, in all its complexity. However, this should be tempered by explicit focus on some forms to allow for repeated engagement. The question of which forms will be addressed further when we discuss Observation 6.

OBSERVATION 4: LEARNERS' OUTPUT (SPEECH) OFTEN FOLLOWS PREDICTABLE PATHS WITH PREDICTABLE STAGES IN THE ACQUISITION OF A GIVEN STRUCTURE

This observation refers to the systematic nature of interlanguage development, based on research on specific structures, such as question formation and negative sentences. As we have seen previously, the morpheme order studies show stage-like development in both native and second language development. From this research there is a tendency to generalise to say that *language* develops in systematic stages. But as we have said repeatedly, *language* is a complex and multi-faceted phenomenon. While it is uncontroversial that there are developmental stages in a very broad sense, there is no documented research showing that all of language is entirely systematic. In other words, though this observation seems to hold at very general and at some very specific levels, there is a rather large middle ground which research has yet to address in this regard.

To illustrate more specifically, at the very general level it is well documented that learners acquire contentful words like *table* and *run* before they learn function words like *the* and *of*. Similarly, they can produce words and phrases before they are able to produce grammatically well-formed clauses, which, in turn, precede complex clauses. And at the other end of the spectrum, there is research on some very specific structures that shows developmental stages. When acquiring negation in English, for example, learners will first add the negative word *no* to the front of a predicate to say things like *no like coffee* before they systematically add a subject, *I no like coffee*, which precedes the final stage in which they correctly include an auxiliary verb: *I don't like coffee.*[5] So for some specific structures there are predictable stages, but there is no research (yet) to show clear developmental stages for all aspects of language. Moreover, the interest in stages has been limited mostly to formalist research, with very few researchers even asking whether this idea of definable 'stages' applies beyond grammar to areas of language function and use.

So what is the use of this observation in the language classroom? If the observation could be empirically shown for all aspects of language at all levels, then the implication would be to strictly follow the developmental stages. Since it is not, teaching in strict stages is only reasonable in a broad sense of moving from the more simple to the more complex and for the limited range of specific language structures which have been researched, like negation.[6] Yet, systematicity in language development, generally speaking, has implications for error correction. If you know that a particular language point is not likely to develop until a later stage in the learner's proficiency, this would suggest that some errors are better left unremarked, with focus instead on errors at the current stage. If, for example, your learners say *no like*, it would make more sense to encourage them to add subjects to their negative statements than to insist on statements with subjects and auxiliary verbs since we know each of these represents a different stage in the development of negation.

You may wonder whether teaching a more complex, final stage might help the learner to go through the intermediate stages more quickly. There is research that investigates whether learners can know a less 'marked' structure if they are taught the more complex corresponding 'marked' forms. Results of research in markedness show that some learners who were taught more complex forms first were able to learn the simpler forms in the process. Unfortunately, however, the results of this kind of research are mixed, suggesting that it may be unrealistic to expect this from all learners in all contexts or for all aspects of language.[7] Returning to our main point about error correction, you may want to expose your learners to complex forms, but it may be best to refrain from correcting those errors that reflect a natural stage in the learner's development.

It is also worth considering that an error may not be an error from the point of view of the learner. The learner is developing an ever-changing interlanguage grammar, one that is a system and not a random set of words and fragments. If the learner's current inter-language system includes *I no like coffee* for negative statements, then for this learner, this is the way to make negative statements. It is only an error from the teacher's point of view. Of course, you may choose to appeal to a student's metalinguistic ability to explain that this is an error as a strategy for compensating for their current interlanguage stage. But if you know that this is a natural step in the learner's development, you may instead want to use the limited time you have with your learners to focus on something else and let the learners' systems develop in their own time as they get more input.

Unfortunately, we also know that sometimes errors persist, even though the learner is considered proficient enough to develop a particular aspect of language. Fossilisation is an unfortunate outcome for many learners on varying aspects of language. From a MOGUL perspective, however, if an error persists beyond the level at which we would expect it, the option is to try to compensate for this lack of modular linguistic development by explicit teaching to allow for metalinguistic development of the language point in question. A teacher can bring the point to the learner's attention and work together with the learner to develop strategies to compensate for fossilisation, drawing on the learner's extra-linguistic general intelligence. With practice, a dedicated learner may be able to automatise this knowledge so that his/her production appears native-like. In other words, for any point of language, a motivated learner should be able to overcome shortcomings in their implicit linguistic knowledge by making use of their general intelligence. This kind of metalinguistic monitoring is particularly useful in written production, as both time and visual representation allow a careful writer to edit their language. With enough dedication and hard work, such self-correction may, in time, be achieved in oral production as well. This will, of course, be helped by experienced teachers who can clearly explain shortcomings and remedy them in a supportive and constructive way.

This view of errors as indicators of a learner's current stage of development is more in concert with Sociocultural Approaches than earlier views of errors as indicative of distance from the native speaker target. Identifying a learner's current and potential stages allows for a Zone of Proximal Development perspective which recognises aims which are possible and realistic for the learner. A learner should be supported to enable him/her to achieve within their Zone, instead of being constantly corrected or criticised for their current abilities. In addition to errors, we should not completely discount mistakes. As mentioned in Chapter 1, as a natural part of language production, mistakes may not be worth correcting, especially in an activity in which fluency is the aim. Yet high rates of mistakes may signal that the learning environment is causing undue stress to the learner to the point where s/he is not able to perform to her/his highest potential. If this is the case, it may signal a need for the teacher to make changes to the classroom environment to provide a more supportive environment that scaffolds the learners as they develop.

OBSERVATION 5: SECOND LANGUAGE LEARNING IS VARIABLE IN ITS OUTCOME

Against the background of systematicity and developmental stages is the unavoidable fact that second language learning is variable in its outcome, a fact that is even more pronounced the older the learner is when first exposed to a language, as pointed out in Bley-Vroman's Fundamental Difference Hypothesis. It is clear that not all learners arrive at a well-developed competence, sometimes even after years and years of effort and exposure. Discussion of this observation first needs clarification of the distinction between 'rate' and 'route'. Seminal early research showed that beginning adult second language learners developed interlanguage proficiency faster than child L2 learners did: in other words, at a more rapid rate – at least initially.[8] But this conclusion should not be used to make assumptions about route. Observation 4 tells us that developmental route is not so variable. The other important finding of the research about rate is that, in the long term, the children were able to acquire a higher level of proficiency than the adults. Second language learning is indeed variable in its outcome.

One clear implication, then, is that a teacher should take age into account. Adults have a more developed cognitive system and a richer amount of experience than children. As experienced learners, adults will have developed learning strategies that they can employ for metalinguistic learning. They may also be more motivated if they have chosen to learn a language, or need it for personal or professional reasons. These affective factors can all contribute to learners exposing themselves to more input and/or actively developing learning strategies for metalinguistic development. Of course, we would do well to keep in mind our earlier discussion about critical periods, which tells us that there is no specific cut-off for language development, and that some aspects of language seem to be affected by age more than others. Indeed, there is no cut-off for learning new vocabulary; nor does basic clausal word order seem to be affected by age. Development of inflectional morphology and phonology, on the other hand, seem to be very susceptible to differences in age.[9]

You may, however, be thinking that even among learners of the same age group there can still be much variability. In addition to the affective factors we have briefly mentioned, there is another clear factor that will lead to variable outcomes in second language learning: the learner's native language. It is widely accepted that learners come to the task of learning a second (or third) language from the starting point of the basic structure of their existing language(s), or, in other words, that there is **Full Transfer** of the first language. Schwartz and Sprouse (1996) argue that L2 development is a matter of restructuring the L1 grammar when that grammar cannot make sense of the L2 input.

Think about how MOGUL presents the learner as having a complex collection of knowledge that is activated in response to any and all linguistic signals. This means that in response to target language input, the learner will use whatever aspects of target language knowledge that they have, as well as all of the native and other language knowledge that they have. The existing L1 knowledge should prove very helpful when it comes to extra-linguistic features that do not vary much among languages, such as tone of voice. It may even help out in some areas of core grammar – for example, adjective + noun or noun + adjective order – depending on whether there is a match between the languages. But it is not likely to be of much use in all aspects of language. The shapes of particular words, for example, are likely to be of little use, since these differ from language to language.

This view of native language transfer may seem obvious, but it quickly becomes more complicated. One widely accepted learnability problem which illustrates the complexity (and importance) of the effects of L1 transfer is to do with what has come to be called the **Subset Principle.** You will remember from our discussion of the Null Subject Parameter in Chapter 3 that in some languages subjects are required for grammaticality while in others they can often be left out, depending on either discourse or inflectional morphology. Thus, a 'null subject' language like Spanish or Japanese allows two grammatical options: a sentence with a subject or the same sentence without. Since English is not a null subject language, it only has the one option of sentences with subjects. In linguistic terms, this is seen as a parameter with +null subject and −null subject settings. Crucial for understanding the Subset Principle is the relationship between the two settings. We can characterise a −null subject-type language as a subset of a +null subject-type language because both share the option of expressing subjects (=subset), but only +null subject languages have the second option of subjectless sentences (=superset) as well.

The Subset Principle is a universal learnability principle that applies to all parameters that can be configured in this kind of way. It states that, initially, learners will automatically assume the more restrictive subset for a parameter, the one that allows only one option. In other words, learners are initially conservative. If there is positive evidence in the input that the other option is allowed, the developing grammar will expand to include the other option. This principle is one of a set of learnability principles that tries to explain how very young children can acquire such complex linguistic systems without the aid of instruction or negative evidence. So what does this mean for the second language context? We have just said that L2 learners start learning based on their L1. So, for example, if a learner has an L1 grammar with a subset setting – in other words –null subjects in English – then when they try to learn a +null subject language, like Spanish or Korean, they will correctly assume that the language allows sentences with subjects; and as soon as they encounter sentences without subjects their interlanguage grammar will develop to include this added option.

Lydia White (1989) went further to ask what happens when a +null subject language speaker tries to learn a –null subject language? Based on their existing L1 grammar, a Spanish speaker, for example, will assume that English has subject and subjectless sentences, like Spanish. The question is, how can the learner *unlearn* the L1-based grammatical rule for subjects? Logic tells us that there are no examples of something that does not occur in the input. The answer, then, is that this is an area in which a teacher needs to give explicit metalinguistic instruction for the learners because exposure to input alone is not going to be enough. Through metalinguistic awareness (in other words, explicit instruction), learners can know what is correct and not correct in a language and with deliberate effort can compensate for this kind of learnability problem.

In sum, second language variability can be attributed to differences in rate, age, amounts of exposure and affective factors. In addition, differences in the existing L1 of learners can have fundamental effects on the development of the grammatical properties of the L2.

OBSERVATION 6: SECOND LANGUAGE LEARNING IS VARIABLE ACROSS LINGUISTIC SUBSYSTEMS

From **inter-linguistic variation**, which addresses differences between languages, we now turn to **intra-linguistic variation**, which refers to differences within a single language system. We have made a broad distinction between core modular linguistic knowledge and non-modular knowledge. And we have characterised modular knowledge as distinct, meaning that it is implicit, automatic and not subject to awareness or deliberate change. But at the same time, drawing on MOGUL, we have said that non-modular knowledge can develop to a level of automaticity. So is there any difference, then, that is relevant to language teachers, aside from just being aware of the academic debate that underlies linguistic theorising?

The answer, of course, is yes. The language module is associated exclusively with implicit acquisition, and is, by definition, beyond the individual's control. As we have already suggested, to facilitate modular development teachers should take a more 'natural' approach: exposing learners to real, natural examples and encouraging them to interact in the target language in order to foster natural, implicit modular language development. Non-modular, general knowledge, by contrast, can develop both through explicit, deliberate learning and incidentally, or implicitly. So in addition to providing the learner with a natural language environment, a good teacher will explicitly teach those areas of language which are non-modular and ask their students to do healthy amounts of practice.

This leads us to the question of which 'areas' are which. Linguists have long debated which areas of language are 'core' and which are not. Fortunately, developments in psycholinguistic and neurolinguistic research have allowed for more empirically based arguments about different aspects of language. As this book is about second language learning and teaching, we will limit our discussion to findings in SLA, acknowledging that this area is currently cutting-edge research, with much work still to be done. The general findings in this line of research are that learners seem to be able to master meaningful aspects of language such as vocabulary and aspects of semantics, but have more difficulty with some of the more grammatical aspects. Learners are able to come to grips with a new language in terms of its semantics, pragmatics and the inventory of words. In other words, learners can readily master the more conceptual-based aspects of a language which, in MOGUL, are part of general cognition.

This ability contrasts with the complex picture emerging from research on acquisition of grammar, which, on the face of it, seems contradictory. On the one hand, second language learners seem to be able to acquire the very core properties of syntax, properties which, within MOGUL, would certainly be considered 'modular'. These core properties of syntax include properties like subject-verb-object word order and other grammatical structures like question formation and negation. But at the same time, they seem to have difficulty with other grammatical properties like subject-verb agreement, articles and passive sentence structure, to name a few examples in English. This contradiction has caused much debate, and may be the reason why some researchers have concluded that second language development is fundamentally different from first.

There is a very recent proposal which may help us to understand this problem more clearly. Slabakova (2008) has brought together a large body of research and observed that the one thing the 'unacquirable' grammatical structures seem to have in common is functional morphology. She hypothesises that grammatical function words/morphemes cause a 'bottleneck' for acquisition. They are a problem for acquisition because they are extremely complex and often there is no casually observable connection between form, function and meaning. If you have tried to teach articles, you will know that, even though there are general rules that work most of the time, there are also problematic 'exceptions' that seem to defy explanation. Another common problem with functional morphemes is that one form can have lots of functions. The -s in English, for example, is used for verbal agreement, plurals and possessive structures; and its phonetic realisation also varies, from /s/ to /z/ to /əs/, depending on the preceding phonetic form. This does not mean that they cannot be explicitly learned, but it does mean that they are not easily learned for all of their functions and with all relevant grammatical distinctions. The **Bottleneck Hypothesis** put forward by Slabakova proposes that these bits of language are problematic for natural, implicit acquisition because they hold a large, complex bundle of grammatical features and functions without any clear connection to meaningful conceptual notions. One strength of this hypothesis is that it is based on a large and growing body of existing data, including the well-known case studies confirming learners' continued difficulty with functional morphology that we discussed in Chapter 3.

The implication of the observation that different domains of language develop differently is that we should teach the different aspects of language differently. If learners can readily acquire both meaning on the one hand and the very core properties of syntax on the other, then we would do well to provide learners with plenty of rich exposure and create a learning environment in which they are actively engaging with language to allow for implicit development of these aspects of language both in the language module and in general cognition. At the same time, we should expect problems where language depends on function words/morphemes.

Yet we should not despair. Slabakova argues that, eventually, these things can be acquired. A MOGUL approach suggests that, instead of waiting for acquisition to occur eventually, these areas can be explicitly taught. Intelligent, motivated learners can consciously learn the form–meaning connections of function words/morphemes and practise them until they begin to occur automatically. This is especially possible for grammatical forms that follow more straightforward form–meaning patterns. For example, the 3rd person -s in English is a fairly dependable rule, with a limited set of exceptions. With ample practice, a learner should be able to master this. The problem is that some areas of language are very complex, with linguists still debating their exact properties. There are several analyses of the grammatical properties of articles in English, for example. This makes it difficult for teachers to be able to teach these properties fully. Fortunately, this is an extreme example. Most of the grammatical forms do follow a fairly clear set of 'rules' which are generally accurate and can be explained and learned by students.

So where does this bring us? Because language learning is variable across linguistic subsystems, we should firstly be aware of the linguistic particulars of that variability. Then we should make decisions about the type of input, to include both 'natural' and explicit presentation of the target language. Most important is the question of how we teach. This observation says that you are better off using your limited class time explaining the rules for functional morphology than for syntactic structure. Yet MOGUL tells us that explanation is not likely to be enough. Students will need to work hard to understand them and practise them for the repeated activation required for learning. Returning to the other broader generalisation, you will also want to explicitly teach 'meaning', which comes from experience and use of language. Students can readily develop a large inventory of words; so teach vocabulary. Students can also learn how to use the language appropriately; so teach differences in formality, registers, genres, and even dialects. But throughout, make sure your learners get plenty of natural input both inside and outside the classroom.

In sum, as expert teachers, we need to develop our understanding of linguistics so that we can take different aspects of language into account in our language classroom. Aspects of language that are modular should be singled out from aspects that are not. Core syntax and subtle aspects of semantics can be acquired. The more experience-based aspects of non-modular language can be readily taught and learned. The more complex aspects of function words/morphemes need as much explanation as possible and lots of practice. They may also require an acceptance by teachers and learners that there may be limits on how well they can be mastered. By knowing what kind of knowledge we are dealing with, we can then make decisions on how to teach (or not teach) that knowledge.

OBSERVATION 7: THERE ARE LIMITS ON THE EFFECTS OF FREQUENCY ON SLA

In this discussion of observations we have mentioned the importance of frequency several times. And the Acquisition by Processing Theory of MOGUL defines learning as strengthening of linguistic forms through repeated activation. Yet while there are neurological studies on processing, there is little research on the neurological basis of learning itself. The existing psycholinguistic research may be more indicative. There is a large literature on priming which shows that the activation of one word allows for faster recognition of related words. The explanation is that the brain is a complex network of associations; repeated activation of a word leads to higher resting levels, which in turn give rise to faster activation. This can be seen as 'learning'. The clear implication of this kind of research is that there is a strong role for frequency in language development. But this observation singles out the *limits* of frequency. If learning happens through repeated activation, why is it not the case that extensive exposure and practice is enough for successful language development?

To make sense of this, it is important to know that this kind of research has mostly been limited to the level of words.[10] There is ample evidence for the storage of words in associative networks. Given the complexity of language, it is difficult to conduct valid neurolinguistic or psycholinguistic studies that truly isolate other aspects of language. Unfortunately, some researchers have used the findings from word-level studies to generalise to language in general. Yet it should be very clear by now that language is much more than a list of words. So, one reason why there is a limit on the effect of frequency in language development is that some areas of language development require more than repeated exposure. If we think about the complexity of language, we can appreciate that there are many complex systems involved in language processing. Aside from the complex morphosyntactic properties of any utterance, processing involves either audio or visual systems as well; this will by necessity implicate systems for decoding pronunciation or writing systems, respectively. And all this says nothing of the content of the message that must be decoded all in the same instant.

One conclusion, then, is that there are limits to the effects of frequency because of the sheer complexity of the processing load on the learner. VanPatten goes further to argue that language development depends on processing constraints. In his **Input Processing** approach, development occurs when the learner's limited processing abilities initially lead to a misinterpretation. If led to the correct interpretation instead, then learning occurs.[11]

Another implication is that the teacher should not only provide ample and frequent input, but make sure that particular linguistic features in the lesson are salient as well. After all, even though a new bit of language may be very frequent in the input, if it is not picked up on by the learner, then frequency is irrelevant. Much has been made of the role of 'noticing' in language development.[12] Yet, as pointed out by Truscott (1998), even though teachers and researchers alike understand this idea of noticing intuitively, there is no theoretical or psycholinguistically based definition of what noticing is exactly. For this reason, some have suggested that teachers should not concern themselves with what may (or may not!) be happening in the learner's brain. Instead, a good teacher will give much time and attention to those things they can control: namely, the nature of the input. Sharwood Smith (1993) proposed **Input Enhancement** as a way of making desired linguistic features more salient to the learner. Enhancement can be done in a number of ways, from making the target feature(s) bold or underlined in a text, to asking students to pick out the feature(s).

If we also bear in mind the psycholinguistic research on priming, we may want to point out related or associative forms in our teaching. Emphasising associations is clearly a good idea for teaching vocabulary, and it will be effective for teaching collocations like *weather forecast*. Whether it is useful for more grammatical forms is still a matter of research. Additionally, whether association facilitates more pragmatic or cultural aspects of language is also an open question. Given the limits in research, you may want to explore the effectiveness of salience and association for different aspects of language. Or, you may want to remain faithful to the research to date and teach different aspects of language differently. As such, teaching by association with frequent exposure and repeated activation may be the way you teach words and fixed phrases, with consideration of processing constraints for other grammatical aspects of language.

As a final note, we must not forget that processing refers to a meaningful activity. Frequency alone says nothing about meaningful processing. We will discuss the importance of interaction when we discuss Observation 9, but will simply point out here that the limits of frequency are also explained if that frequency only occurs in meaningless activities.

OBSERVATION 8: THERE ARE LIMITS ON THE EFFECT OF A LEARNER'S FIRST LANGUAGE ON SLA

In Chapter 2, we discussed how Contrastive Analysis is intuitively appealing, but has been shown to be problematic conceptually and empirically for many aspects of language. In other words, research does not show that it is necessarily easier to learn morphosyntactic features that are similar in the first and target languages; nor is it necessarily harder to learn those that are different. Yet we have seen that there are transfer effects in second language development. In Observation 5 we discussed how the native language can be the source of a learnability problem in second language development in certain areas, using the Subset Principle as an example. These two points tell us that we should be aware of the first language as a factor in second language development, but that there are limits on the effect.

The implications for language teaching reinforce an emerging theme: there are many points of which a good teacher should have awareness, while also recognising that it is only one factor among many. The existence of the first language is one major difference between native and second language development. The MOGUL framework presents a picture in which that first language is ready for activation, in response to any linguistic input. But we now have a growing number of other factors which may limit the effect of the first language. Salience, as mentioned above, is likely to affect activation. When we are teaching the appropriate use of some language form, for example, the target language context is likely to be the more salient context for a learner than a native language context. This may keep the native language from being activated, thereby limiting the effect of the first language.

This conscious, or explicit, attention to language stands in contrast with a more implicit process whereby the first language may facilitate or inhibit development. Yet, we know that even in terms of core or modular language, there are limits on language transfer. There is the possibility of UG-constrained modular development; the research shows a degree of systematic development regardless of the native language of the learner. This suggests that more universal principles of development may at times outweigh language transfer. Though our approach has been exclusively limited to the properties of language, the importance of the native language will also vary from one teaching context to another. While it is common for language teachers in a second language teaching setting to have students from a range of first language backgrounds, for example, a foreign language teacher may find all the students share a mother tongue. We will bring in these more practical issues of classroom teaching as this book progresses.

Between the theoretical issues of language and the practical issues of the classroom, there are other issues related to the first language. There are, for example, some well-known stereotypes associated with particular groups of language learners. Many of these stereotypes are likely to be more of a product of particular educational practices than properties of the native language itself. For example, for adults coming from an educational system that relies heavily on rote memorisation, it is not surprising that learners have highly developed memorisation skills. Similarly, for those coming from an educational system that makes heavy use of orality or, conversely, literacy, it is not surprising to find that these learners have disproportionately developed abilities in speaking over writing, or vice versa. As a teacher, you can tap into existing learning strategies to enhance language development while at the same time actively working to develop the less-developed skills, as appropriate. We will close this discussion by reiterating that the native language is only one of a range of factors that are implicated in language development. A good teacher will have an awareness of the learners' native language, but will not accommodate L1 transfer blindly since the effects are limited.

OBSERVATION 9: THERE ARE LIMITS ON THE EFFECTS OF INSTRUCTION ON SLA

We have already drawn the conclusion that there is a degree of 'natural' acquisition in SLA, and we have discussed incidental learning. Both of these conclusions suggest that the power of instruction is limited. But this observation makes reference to another very important factor in language development, the role of learner interaction. This is captured by Michael Long's **Interaction Hypothesis**, which argues that language development depends on learner interaction because it is not only the challenge of making sense of but also making sense in a language that facilitates language development.[13] Long's view is that second language learning does not depend on just internal or external factors, but instead on the learner's active engagement with the language.

This may seem like an obvious point from the advantage of present views of language teaching. However, it was an important contribution at the time when it was proposed as an advancement on Krashen's Input Hypothesis. Like Krashen, we have highlighted input; yet it should be clear that input is only one of a number of important factors, and, as argued by Long, certainly not sufficient on its own for successful language development. Instead what matters is what learners do with the input to which they are exposed. Also proposed at this time to counter the Input Hypothesis was Merrill Swain's **Output Hypothesis**.[14] Swain researched Canadian immersion language programmes which showed that L1 English children who did their education through the medium of French had very good comprehension abilities, but were less proficient in writing and speaking. This led her to conclude that language production is not just a pedagogic by-product of language teaching, but is necessary for language development, especially when it comes to language production.

Long's Interaction Hypothesis captures both input and output, relying on the dynamic process of **negotiation of meaning**. As learners struggle to understand input and as they strive to produce output, the process itself will translate into language development.[15] It is this negotiation of meaning that makes input comprehensible, and this that enables learners to 'notice' gaps in their interlanguage. Students must actively work to make sense of the input from both the teacher and their fellow students. And they must modify their output in order to be understood.

This emphasis on the learner means that the effect of instruction is limited. The implication, most broadly speaking, is communicative language teaching. Communicative activities require interaction. A more specific application of the Interaction Hypothesis is **task-based learning**. A **task** is an activity between two or more learners with a goal that is not linguistic, but instead designed to require the use of particular linguistic features. So, for example, asking one student to refer to a map to direct another student who cannot see the map has the goal of manoeuvring to a destination, but depends on the use of language. More specifically, this task requires the use of imperatives as well as the prepositions and adverbs needed for giving directions.

Task-based teaching establishes a natural platform for Focus on Form. In carefully devising tasks, a teacher can create situations which require the learners to use particular forms which may be new to them. We will discuss task-based learning and teaching further in the next chapter, but will close by saying that when we say the effect of instruction is limited, we are especially referring to limitations of explicit language instruction, such as traditional Focus on FormS techniques.

OBSERVATION 10: THERE ARE LIMITS ON THE EFFECTS OF OUTPUT (LEARNER PRODUCTION) ON LANGUAGE ACQUISITION

This observation clarifies one of the points from the preceding observation. As we just saw, output is an important feature of language development. Negotiation of meaning requires modification of output, which can, in turn, challenge learners to use their full range of linguistic resources. Moreover, learners might need to be pushed to produce forms that challenge their current level in their output. Otherwise, there is a tendency for learners to avoid difficult language structures. Research in **avoidance** shows that high accuracy levels in language production among some learners may disguise actual ability, as they may be using a strategy to avoid more difficult language constructions.[16] A learner who is pushed to produce difficult language will not be able to engage readily in avoidance.

The observation that production is limited is given because there is no research that directly shows that the act of producing language leads to higher or better language ability. Even though research in immersion classrooms shows that learners who do not regularly produce language had limitations in their production, this does not mean that those who do produce language will necessarily be more accurate or have higher levels of fluency. Production can be seen as a reflection of the learner's ability at any given point in time; it has not been shown to be an agent for change itself, at least not change to the learner's implicit interlanguage grammar.

There may be differences between the effect of output on explicit vs implicit knowledge. It may be that output has more of an effect on the status of explicit metalinguistic knowledge. Through practice, particular phrases may be memorised, leading to increased speed of production, or automatisation. While this may be useful for single words or set phrases, reliance on rote repetition will be limited for real language in real time, since language is creative and not just a list of set phrases. It is also the case that output is generally understood to refer to meaningful production and not rote repetition. Thus, practice in these terms would refer to a kind of self-rehearsal, more than rote repetition. Rehearsal could very well prepare a learner for a specific interaction, as the learner could draw on metalinguistic knowledge to prepare relevant vocabulary or phrases. Additionally, a learner could think through specific grammatical rules underlying the sentences they plan to use. This is the logic behind Krashen's famous Monitor Model. Learners are able to monitor their production, drawing on the current state of their acquired knowledge and modifying their output based on their explicit metalinguistic knowledge. Of course, the real-time pressures of spontaneous speech may limit the effectivity of monitoring, but adept development of strategies coupled with memorisation of phrases may be enough to allow for a seemingly native-like proficiency.

The conclusion is not that output is not useful for the learner; it is only the observation that the effect of output on acquisition is limited. The implication for teaching is that for language activities that are not constrained by time, monitoring may be very helpful. And though learner rehearsal may not actually lead to language acquisition, it may lead to more successful interactions, which, in turn could lead to increased levels of automaticity and increased levels of confidence. Another implication for teaching is to do with error correction. If output reflects the current level of language, an error in output may reveal an underlying rule which the teacher could draw attention to, working with the learner to develop specific strategies to overcome it. With increased awareness, explicit instruction may help the learner to self-correct for more effective fluency.

CONCLUSION

In this chapter we have discussed VanPatten and Williams's ten generalisations about second language development, looking for implications for the classroom. One important point to note is that the implications presented here are logical conclusions; not all are empirically based. Applied generative SLA in particular is one area which is in much need of empirical research.

One theme that has clearly emerged from our discussion of these observations is complexity; language itself is complex, and the process of language development is complex. Knowledgeable teachers need to take on the complexity of language and language development – in addition to the many other practical factors and constraints that accompany any language teaching context. A second theme also emerges: there is a clear role for teachers and teaching in successful language development.

Language development is not just a matter of language exposure; teachers must decide what the input will be and how to expose the learner to it. Language development is not just a matter of output; teachers must make that output meaningful and it should require use of language that challenges learners, whatever their current level. MOGUL can help a teacher to sort through the balance between 'natural' and complex implicit input and explicit instructed input. Research to date suggests that learners can acquire aspects of meaning, including pragmatic knowledge, the meaning of words and more subtle aspects of semantics which even linguists have difficulty explaining. Core properties of syntax such as word order and sentence formation can also be acquired. This suggests that these are areas which will develop in response to rich, authentic input. Other areas of language, such as native-like pronunciation and functional morphology, seem beyond the reach of natural acquisition except in exceptional cases. These are areas that will need more explicit instruction.

Given the limited time constraints of most language classrooms, teachers would do well to decide selectively what to use their time teaching on explicitly. Moreover, while there is much variability among learners, there seem to be constraints on the extent to which older learners can acquire language to native-speaker level. MOGUL reminds us that explicit language knowledge can compensate for implicit language knowledge, however. Learners can develop metalinguistic knowledge about areas of language that have the potential for implicit development. With practice, this metalinguistic knowledge can become automatised so that it allows for fluency. With this understanding of language and language development, we now turn to more explicit discussion of the classroom as we continue to apply these ideas to classroom teaching.

FOR DISCUSSION

1. Think of your own experience with teaching (or learning) a language. Can you come up with examples from your personal experience that support each of the observations?
2. Again based on your experience, can you add any observations about language development to those discussed in this chapter?

3. The ten observations have been discussed with little regard to particular contexts or types of learners. Consider each observation from the point of view of each the following variables to discuss the extent to which they are relevant.

   a. age
   b. proficiency
   c. native language
   d. number of languages learned
   e. learning environments: for example, naturalistic vs instructed
   f. reasons for learning language: for instance, motivation.

4. Can you think of any other factors that might affect the development of language?
5. Thinking of your own experience as a teacher (or learner), what have you done in the past to address (some of) the observations for more effective language development?
6. Consider each observation from the point of view of a language teacher. What could you do to take each into account? Are some easier to address than others?

NOTES

1. Stephen Krashen has devoted much of his more recent career to researching the effectiveness of 'sustained silent reading', which, he argues, has enormous potential for bolstering learners' second language ability. See Krashen (2004). There is also research showing the role that reading can play in the development of vocabulary. See Nation (2001).
2. See Schwartz (1993), who defends the position that learned and acquired knowledge are and remain distinct.
3. See the edited volume by Doughty and Williams (1998) for a discussion of Focus on Form and its relationship with Focus on Meaning and Focus on FormS.
4. The work of Dekydtspotter and colleagues (see note 11 of Chapter 3) is all within the realm of semantic interpretation, as is the work of Marsden.
5. Early research on the development of negation in L2 English focused on child L2. See Wode (1977) for research on German native-speaker children, and Schumann (1979) for research on Spanish native-speaker children, both acquiring English negation. Hyltenstam (1977) also finds stages of development in acquisition of negation for L2 Norwegian learners. Later work researched negation as one property of a larger parameter cluster. For example, see White (1992) for research in L2 English, and Yuan (2001) for L2 Chinese research.

6. Stages of development constitute an area of L2 research that is in need of more study. The most developed line of research in this direction at the moment is Pienemann's Processability Theory and associated work in Teachability. See Pienemann (1998, 2005).

7. The best-known research in this area is based on the Accessibility Hierarchy for relative clauses (Keenan and Comrie 1977). The original study showing that learners who are taught a more difficult, or marked form, is Gass (1982). Since then numerous studies have been done, some confirming and others disconfirming this result. For a more recent study, see Ammar and Lightbown (2003). Not surprisingly, additional research has led to the realisation that there is much complexity in terms of the language facts, which may affect overall results.

8. Research by Snow and Hoefnagel-Höhle (1978) included English speakers learning Dutch in an immersion setting. The adults were all middle-class, educated professionals. Despite the possibility that these learners were unusually diligent and motivated, the larger point still holds: rate of development is distinct from route of development. See also Wode (1978).

9. Flege, who researches L2 phonology in general, has also done work on age and phonology; see Flege (1999, 2009) in particular.

10. See Paradis (2004) for a discussion of how most of the research in neuroimaging is limited to words.

11. See VanPatten (1996, 2004) for more detailed discussion.

12. The Noticing Hypothesis was proposed by Schmidt (1990, 1993) and was subsequently adopted by many notable researchers. See, for example, Ellis (1994), Long (1991) or Robinson (1995).

13. See Long (1981, 1983) for the original formulation of the Interaction Hypothesis and Long (1996) for an update.

14. See Swain (1985) for the original formulation of the Output Hypotheses and Swain (2005) for a recent discussion.

15. Another significant contribution from Michael Long has been to inspire a research agenda that analyses interaction among native and non-native speakers. This has led to a large body of literature on feedback techniques such as repetition, clarification and expansion. While much of the early research was conducted in artificial contexts, more recent work has studied real classroom interaction. See Keck et al. (2006) for a meta-analysis of research on interaction and Russell and Spada (2006) for a meta-analysis of research on corrective feedback.

16. Schachter (1974) took a Contrastive Analysis Hypothesis approach to argue that avoidance occurs when there are differences between the native language and target language. While this argument has been much debated since then (see Laufer and Eliasson 1993, for example), there seems little doubt that avoidance of particular forms is a common feature of L2 production.

6

APPROACHES TO ENGLISH LANGUAGE TEACHING

༄

INTRODUCTION

In Chapter 2, we took a historical perspective, exploring how differing views about language and language development have translated into approaches to language teaching in Europe over the ages. We saw that the influence of classical language in the early years of language teaching meant that the method of teaching Latin was adopted for teaching other European languages. This Grammar Translation method was challenged, however, by the Reform Movement, which looked to native language development and proposed the Direct Method, requiring exclusive use of the target language in the classroom. In some ways, this quite radical approach was ahead of its time. The enormous difference between Grammar Translation and the Direct Method no doubt contributed to the latter's failure, since change tends to happen much more gradually.

The prevailing viewpoints of the growing academic fields of linguistics and psychology from this time left a mark on the language teaching field. A structuralist view of language provided a list of grammatical structures to consider alongside grammarians' language rules. And the emerging behaviourist view of habit formation encouraged teachers to adopt an approach which depended heavily on repetitive practice and drilling. The progressive contribution of the Oral and Situational Approaches was not only to emphasise spoken language, but also to recognise that language should be presented in meaningful contexts. Less progressive was the behaviourist influence, as the Oral Approach in the UK and the Situational Approach in Australia looked very much like the Audiolingual Approach in North America in terms of classroom practice, relying heavily on repetition, memorisation and drilling.

This was the situation in English language teaching when the so-called Chomskyan Revolution in linguistics took place. Generative Linguistics discredited the behaviourist view of language and native language development, arguing that language is comprised of universal principles which children possess innately at birth. We ended Chapter 2 by exploring the effects of this development in SLA. We saw how the idea that language is a system has also been supported by SLA research, with investigation into second language learning as a systematic process. Unfortunately, the early practices of Error Analysis and Contrastive Analysis did not support the overly optimistic view that merely identifying where native and target language are the same and different would be enough to determine which areas of second language development are easy and problematic, respectively. In the last chapter we explored the implications of more current understandings of second language development for language teaching. In this chapter we ask how these implications translate into approaches to language teaching in the more recent period leading up to the present.

Firstly, however, we need to clarify some terminology. There is a widely held distinction between method and approach. An **approach** to teaching refers to the conceptual principles, views or assumptions that underpin the way one teaches. These beliefs may be explicit and supported by research, or they may be deeply held intuitions of which a teacher is not even explicitly aware. In terms of language teaching, it includes the understanding of what language is and how it develops; this influences a teacher's fundamental decisions. One main aim of this book is to explore some of these fundamental assumptions in order to challenge you as a teacher to be explicitly aware of your understandings and beliefs. These beliefs will affect your choice of method. **Method** refers to the way the language is taught, the type of activities and how these are structured and presented.[1]

The following exemplifies these two terms: if I held a structuralist view of language, this would affect my overall approach, as I would view my task as being to teach sets of language structures, emphasising grammatical rules and correct forms. And if I had a behaviourist view of language development, I would want to appeal to memorisation and repetition. Thus, the method I would choose would be Audiolingualism. In this chapter we will be looking at both approaches and methods in language teaching. At times, we will also make reference to more specific **techniques** of classroom teaching, like lesson planning and error correction, for example. However, these more specific aspects of teaching are more the subject of the last couple of chapters of this book.

'DESIGNER' APPROACHES

In this section we will briefly survey what I will call 'designer' approaches, exploring a range of language teaching practices that have been devised in order to translate specific beliefs about language or language development into classroom practice. And, as there are limits to what one book can do, we will limit our discussion to English language teaching. The period from the 1960s to the 1990s saw much experimentation as new developments in language study inspired new and creative approaches to language teaching. Unsurprisingly, new ideas tended to influence the profession locally, at least in the first instance. Thus, in the early part of the 'modern' period there were differences in North America on the one hand and the UK and Australia on the other. As we will see at the end of this section, however, by the 1990s the differences had all contributed in their own way to a more general trend among English language teaching professionals globally.

We start this discussion of designer approaches in North America. The Natural Approach of Krashen and Terrell (1983) was based on what has come to be known as Krashen's **Monitor Model**.[2] An attempt to apply the new ideas coming out of Generative Linguistics to language teaching, the Monitor Model included five hypotheses. The first, the **Acquisition-Learning Hypothesis**, made the very useful distinction between implicit and explicit learning, with acquisition as subconscious, implicit development of language and learning as the conscious, explicit process. A speaker draws on acquired knowledge without thinking about it, while learned knowledge is explicit meta-linguistic language knowledge. Additionally, acquisition is associated with the language module and learning with general cognition. For Krashen, the two are distinct processes; learning cannot become or affect acquisition. The acquisition-learning distinction was appealing to teachers since there is a well-known tendency for learners to 'know' a form, but still make mistakes. With Krashen's distinction, we can say that they have learned the form, but they have not acquired it.

The second hypothesis is the **Monitor Hypothesis**, whereby learner output, which originates from acquired knowledge, can be consciously 'monitored', making use of learned knowledge. In order for a learner to use the Monitor, however, there are some requirements. There must be time for reflection during output; the learner must pay attention to the form of the output; and the learner must have enough explicit knowledge of the relevant language rules in order to self-correct.

The next two hypotheses are closely related. The **Natural Order Hypothesis** specified that rules of a language are acquired in a 'natural' order. For this part of the Monitor Model there was little discussion of differences between native child language development and adult second language development. Krashen put much stock in the research he did on morpheme orders, which showed very little differences between in language development in terms of age or native language – at least for the development of English functional morphemes.[3] For Krashen and the Natural Approach, then, language development followed a natural order depending more on an internal syllabus than on instruction. Because there is a natural order, acquisition must proceed from stage to stage. The **Input Hypothesis** asserted that, instead of explicit teaching, what is really needed is lots of input 'appropriate' to the stage of the learner. More specifically, learners need **comprehensible input**, also known as $i + 1$, where i is the current level of the learner and 1 is the stage just one step beyond the current level. The role of the teacher in the Natural Approach, then, is to provide sufficient amounts of input at the right level of development. The final piece of the Monitor Model puzzle is the **Affective Filter Hypothesis**. Recognising that adult language development is different from child development, Krashen suggested that adults have a 'filter' which determines how much of the comprehensible input is 'allowed' into the language module. In Krashen's terms, the filter would be raised if a learner had little interest and motivation or if other affective factors led to a less than ideal learning environment. In addition to child–adult differences, this filter can explain individual variation among adult learners since learners differ widely in terms of affective factors. Like many aspects of Krashen's ideas, this affective filter idea may be intuitively appealing, as it seems to capture what we as teachers experience with our learners. The problem, however, is that there was and is no principled basis for it – there is no theory in psychology or linguistics which includes any kind of filter like this, nor is there any empirical way to prove that such a filter might exist.

Based on these basic tenets, Krashen and Terrell developed the Natural Approach, which emphasised comprehension first, putting much stock on input from the teacher. While this input was expected to be graded, following a natural order, in reality the approach was not able to specify what that order might be. Instead, the emphasis was on sufficient input with ample time for learners to acquire before producing language. At low levels, learners were allowed to go through a silent period, much as native language learners do. With early production, errors were to be ignored in order to encourage fluency. The emphasis on fluency meant classroom activities that were communicative in nature. Also essential in this approach was a commitment to a very supportive atmosphere in order for affective filters to be lowered as much as possible.

While Krashen is to be respected for trying to relate work in theoretical linguistics to language teaching, he went beyond what the theory could actually support, both empirically and conceptually. And the Natural Approach itself was not quite the success in the classroom for which he might have hoped. Second language development in the classroom cannot be left entirely to 'natural' tendencies. Unfortunately, the Chomskyan 'revolution' in linguistics did not have the revolutionary effect on classroom teaching for which some applied linguists may have hoped. In fact, the failings of the Natural Approach brought to mind the much earlier failings of the Direct Method. The problem is that second language learning is different to first. Adult language learners, for example, do not necessarily go through a silent period as young children do. Yet, despite the failings of his Monitor Model and Natural Approach, Krashen made an important contribution and his ideas remain influential. As has been made evident in this book, generative research does have an important role to play in informing classroom language teaching. But as we have seen, this requires a much more sophisticated understanding of what is happening in language development than the picture painted by the Monitor Model.

Krashen's ideas contrast with approaches that had developed in other parts of the world. The predominant view of language in Australia and the UK in the 1970s and 1980s was the functionalist view of Halliday. Building on the tradition of the Oral/Situational Approach, David Wilkins (1976) proposed the **Notional Syllabus**. As reflected in the title, language in this view is seen as a set of conceptual notions. Examples of notional categories are time, quantity or location. However, as a syllabus based only on notions is a bit limited, connections were made between notions with specific language functions, such as requests, denials, offers, apologies, and so on. Devising a syllabus in terms of notion and function provided a concrete step away from the traditional reliance on language structure as an organising approach to teaching. This allowed for a genuine shift to teaching language in context. After all, a lesson devised around a notion such as location and a function such as requests leads very naturally to activities that embody language in use. This gave rise to the type of textbook that is still popular as a format for modern textbooks, with lesson titles like 'At the train station' or 'Asking or directions'.

The move to a notional syllabus was well received and reasonably successful, as teachers and learners alike recognised the importance of meaningful language learning. All of the approaches of the post-war period were trying, in their own way, to move away from the traditional tendency to teach language as a static set of grammar rules. This tendency was (and still is!) seen in the PPP approach to lesson planning, which lends itself to teaching specifically identified language points or rules and then asking learners to practise and produce them. While PPP can be extended to more functional features of language, it is, in effect, inherently structuralist, as it breaks language down into structures for presentation.

In addition to approaches to teaching based on particular views of language, there have been designer approaches that develop other pedagogic principles. While we will not discuss any of them in great detail, we will try to give a flavour of some of the so-called 'alternative' approaches that have been proposed.[4] Perhaps the best known of the designer approaches is the **Silent Way**, devised by Caleb Gattegno. The main idea of this approach is that learners should produce as much language as possible, and teachers should be as silent as possible. This approach to teaching language adopts the widely accepted pedagogic principle that learning occurs through problem-solving and discovery, and not through the teacher simply telling students what they ought to know. The Silent Way does recognise that some spoken input is needed. At times, teachers do model new language forms, but the majority of the lesson requires learners to work out language rules, to repeat new target forms and both to self-correct and peer-correct. With limited oral input, the Silent Way makes much use of physical objects, body language and gestures. Obviously, this view sees classroom second language learning as very different from native FLA. Proponents of the Silent Way insist that this difference should be explicitly recognised.[5]

The Silent Way stands in stark contrast to **Comprehension Approaches** like Krashen's Natural Approach, which emphasise the understanding of language over production, at least initially. **The Learnables**, devised by Harris Winitz, also de-emphasises learner production. This approach depends exclusively on pictures accompanied by sound. Mimicking the child experience, learners are expected to learn by looking and listening.[6] Another comprehension approach, James Asher's **Total Physical Response (TPR)**, highlights the importance of kinetics; learners learn language by reacting physically to language input. TPR develops the ideas of educational psychology in which learning is rooted in stimulus–response cycles. By asking learners to respond physically to language commands, the right brain is engaged for motor functioning and the left brain for reasoning.[7] As in the Natural Approach, learners are not expected to speak until they are ready. For advocates of comprehension approaches like the Learnables, TPR and the Natural Approach, the absence of pressure to produce language will reduce stress and facilitate learning.

The idea of reducing stress is taken even further by **Suggestopedia,** developed by Georgi Lozanov, a Bulgarian psychologist with an interest in yoga. Relaxation to allow the learner to be primed for learning is essential in this approach. A Suggestopedia classroom is immediately identifiable by its comfortable chairs, candles and music, used to create a relaxed atmosphere. Coupled with this idea of 'psycho-relaxation', however, is the importance of the teacher as an authority figure. The idea is that learners will be more susceptible to learning if they enter a more child-like state, which will happen if the teacher carries authority. Another child language-inspired requirement is that the teacher exaggerates intonation when speaking, emphasising the rhythm of the language. In terms of the actual lesson, the procedure is to use what is referred to as a Séance or Concert Session, in which the teacher 'performs' a dialogue which students follow, looking at a script. The script may have notes or even native language translations, and particular vocabulary or difficult grammar will be identified and taught. The dialogue is then delivered again, but this time the students listen without the aid of a text. At the end, students leave the class in silence, absorbing the day's lesson for themselves.[8]

Another approach based on ideas from psychology and, more specifically, counselling is the **Community Language Learning** of Charles Curran. In this approach, the teacher is a counsellor and learners are clients. Language is a social process of collaboration and community development. Learning will occur if the whole person is engaged, not just their intellect, but their emotions and feelings. Modelling the stages of development from childhood to adulthood, learners are expected to feel insecure in early stages before being able to assert a degree of independence. In doing so, they will begin to establish an identity in the new language. It is only at more proficient stages that the learners will be able to accept criticism, and so error correction should be avoided until then.[9]

The final designer approach that we will consider here, **Rassias**, is named after its founder, John Rassias. For Rassias, language is a cultural artefact which must be learned from within the social context of the target language. Since there is no such environment in the usual foreign language teaching setting, it is important for the teacher to create an immersion environment which mimics the target language environment as far as possible. This aspect of the approach requires skills in drama, as there is a degree of 'acting' involved. It also requires much enthusiasm and energy from the teacher, who is expected not only to create an authentic environment, but also to eliminate the inhibitions of the learners so that they can take part in their new environment. In practical terms, there is also use of repetition and drills, but in such a way that the emphasis is on positive reinforcement, not rote memory.[10]

This idea of creating a target language environment is an attempt to create an immersion situation when immersion is otherwise not possible. Total immersion has been advocated as the most effective way to promote language learning. In an immersion programme, content classes such as geography and science are taught through the medium of the target language while the target language itself does not have explicitly dedicated class time. Because immersion is the closest setting to a native environment, it might be expected that this would be the most successful of language approaches. However, as we saw in the last chapter, it has been found that such programmes do not necessarily result in higher language ability than tradition language classes, especially in terms of learners' ability to produce language. Nevertheless, it remains a viable option and should be considered as an option if the circumstances allow it.

Immersion programmes are normally associated with primary level schooling. When implemented at secondary levels or above they tend to take the form of Content-Based Instruction (CBI). Again, the idea is that the object of the lesson is some meaningful content, like biology, for example. But this content is taught through the medium of the target language.[11] Because the nature of the content for adults is likely to be relatively advanced, CBI is often associated with advanced levels of language learning as well. Thus CBI is a type of **English for Specific Purposes (ESP)**, in which English classes are tailored to the specific needs of the particular set of learners.[12]

While all of these approaches are based on pedagogically relevant principles, they vary in terms of their emphasis and understanding of what language is, how language develops and what best fosters this development. Unfortunately, one thing they all have in common is that no single approach or method is appropriate for the range of language classroom settings that exist. And even within the particular context for which it may be designed, no approach has shown itself to be foolproof. Against this somewhat pessimistic conclusion, however, is the more optimistic development of a general trend within modern language teaching circles. This trend is for a Communicative Language Teaching approach to language teaching.

CURRENT TREND: COMMUNICATIVE LANGUAGE TEACHING

The development of **Communicative Language Teaching (CLT)** is often seen as a natural outgrowth of the functionalist view of language. Notably, however, even though there is a fundamental difference between the generative view that developed initially in North America, and the functionalist view originating in Australia and the UK, both have reasons for agreeing that CLT is an appropriate approach to teaching. For generativists, language is 'natural' and language acquisition occurs in response to 'real' or positive input. For functionalists, language is a tool for making meaning and language will develop through interaction and use. As we will see, authentic input and interaction are two basic features of CLT.

In fact, CLT has not developed only out of these two linguistic approaches. Many of the features of CLT are a natural outcome of a broader trend in education as well. **Progressivism** in mainstream education is a twentieth-century trend which emphasises the needs of students as individuals; it promotes the idea that active learning through doing and discovery is more effective than the passive absorption of bodies of knowledge.[13] Another reason for converging on CLT is simply the passage of time. While language specialists have been calling for a shift away from the teaching of language structures for a very long time, in practice, fundamental change is often slow. The call to teach notions and functions, for example, looked progressive, but in practice it tended to result in lists of phrases that were often drilled and memorised. In fact, the early attempts to make language teaching more communicative also tended, in reality, to atomise language and teach lists and rules. In time, however, the consensus has led to an emergence of genuinely communicative practices.

CLT is an approach, and not a method. It adheres to a range of principles, which in turn give rise to particular teaching methods. We will discuss the main basic principles underlying CLT. The first basic premise is that language is communication which develops through use. Because of the importance of language use, it may be more appropriate to refer to students as language users than language learners. Accordingly, **fluency** is emphasised over the more traditional focus on **accuracy** in terms of grammar, pronunciation and word choice, for example. CLT is often willing to overlook accuracy at the level of detail for the sake of promoting fluent use. Learners are encouraged to speak without worrying too much about 'correct' forms, as long as communication is successful. This is not to say that errors are entirely ignored, but they are often seen as secondary to the more important aim of maximising language production. Fluency is generally associated with production; yet the ability to understand spoken speech in real time as well as target-like reading speed can be seen as other aspects of fluency which should be promoted and developed. Additionally, in practice the emphasis on fluency over accuracy tends to be true more for spoken than for written production, as many CLT practitioners will overlook inaccuracies in speech which they would correct in writing.

This accuracy vs fluency issue is closely related to the question of **process vs product**. Since communication is basic to CLT, there is an emphasis on process over product. In other words, value is given to the act of making meaning rather than to the particular choice of output in terms of form. This is because of the importance of interaction in CLT. As we discussed in Chapter 5, Long's Interaction Hypothesis calls for learners to negotiate meaning. By engaging in actual communication, language-learning users will have to work through gaps in their comprehension and production. This hard work requires strategies for overcoming communication breakdown, which in turn entails a degree of self-awareness and self-reflection. In other words, learners will benefit from a sophisticated understanding of and control over the processes involved in language. Or, to use a term recently coined by Swain (2006), learners develop competent skills in the process of **languaging**. This hard work of making meaning in interaction is the basis for language development.

Another basic characteristic of CLT, which we have already touched on, is the importance of language meaning instead of the more traditional focus on grammar rules. Language lessons should revolve around meaningful activities. While involved in meaningful activities, learners will be receiving input which can lead to incidental learning and natural acquisition. And we know from empirical research that learners can acquire both core aspects of syntax and very subtle properties of semantic interpretation. In order to make sure tasks will be seen as meaningful, a CLT practitioner will need to be aware of the learners' language learning needs. **Needs analysis** is an accepted practice in CLT at many levels. This could include formal assessment that takes place before a course is designed, but in most CLT settings, it happens more informally, as teachers are expected to gauge the needs of their learners from day to day, and plan lessons accordingly.[14]

While the emphasis is on meaning, there is some room in CLT for the more structural aspects of language. Any explicit teaching of language rules, however, should occur only in the context of use. In other words, there should be Focus on Form, as we discussed in Chapter 5. This means that any problems with or questions about language forms or structures should be addressed as they arise. If they are explicitly introduced by the teacher, this should not be done outside of mean-ingful language tasks. And when teachers are explicitly teaching them, language points should be taught in terms of their meaning and use. To illustrate, if the passive comes up in an English class as an area of difficulty, the teacher should highlight the usefulness of omitting or sidelining the subject of a sentence in order to achieve an effect in the message; the passive should not be taught purely as a grammatical rule that applies to active sentences. In a classroom that is strictly CLT, attention to form will occur only if there is breakdown in communica-tion or if a learner is unclear about some point of language. In CLT, there should never be Focus on FormS.

It is easy to understand why the emphasis on meaning and com-munication in CLT leads to an uneasy feeling about error correction, or what I will refer to as **selective error correction**. In the interests of promoting fluency, it is not a priority to correct every non-targetlike feature of learner production. Moreover, a proponent of CLT does not want to distract the student continuously from the communicative message in an interaction, whether between learners or between the teacher and the student. There is also a sense in which too much correction may easily discourage and thereby de-motivate the student. For these reasons, error correction is often restricted to Focus on Form-type situations – in other words, only when the error leads to a breakdown in communication.

This is especially true in terms of spoken language production, but can also apply for written forms. In response to a written piece of work, CLT teachers should comment on the ideas and/or overall message of writing. The extent to which they also comment on the grammar, vocabulary and spelling is likely to vary, unless these errors lead to an inability to make sense of the written message. While hesitation to correct errors is compatible with other principles of CLT, it is also supported by a view which sees language development as occurring in natural stages, as it may be more useful to overlook errors which signal a level of development yet to be achieved.

Another feature of CLT is the use of 'real' or **authentic materials**. In their true form, authentic materials will be spoken and written texts taken from non-pedagogic sources: in other words, **realia** such as magazines, brochures and 'real' video or audio broadcasts. In practice, mainstream language textbook writers usually create texts that are 'typical' examples, but written specifically for learners. This enables closer control of specific vocabulary and grammatical forms. CLT materials are also devised for authentic language tasks, generally known as 'gap' tasks. **Information gap** tasks require language-learning users to gather information. Materials such as role play cards can be written to simulate 'real' situations to form the basis for gathering information. Language teachers dedicated to unfabricated authentic materials could bring in cultural artefacts. For example, with maps and train timetables, students could then be asked to create a package holiday brochure. This type of 'real-life' language activity is communicative and will be more meaningful to the language-learning users than traditional exercises.

Because learners are engaged in 'real' activities, using authentic sources, a CLT approach is also characterised by an **integrated skills** approach. In other words, a single activity or set of activities in a CLT classroom is likely to make use of all four skills: speaking, listening, reading and writing. The more traditional practice of teaching each skill separately does not sit well with an approach which mimics real-life interaction. After all, speaking without listening is very odd, and rarely occurs in natural settings. Though you may question the interdependence of reading and writing, good writers are very much aware of their readership, just as sophisticated readers are aware of the potential biases of the writer. For CLT, the emphasis on genuine communication means structuring classes in terms of activities that require a range of skills, instead of singling out a particular skill as the only aim of the lesson.

Communicative tasks also require **active learning**, not passive reception of knowledge. Gap tasks, role plays and debates are examples of active learning that require interaction among language-learning users. This will result in higher levels of engagement with language by the learner, which in turn will lead to more active processing. As made clear in MOGUL, this is what is needed for language development, whether implicit or explicit. The emphasis on learning from others through interaction makes the use of groupwork very common in CLT classrooms. **Cooperative language learning** requires learners to work together for greater improvement in individual learning. In addition to offering increased opportunities to use language, cooperative learning allows students to learn from each other. If properly conducted, groupwork can also create a supportive atmosphere for learners, thereby nurturing learners and encouraging them to challenge themselves to their fullest potential.

CLT is also compatible with a sociocultural view which sees language as tied to cultural practices and contexts. In order to promote a connection between language and culture, a CLT classroom can try to create the atmosphere of the culture where the target language is spoken. This can be done physically with cultural artefacts such as pictures, photos, magazines, books, and music. Many CLT practitioners will also try to foster the development of a second language identity by giving language-learning users a name in the target language.[15] Of course, any attempt to create a genuine target language atmosphere requires the (exclusive) use of the target language by the teacher, not only during formal instruction but also in the informal interactions that take place, as well as an insistence that learners use only the target language while in class. This will maximise the amount of natural input that learners receive in class.

Another way to maximise quantities of input is to promote **learner autonomy**. While the concept of autonomy can mean different things to different people, the general idea of learner autonomy is that language-learning users should take ownership of their language development instead of relying heavily on the teacher and/or the classroom materials. An autonomous learner will take responsibility for their own learning by increasing opportunities to engage with language and taking steps to improve in the particular areas in which they need more development. After all, the time constraints on most classroom settings means that learners need to devote time to the language outside class as well.[16] Learner autonomy is compatible with the idea of **reflective learning**. A reflective learner will take time to monitor their strengths and weaknesses in order to decide on the areas to which they will devote more time and attention. A CLT practitioner will train learners to be reflective in order to promote autonomous learning. Once this is achieved, the teacher can act more as a facilitator, enabling learners to progress in ways that are most appropriate to their individual needs. The most common technique associated with reflective learning is the **learner diary**, journal or blog, in which learners are asked to record their thoughts and observations about the process of learning as they experience it.

The overall view of the learner in CLT is very much in the tradition of progressive education. In other words, it takes a **humanistic** approach with an acute awareness of the needs of the individual learners in the classroom. This type of learner-centeredness is a part of the larger trend in education that views learners as people with emotional needs that affect learning as much as, or perhaps even more than, their intellectual capacities. A view of a learner as a whole person with beliefs and desires rooted in personal experience, instead of an empty vessel to be filled with knowledge, fits comfortably with an approach which sees language as a tool for making meaning and a means for participating in a social context. Similarly, it is proposed that learning should be seen in terms of participation in the act of learning instead of acquisition of a body of knowledge.[17] The humanistic emphasis on fostering personal development supports cooperation over competition in the classroom and moves away from predetermined goals which all language-learning users are expected to achieve in unison.[18] After all, we know that there is considerable variability in second language development.

The recognition of individual differences and needs may be one reason why one specific teaching method for CLT does not exist. As should have become clear from this discussion, CLT is an approach to teaching, not a method. It embodies a range of beliefs and understandings about language, language development and learning in general that have developed over time. One reason why it has been widely endorsed is because of its broad appeal. Yet, the fact of being an umbrella term is also one of its greatest weaknesses. With CLT as an approach, a teacher must look elsewhere for specific methods for teaching. The combination of a consensus supporting CLT with an absence of a single specific teaching method has led to what is now generally accepted to be the 'Post-Methods Era'.

POST-METHODS ERA

The emergence of the Post-Methods Era is not surprising, given the complexity inherent to language teaching. From a linguistic point of view, strict adherence to a single aspect or view of language is going to result in limitations, as any one view leaves out other crucial aspects of language. Add to this the complexity of pedagogic issues and the demands of particular educational agendas, and it is no wonder that there is no agreed method for language teaching. Since there has been no single, universally appropriate, foolproof method for language teaching, a good language teacher in the Post-Methods Era will adhere to the general principles of CLT and pick and choose from a range of methods, mixing them up as appropriate to the particular context and to keep the class interested and engaged.

Though there is no single accepted method, the one very useful and flexible method that we will adopt for the rest of our discussion is Task-Based Learning and Teaching (TBLT), briefly introduced in the last chapter. TBLT has been endorsed by a range of applied linguists, from those taking classroom practice as a starting point for thinking about teaching to those preferring to start from questions of theory, asking how findings from research in SLA should manifest themselves in the classroom.[19] TBLT sits well not only with the basic tenets of CLT but with the generalisations that have emerged from research in SLA as well. A task is a meaningful activity which requires active engagement with language. Though the task may lend itself to particular language forms or sets of vocabulary, these formal aspects of language will support the task instead of taking centre-stage in the lesson. Thus, for example, a task will be designed with an objective such as 'to design a tourist brochure', and not 'to learn the grammar of descriptive adjectives'. In other words, TBLT is about purposeful activities that emphasise communication because learning happens through interaction and use of language and acquisition occur in response to rich input. TBLT activities are usually authentic, though they may be modified to facilitate communication or to highlight particular features of language. And, crucially, tasks are things that learner do; learners as active participants in a TBLT classroom are engaged so that there is a maximal level of processing, as required for language development.

One notable feature of TBLT, then, is the roles of the teacher and the student, the former as facilitator and the latter as active participant. In observing a TBLT classroom, it may seem as though the learners are doing all the work while the teacher is sitting by. But, in fact, good TBLT requires a considerable amount of work from the teacher from preparing to implementing and following up the task. Ideally, a teacher will have a predetermined syllabus with clearly defined tasks. A principled task-based course will include a series of tasks with intentionally targeted aspects of language which will be sequenced, based on findings in SLA research that show developmental paths in second language development. Of course, the tasks will consider the interests of the students and the appropriateness of the content of each task for the particular pedagogical context as well. But we will limit the extent to which we become distracted by these other pedagogical considerations.

Looking more closely at specific linguistic aims for illustration, tasks requiring simple declarative sentences should precede tasks that emphasise question formation. Yet at the same time, because development does not happen in lock-step fashion, target items introduced, or seeded, in one lesson will be included again, or recycled, in later lessons for reiteration and reinforcement. Additionally, a principled TBLT syllabus will recognise that language develops differently across linguistic subsystems. Though this will affect syllabus design and task-ordering, this point will inform decision-making by the class teacher as well. For example, since word order facts seem to be acquired implicitly, there is little point in correcting word order errors at early stages of development. By contrast, the meaning and use of words, for example, can and should be taught through explicit instruction. These are prime candidates, then, for pre-task teaching.

At the same time, we know that a fair amount of SLA happens incidentally. In TBLT learners are exposed to authentic input containing plenty of examples of linguistic points that push the learners' development. Since the prime emphasis is on meaning, the particular language points are often not addressed explicitly until post-task activities, once the task is finished. In other words, TBLT lends itself to a Focus on Form approach as well. This makes good sense, considering the observation that there are limits to the effects of frequency in the input. In TBLT, teachers expose the learners to generous amounts of rich input, followed by explicit instruction. Whether linguistic forms are also introduced in pre-task activities, and the way any such forms might be introduced, will vary, depending on the needs of the students and the nature of the 'forms' in question. One danger inherent to the pre-task, task, post-task structure of a TBLT lesson is that the first and third stages can very easily turn into old-fashioned traditional teaching. Yet, if the true aim of the lesson is the successful completion of task itself, then the pre- and post-task activities will be subordinate to that task. And learners will see the importance and value of them as a necessary component for completing the task.

Of course, by definition, the task itself must be meaningful and engaging. This core feature of TBLT recognises that exposure to input is necessary for SLA and that there are limits on explicit instruction. The aim of TBLT is to promote interaction and facilitate active engagement with language. But the hard work on the part of the learners does not mean that teachers can take a break and relax during the task. Instead, the teacher must remain engaged, continuously monitoring the learners and noting difficulties as they complete the task. During this phase a teacher must decide how to address language problems or errors that arise. There are times when it may be appropriate to give individual learners specific feedback or correction in real time, as they engage in the task. But if such error correction is likely to have a detrimental effect on the communicative act, then it may be more appropriate to note errors for later discussion. Waiting to address common errors being made by a number of students instead of pinpointing particular students will be less likely to isolate and perhaps alienate individual learners as well. This kind of feedback or error correction can form part of the post-task lesson.

In summary, TBLT follows a three-step structure of pre-task, task and post-task. Adhering to current understandings of both language and language development, within TBLT the full complexity of language can be addressed. In preparing students to do the task, particular language points can be identified and highlighted by the teacher, whether vocabulary, grammar, pronunciation, or pragmatic or cultural points. During the task, the teacher manages the interaction among students, pushing learners to challenge themselves and intervening when communication breakdown cannot be resolved by the learners. The post-task phase will involve some form of reporting on or responding to the completed task by the teacher. In doing so, a skilled teacher will highlight the language points s/he has identified for this task and reinforce new vocabulary as well as relevant cultural points.

The importance of communication is clearly central to Task Based Learning. Despite this, however, there have been critics who caution against an over-emphasis on production. Michael Lewis (1993, 2000) and proponents of the **Lexical Approach** point out that learners need to do more than practise using their current stores of knowledge; they need constantly to expand that store in order to develop. Specifically, teachers should teach words, but not as vocabulary items in isolation. Instead, all words should be taught in terms of how they are used and, crucially, in the context of the other words with which they tend to appear. This approach echoes the cognitive emphasis on semantic networks. Words and phrases pattern together as collocations and colligations. Therefore, words should be taught as patterns, from two-word collocations like *inspire confidence* to clausal colligations like *laugh all the way to the bank*. For the Lexical Approach, the store of knowledge which learners need to increase is their store of collocations/colligations.

In this approach words and the patterns that they form are the basic units of language. Strong proponents, such as Lewis, take the extreme position that language is exclusively made up of sets of words and there are no grammar 'rules' or constraints. Language is a collection of words which language users tend to express following the patterns they hear. For example, though the sentences in (1) are 'grammatically' correct in English, in fact chances are that a native speaker would actually use the variants in (2).

1. a. I comprehensively agree.
    b. I wonder what his different motive is.
    c. The gangster shot the man repeatedly until he died.
    d. That was decidedly five years ago.
    e. I don't agree, but that's next to the point.
2. a. I totally/completely agree.
    b. I wonder what his ulterior motive is.
    c. The gangster shot the man dead.
    d. That was a good five years ago.
    e. I don't agree, but that's beside the point.

As illustrated here, collocations occur at the level of individual words (2a, b), or at the level of the clause (2c). Moreover, they can be fixed phrases (2d, e) which have no grammatically equivalent alternative, or they can have a degree of flexibility as in (2a).

The Lexical Approach is supported by corpus linguistics with enormous databases that allow linguists to study examples of 'real' language actually produced by speakers instead of an idealised assumption of what constitutes language.[20] Corpus linguists argue that collocations form the basis of a much more significant percentage of language that speakers actually use than perhaps has been acknowledged by mainstream linguists of the modern period. The Lexical Approach also finds support from acquisition research on the role of **formulaic language** in language acquisition, which shows that learners take in and produce **unanalysed chunks** for a communicative effect, without necessarily knowing each item in the 'chunk'.[21] This happens in beginning English classes when learners use phrases such as *I'm a student* without realising that the sentence includes four distinct words.

In many ways, TBLT and the Lexical Approach make a natural combination. The Lexical Approach provides lists of phrases for the teacher to teach. This can be done through both explicit instruction and implicit exposure, and can then be practised by learners in a task-based communicative way. Because knowledge of words lies at the heart of being able to communicate, strong proponents of the Lexical Approach will be content to teach collocations without teaching 'grammar'. Yet, as the discussions of language in this book indicate, most linguists agree that grammar is a real feature of language which must also be taken into account in language teaching, and as a result teachers are urged to take a Focus on Form approach within the broader context of CLT. In the next chapter, we will bring together all of the strands of research discussed in the first half of this book, together with the range of approaches to language teaching surveyed in this chapter to construct a language lesson for illustrative purposes, which we will dissect with questions of theory in mind.

FOR DISCUSSION

1. Consider each of the four main views of language – generative, cognitive, functionalist and sociocultural – in terms of approach to language teaching, identifying methods that would be appropriate or compatible with each approach.
2. Make a list of all the approaches and methods discussed in this chapter. Then organise them in terms of those which do and those which do not have theoretical foundations in linguistics. Discuss the extent to which a theoretical foundation in linguistics is important for language teaching.
3. Consider each of the ten observations about second language development discussed in Chapter 5. For each one, go through the section on Communicative Language Teaching, looking for connections between theory and practice.
4. Choose any language teaching textbook that you have access to (for any language). Can you identify any elements of the approaches and methods identified in this chapter? Where do you see different aspects of communicative language teaching in the textbook?

5. Are some of these approaches and methods more suitable for different kinds of learners? Discuss the options in terms of differences in age, cultural context, type of institution and proficiency.
6. Are some of these approaches and methods more suitable for some languages than others? Discuss the reasons why or why not.

NOTES

1. In defining these terms this way, I follow the tradition in applied linguistics that is attributed to Edward Anthony in 1963 and continues today in widely used textbooks such as Richards and Rodgers (2001).
2. Krashen developed his Monitor Model over a series of publications. See Krashen (1977, 1981, 1982, 1985).
3. See Chapter 3 for discussion of these studies.
4. Richards and Rodgers (2001) use the term 'alternative' for approaches that do not have a basis in linguistic theory. While a number of these 'designer' approaches are alternative in Richards and Rodgers's sense, others are not. Instead, the term 'alternative' is used here to contrast with current mainstream approaches in language teaching. See Richards and Rodgers (2001) for more detailed descriptions of: Total Physical Response, The Silent Way, Community Language Learning and Suggestopedia.
5. For more information on the Silent Way, see Gattegno (1972, 1976). For more information on the notion of learning through discovery, see the work of educationalist Jerome Bruner; for example, Bruner (1961, 1967).
6. See Winitz (1981) for more information on the Learnables.
7. For a teacher's guide to TPR, see Asher (1977). For more on the premises of TPR, see Asher (1966).
8. 'Suggestology' is outlined in Lozanov (1978). See also Scovel (1979).
9. See Curran (1976).
10. For more information about John Rassias and the Rassias Method, see the edited volume by Yoken (2007).
11. See Chapter 17 of Richards and Rodgers (2001) for a clear overview of content-based instruction and immersion programmes, and references for further reading.
12. For early work in ESP, see Hutchinson and Waters (1987). For current work, consult the regularly issued journal, *English for Specific Purposes*, formerly known as *The ESP Journal*.
13. The notion of progressive education is generally associated with philosopher and educational reformer, John Dewey. See Dewey (1938, 1944). For a discussion of progressivism in the current context, see Hayes (2006).

14. Needs Analysis as a formal tool is generally associated with English for Specific Purposes. See, for example, Hutchinson and Waters (1987).
15. For a historical overview of the question of identity in language learning, see Block (2007). For a study of immigrant language learners and issues of identity, see Norton (2000).
16. For a useful discussion and review of literature related to learner autonomy, see Benson (2001). See also Dam (1995) and the volume edited by Little, Ridley and Ushioda (2003).
17. Sfard (1998) has usefully presented this distinction between so-called Participation and Acquisition Metaphors for learning. While she writes in the context of teaching mathematics, the distinction has been readily taken up for language, as teachers are encouraged to see learners *doing* language instead of *having* language.
18. For seminal work on humanism and language teaching, see Stevick (1990).
19. Early well-known examples of TBLT were the Bangalore Project (Prabhu 1987, Beretta 1990) and the Malaysian English Language Syllabus (Kementerian Pelajaran Malaysia 1975). Much has been written about Task-Based Learning. For an early discussion of the principles underlying a TBLT syllabus, see Long and Crookes (1992). For more recent work on TBLT, see Willis and Willis (1996, 2007), Ellis (2003), Nunan (2004), and the edited volume by Van den Branden (2006).
20. For examples of work in Corpus Linguistics see Biber, Conrad and Reppen (1998), and the edited volume by Cowie (1998).
21. See the work of Nattinger and DeCarrico (1992); Myles, Hooper and Mitchell (1998); and Wray (2002). For a review of literature on formulaic language, see Weinert (1995).

7

PUTTING THEORY INTO PRACTICE

⌒

INTRODUCTION AND CONTEXT

This book began with abstract concepts based on linguistic theory, before moving to questions of relevance to language teaching. Though we have surveyed a range of linguistic approaches to language, we have emphasised mentalist points of view, looking for areas in which there is general agreement, and giving most of our attention to the most formal of the linguistic approaches – the Generative Approach. The ambitious aim of this book is to show the research into abstract questions of language and the cognitive processes underlying language development are relevant to the language teacher.[1]

These last two chapters move into the classroom itself. In this chapter, we will consider an actual lesson plan which makes use of current approaches to language teaching, putting into practice the methods endorsed in the last chapter. We will then discuss the salient features of the lesson plan, making reference to the themes that have emerged from the discussions of linguistic theory and language development. In order to create a lesson, however, we must first specify the profile and context of the class. For the purposes of our discussion, we will try to define a 'typical' language-teaching context in which to situate our lesson plan. In the next and final chapter of this book we will then modify the context in order to highlight some specific concerns that are particular to different groups of learners and that draw in particular areas of research.

Of course, there is no such thing as a 'typical' language-teaching context. Every context has its particulars in terms of aims, funding, personalities, culture and political climate, to name a few. Indeed, every class is unique. For the purposes of illustration, however, we need to specify context for our lesson. Accordingly, I propose an **English as a Foreign Language** (EFL) context because it has the broadest appeal. The theoretical points made in this book are relevant for the teaching of any language. It seems safe to assume that, globally, most language teaching takes place in a foreign context, not a second language context. For this reason, the lesson discussed in this chapter is intended to be taught in a country where English is not the dominant or official language, in contrast with an **English as a Second Language (ESL)** context in which the target language is also an official language of the country where it is being taught.

Again, appealing to the broadest context possible, our EFL class is envisioned as a core language class of highest/oldest level in a state-funded secondary school, with a class size of thirty-six, all approximately aged seventeen and evenly split between girls and boys. Assuming a national curriculum in which English is introduced at least in a limited way at primary levels, these students are assumed to be at a 'lower intermediate' level of proficiency. In order to specify what is meant by lower intermediate, I will refer to the Council of Europe's *Common European Framework of Reference for Languages* (CEFR), as it provides a useful articulation of language levels with a degree of detail. The learners in our context are at the lower end of the CEFR's 'Independent User' category, or B1. Quoting the CEFR document, this means that their global ability in English is as follows:

> Can understand the main points of clear standard input on familiar matters regularly encountered in work, school, leisure, etc. Can deal with most situations likely to arise whilst travelling in an area where the language is spoken. Can produce simple connected text on topics, which are familiar, or of personal interest. Can describe experiences and events, dreams, hopes & ambitions and briefly give reasons and explanations for opinions and plans. (CEFR, p. 5)

In order to provide a bit more detail, Table 1, again quoting the CEFR (p. 6), shows the Council of Europe's 'self-assessment grid' for a B1-level learner in terms of Reception, Interaction and Production.

In terms of linguistic ability, the CEFR describes a B1-level learner as having 'enough language to get by, with sufficient vocabulary to express him/herself with some hesitation and circumlocutions on topics such as family, hobbies and interests, work, travel, and current events, but lexical limitations cause repetition and even difficulty with formulation at times' (p. 27).

A summary of the context is given below.

Summary of class profile and context

- National context: English as a Foreign Language (EFL)
- Type of institution: State-funded secondary school
- Number of students: 36
- Gender: evenly mixed
- Approximate age: 17 years old
- Proficiency level: Lower intermediate/CEFR B1
- Class time: 50 minutes daily

Reception		Interaction		Production	
Listening	Reading	Spoken interaction	Written interaction	Spoken production	Written production
I can understand the main points of clear standard speech on familiar matters regularly encountered in work, school, leisure, etc. I can understand the main point of many radio or TV programmes on current affairs or topics of personal or professional interest when the delivery is relatively slow and clear.	I can understand texts that consist mainly of high-frequency everyday or job-related language. I can understand the description of events, feelings and wishes in personal letters.	I can deal with most situations likely to arise whilst travelling in an area where the language is spoken. I can enter unprepared into conversation on topics that are familiar, of personal interest or pertinent to everyday life (e.g. family, hobbies, work, travel and current events).	I can write personal letters describing experiences and impressions.	I can connect phrases in a simple way in order to describe experiences and events, my dreams, hopes & ambitions. I can briefly give reasons and explanations for opinions and plans. I can narrate a story or relate the plot of a book or film and describe my reactions.	I can write straightforward connected text on topics which are familiar, or of personal interest.

Table 7.1   CEFR Self-assessment grid for B1 level proficiency

With the class profile and context now defined, we need to provide some context for the lesson plan that follows because no lesson occurs in isolation, but instead follows the lesson that came before, and points to the lessons to follow. In any pedagogically sound context, it will be situated within a syllabus following a curriculum. Presenting a curriculum and detailing an entire syllabus would take us far beyond the scope of this book. However, we need a degree of context for our lesson plan. Thus in Table 7.2 we have included a rough sketch of a syllabus, also including a very general idea of linguistic aims, for illustration.

Unit Topic	Target competence	Grammar	Pronunciation	Vocabulary
Identity	Fluency	Simple vs complex sentence structure	Consonant contrasts	Connecting words/ phrases
Interviews	Strategic	Questions; auxiliary verbs	Intonation	Phrases for clarification
Newspapers	Discourse (written)	Sentence structure: punctuation	Consonant clusters	Phrases for description
Meeting new people	Pragmatic	Verb tense	Long and short vowels	Phrases for starting, ending and changing conversations
Travelling abroad	Strategic	Negation	Word stress	Synonymous and antonymous phrases
Tourist attractions	Discourse (spoken)	Complex noun phrases	Phrasal stress	Phrases for location
Animal rights	Pragmatic	Modal verbs	Using stress for emphasis	Phrases for interrupting
English in the world	Fluency	Demonstratives	Sentence stress	Phrases for categorising

Table 7.2   Overview of syllabus

The fundamental organising principle of the syllabus sketch in Table 7.2 is form and function. With function in mind, there are eight topical units, and in terms of form, specific points of linguistic competence are listed, including grammar, pronunciation and vocabulary. As shown in the second column, each unit emphasises one other aspect of communicative competence beyond linguistic competence (as discussed in Chapter 4). Attempts have been made to ensure the linguistic points are related to the topic and the chosen communicative competence.

Consider the first unit of the syllabus. Because it is the first lesson, it is based on the theme of identity, allowing the class become familiar with each other. Linguistically, the focus is on basic sentence structure, with an emphasis on connecting phrases to show how simple sentences might be combined to make complex sentences. The expectation is that at this level, students should be able to create grammatically accurate sentences to describe themselves. However, in the interests of promoting communicative competence in general, the lessons at the start of this unit are designed to promote fluency in an attempt to set an early tone of active production in the classroom. To facilitate production, the associated pronunciation focus is also very basic. Though the focus is listed as 'consonant contrasts', the assumption is that the teacher would focus specifically on consonants of particular difficulty to the students in his/her particular class, anticipating native language transfer. In sum, this introductory unit is designed to build confidence and promote communicative competence, as a starting point for the course to come.

Within each unit there are specific lessons with more specific aims. The lessons included in the sixth unit from the above overview are given in Table 7.3, in order to provide more context for the single lesson plan that will be considered in detail in this chapter.

Unit	Lesson topic	Language focus	Example	Main task
Tourist attractions: the zoo	Animals and zoos	New vocabulary; complex noun phrases	the giraffe eating leaves	Catalogue of zoo animals
	Animal habits	Habitual expressions and expressions for current activity	usually sleeps, is sleeping now	Showcase an animal
	The zoo: a map	Expressions for location; phrasal stress	near here, far away	Design a layout for the zoo
	Animals at risk	Simple imperative phrases	visit our zoo, learn about animals	Make a brochure to promote awareness

Table 7.3 Example of lessons within one unit

The theme of this unit is 'Tourist attractions', with particular focus on 'The zoo'. Learners at this level should already know general vocabulary for animals to be found in a zoo, such as *tigers* and *bears*. The linguistic focus in the first lesson is complex noun phrases, starting with pre-modified phrases such as *the hungry tiger* and introducing post-modification, such as *the tiger sitting under the tree*. The task is for the class to put together a catalogue of zoo animals, with basic descriptions. This forms the basis of the second lesson, in which learners are asked to choose an animal to showcase in a bit more depth.

Building on post-modified noun phrases, the second lesson of this unit reinforces the differences between habitual verbal expressions like *usually eats leaves* and progressive verbal expressions like *is eating a leaf*. Throughout this unit, the attention to pronunciation goes beyond the segment level to focus on phrasal level stress. The emphasis on complex noun phrases and verbal clusters allows for this quite naturally. Because the communicative competence for this unit is spoken discourse, attention is paid to the role that word stress within the phrase plays in conveying emphasis in spoken interaction. To get a real sense of lessons sketched, much more would need to be said. The aim here, however, is to provide a backdrop for the lesson to be considered in the next section. Thus, we will cut short this description of the first two lessons of this unit and move on to discuss the third lesson in more detail.

A POST-METHODS LESSON PLAN

This lesson is task-based with pre- and post-task activities designed to draw attention to the language-particular aims of the lesson. While the communicative competence theme for this unit in general is spoken discourse, the particular aims of this lesson are informal phrases for seeking clarification from peers and the role of word stress for clarification in spoken interaction. The lexical expressions highlighted in this lesson are adverbial phrases. This makes a natural next step after discussions of complex noun phrases and present simple vs present progressive in the previous two lessons. The main task of the lesson is to design a layout for a zoo. This makes use of the output from preceding lessons, the catalogue of zoo animals and the individual animal showcases, and offers an opportunity to reinforce recently learned vocabulary.

The lesson plan itself follows a simple standard format appropriate for most teaching contexts. The procedures are listed with the interaction type and timing specified for each step of the lesson. Also listed are the specific aims of this lesson, the task itself, the materials that will be needed during the lesson, and the aspects of language that will be attended to by the teacher for corrective feedback.

LESSON PLAN

Lesson 3: A map
Unit 6: The zoo

Aims
Linguistic aims
Lexical
  - Students will be able to use location adverbs correctly
    e.g. near, here, away from, separate, next to, etc.
Pronunciation
  - Students will be able to use phrasal stress patterns
    e.g. NEAR the entrance vs near the ENTRANCE

Spoken discourse aims
  - Students will be able to use stress patterns for communicative purposes
    e.g. NEAR the entrance vs near the ENTRANCE
  - Students will be able to ask for clarification during peer interaction
    e.g. what did you say? huh?

Task aim
  - Design a layout for a zoo

Areas for corrective feedback
  - Use of location adverbials
  - Use of vocabulary taught today and in recent lessons
  - Use of phrasal stress for natural stress patterns and for emphasis
  - Informal register, appropriate for peer interaction

Materials
  - Cards or slips of paper each with a zoo animal written on it
  - Large pieces of paper
  - Glue or tape

Procedure	Interaction type	Timing
Before the lesson		
Put location phrases on the board with simple symbols for illustration.		
e.g. *the O is near the X*: O ^X		
far away from: O X		
together: OX		
separated from each other: O YZ X		
etc.		
Pre-task		
Animal placement game		
In pairs, each with set of zoo animals cards	Teacher ↔ Class	5 minutes
Listen to the instructions and place each animal	Listening	
accordingly.	comprehension, with	
(e.g. Put the tiger in the middle of your desk.	peer support	
Put the zebra near the tiger.		
Put the elephant far away from the zebra,		
etc.)		
Without making any changes, discuss the layout	Student ↔ Student	5 minutes
of animals with your partner. Would it be a	(Pair discussion)	
suitable layout for a zoo? Why or why not?		
Focus on meaning		
Summarise the most useful points overheard	Teacher	3 minutes
from group discussions (e.g. outdoor vs indoor		
animals; animals needing big cages; group vs		
solitary animals, etc.)		
Focus on form		
If you have a disagreement in a discussion, what	Teacher ↔ Class	3 minutes
expressions do you use?		
Elicit: *I disagree. How about . . . .*, etc.		
There are other methods for making a point.		
Model: How about next to HERE?		
How about BESIDE the exit?		

Task 1

Instructions

Today's task is to design a layout for a zoo. Use the arrangement of the animals on your desk as a starting point. As you discuss the best place to put each animal, pay attention to your use of word stress. [Distribute large blank piece of paper to each pair.]	Student ↔ Student (Pair interaction)	10 minutes

Post-task

Focus on form

Praise the students for attending to stress. Ask: What's the difference? near the ENTRANCE vs NEAR the entrance Highlight the role of stress for clarification.	Teacher ↔ Class	3 minutes
What do you say if you don't understand your classmate? Expect: *Excuse me, could you repeat . . .?* What do we actually say to friends? Model: *What did you say? Huh?* Reinforce: Formal vs informal spoken discourse	Teacher ↔ Class	4 minutes

Task 2

[Form groups of four, combining two pairs.]

Instructions

Consider the two layouts. Put them together to make one agreed layout. Glue the cards to the paper and draw paths, cages, fences, etc. As you work together, consider the strategies you use for clarification: choice of phrase and phrasal stress [Hang the maps on the wall for tomorrow's lesson.]	Student ↔ Student (Group interaction)	15 minutes

Focus on form

Highlight good examples of clarification during group interaction. Tomorrow we are going to bring together the animal showcases and maps to create a brochure for our zoo which highlights animals at risk.	Teacher	2 minutes

Homework

Read anything of your choosing for 30 minutes. If you do not know what to read, search online for websites relevant to zoos and about zoo animals.	Student

DISCUSSION OF THE POST-METHODS LESSON

The lesson has been labelled a 'Post-Methods' lesson because it is, broadly, communicative in its approach, but also emphasises aspects that are associated with more traditional language teaching. And, as will be discussed in this section, it tries to take into account a range of principles from linguistic theory and language development. If we were to consider all of the lessons in the course or even a whole unit, we would see greater variation in method, as different approaches and methods are appropriate for different aims from day to day. In other words, instead of adhering to one single method, we would take an eclectic Post-Methods approach, selecting from the range of options in order to best suit the needs of the learners. This particular lesson makes use of the usefully flexible Task-Based Approach, which allows for Focus on Form and works in elements of a Lexical Approach. This combination allows us to translate into classroom teaching our theoretical understanding of what language is and how language develops.

Form and Function

The most basic principle underlying the above lesson is a balance between form and function. Contrary to a 'meaning only' view, language forms are taught, but in such a way that they are grounded in meaning. So, for example, the teaching of adverbial phrases in the pre-task game requires that students understand the meaning of the phrases. This kind of meaning-based focus on form occurs throughout the lesson. As another example, phrasal stress is a feature of pronunciation – in other words, form – but it is taught in terms of the meaning that it conveys. These points of language form are all situated in the larger class aim of designing a layout for a zoo. True to the definition of a task, this aim is not actually linguistic; however, it is designed to require the use of language and, crucially, to require interaction among the learners. And it is structured in such a way that the particular features of language that have been identified for the day's lesson can be taught. As such, this is not strictly Focus on Form as defined by Long because the focus does not arise incidentally. Instead, the lesson plan is designed to force the pre-identified points to arise – so that the teacher can teach particular forms in this lesson.

One main reason to endorse a pre-determined, or deliberate, Focus on Form approach has nothing to do with abstract theory and everything to do with real-world realities. In many language-teaching contexts, there is real pressure to teach specific forms. This often shows itself in the syllabus, or in the course materials that teachers are expected to use. Even in places where there is a degree of freedom for teachers to choose their own classroom materials, the formal assessments for very many courses are, in fact, very 'form-centric'. A final, related reason is to do with current language teaching practices to be found in much of the world's foreign language-teaching contexts. In many language classrooms around the world, the norm is some variety of the traditional Focus on FormS approach. Moving to deliberate Focus on Form may be a more achievable and appropriate development than incidental Focus on Form. This contrasts with those second language-teaching classrooms which have embraced a strong Focus on Meaning approach. If these find that they need to shift back to include some teaching of forms, an incidental Focus on Form may be a more natural progression.

But deliberately focusing on form is not endorsed only for practical reasons. Both psycholinguistic research and interaction research tell us that intelligent and motivated learners 'notice' patterns and rules. And our theoretical model of language development holds a place for explicit, conscious learning alongside implicit acquisition. Like most processing models, MOGUL tells us that repeated use of forms will raise activation levels leading to language development. Of course, frequency for its own sake, or rote memorisation, is not what we have in mind, but instead repeated use in meaningful contexts. This lesson requires that learners make use of the adverbial forms throughout the lesson, repeating the forms for different (meaningful) purposes.

At the same time, the lesson is 'function'-oriented. For example, when attention is drawn to the phrases students use during discussions within their groups, emphasis is put on using the appropriate register for peer interaction. This is needed to contrast with the formal phrases that are often to be found in published language course books. One challenge facing language textbook writers is the fact that textbooks are, by definition, a written medium. It is natural for a textbook writer to include relatively formal phrases because the medium of a textbook is somewhat formal. Even if a textbook writer presents informal registers, the result is often somewhat problematic. When 'real' language is captured in a clear enough way to include it in a textbook, it can often seem quite stilted and unnatural due to the mismatch between the spoken and written medium. Yet real language use requires the ability to speak from a range of levels from formal to informal. A lesson like this one, with a focus on spoken discourse, requires real-life spoken interaction among peers. Tasks like those in this lesson provide an excellent opportunity to teach features of spoken discourse such as the informal expressions that we actually use with peers when seeking clarification.

At a more general level, on the function side of the form–function equation is the topic-based underlying organisation of this lesson, and all of the lessons. This lesson fits into a larger unit about zoos and animals, a topic which is largely neutral in terms of cross-cultural appropriateness. It also sets the scene for the less neutral unit to come, a unit based on animal rights. While animal rights may not be a concern to some people in some cultures, it is very much a concern among most English-speaking cultures. Keeping in mind that language cannot be divorced from culture and society, the next unit explicitly raises a culturally grounded issue. The way that a teacher approaches our current unit, 'The zoo', could also touch on cultural values to do with the treatment of animals, but it does not have to. In good Post-Methods spirit, some lessons will include more explicit reference to cultural difference than others. In the next section we will deconstruct our lesson further to make more connections with the more abstract theoretical points which we encountered earlier in this book.

Providing Input and Fostering Output

Throughout this book we have focused on points of consensus emerging from subfields of linguistics and applied linguistics which, in the world of academic debate, are very much opposed to each other. By understanding the conflicting views, we as teachers can gain a more sophisticated understanding of our subject matter: language. Yet at the same time, we need to step away from the debate and determine where there is consensus and where there are points that can inform the practical concerns of language teaching. In this book, the emphasis has been primarily on mentalist approaches to language, exploring formal, abstract approaches in particular. In this section we will use the above lesson plan to show how formal views of language can emerge in an activity as practical as a language lesson for a class of intermediate learners. In doing so, we will highlight some of the observations about second language development that we explored in Chapter 5, showing how these can provide a principled foundation for decision-making in preparation for the lesson and during the lesson itself.

In an attempt to ground ourselves in a single framework which unifies a range of approaches, we concluded our survey of approaches to language in Chapter 4 with a description of MOGUL, Modular On-line Growth and Use of Language. In concert with most mentalist approaches to second language development, MOGUL considers input as central to the process. The centrality of input is also why it is the first of the ten observations originally given by VanPatten and Williams (2007): *Exposure to input is necessary*. The unspoken assumption in the above lesson plan is that the entire lesson is conducted in the target language. Arguably, target language-only instruction is possible, even from the very beginning of language learning. At the intermediate level of our hypothetical learners, there is no reason why the lesson cannot be done completely in English. This maximises the amount of input that learners receive. That way, a large amount of the input that comes in the lesson – from instructions on the tasks to discussions of animals and zoos – is authentic, natural input.

In order to try to maximise input, the lesson also includes home-work, requiring reading for pleasure. Emphasising personal reading comes from research showing that silent reading is a valuable source of natural input for learners. It will also foster learner autonomy, as students are encouraged to choose their own reading. The importance of natural input is also a direct implication of the second observation: *A good deal of SLA happens incidentally*. We know from research coming out of both generative and cognitive second language research that learners come to know features of language that have not been explicitly taught. So it only makes sense to facilitate this feature of language development by maximising the students' learning potential through maximal amounts of input, both inside and outside the classroom.

In addition to natural linguistic input, this lesson includes explicit metalinguistic input. By MOGUL there is natural development of linguistic knowledge as a result of natural, authentic input and there is the equally natural development of metalinguistic knowledge through explicit input. For MOGUL, both types of knowledge are 'natural' in the sense that they are both features of the human mental system, depending, as they do, on internal, cognitive mechanisms in the brain. This extends a long-held conviction of linguists working in a generative framework: the language 'module' is associated with implicit linguistic knowledge while the mental component that includes 'general intelligence' is associated with metalinguistic knowledge, or knowledge about language. Importantly, however, both are used by speakers of language (whether native or non-native) when they comprehend and produce language. And the degree of development of both will contribute to the overall level of proficiency and fluency in a language. The dividing line and the exact relationship between the two is a matter of debate. But the existence of two types of knowledge is widely accepted, even among other mentalist views of language. Cognitive linguists acknowledge a distinction between deliberate, conscious, declarative knowledge and automatic, subconscious, procedural knowledge. And though strict proponents of theory will disagree, this implicit, automatic knowledge can be likened to the notion of 'internalised' knowledge found within Sociocultural Approaches.

In sum, all approaches agree that there is an extent to which learners can come to know more than they have been made explicitly aware of in their input, which is the third observation: *Learners come to know more than what they have been exposed to in the input.* Accordingly, in our lesson plan there is a healthy balance between natural language input and explicit language instruction. This facilitates both natural acquisition and controlled learning. As widely acknowledged, the success of learning is often tied up in extra-linguistic factors such as intelligence, diligence, interest and motivation. This is not surprising if an element of second language development implicates intentional, deliberate learning. Simply put, those who try harder are likely to achieve more. Yet, these affective factors could also indirectly affect the natural acquisition potential as well. Learners who allow themselves to be exposed to more (or less) input, depending on levels of interest and diligence, will affect the extent to which incidental acquisition is even possible. By embedding classroom activity in tasks that require the involvement of individual learners and the interaction of learners among themselves, it is hoped that interest will be piqued and motivation will be enhanced, leading to increased levels of all types of input.

A further point crucially related to input is the role of output, as captured in Swain's Output Hypothesis and included in Long's Interaction Hypothesis. Output is important as one part of the processes involved in successful and meaningful language production. The research shows us that this is particularly true if learners are pushed to produce language which is challenging to their current level of proficiency. Accordingly, this lesson plan revolves around tasks that not only require the learner to produce language in group discussion, but which also require the specific production of predetermined aspects of language, challenging the learners to use the new adverbial forms. Moreover, focus on these linguistic aims comes in both in the group discussions and in the ultimate creation of the layout of the zoo.

However, as captured in Observation 10, *there are limits on the effects of output (learner production) on language acquisition.* In addition to input and output, the Interaction Hypothesis includes the notion of negotiation of meaning. When learners encounter difficulty in communication, they will have to attend to the gap in knowledge that caused the breakdown in order to repair it. This process facilitates learning, as it forces attention to language and pushes development as the learner strives to correct the problem. In our lesson plan, the second task includes a focus on phrases for clarification during group discussions in order to encourage the learners to seek repair where there is misunderstanding or lack of clarity. The intention is that focus on phrases for clarification will foster negotiation of meaning, which will, in turn, promote language development.

In addition to type of input, we have discussed the question of amount of input, concluding that the more, the better. While we have suggested that a large amount of input is important in general, we are also concerned with amount of input in terms of specific linguistic forms or constructions as well. Research on the importance of frequency in the input refers to the repetition of specific forms in order to foster learning. As we noted in Chapter 5, most of the research on frequency has been limited to the level of vocabulary. It is this research that underlies the so-called seeding and recycling of adverbial phrases throughout this lesson. Adverbial phrases are taught in the opening animal placement game and then recycled throughout the lesson. In addition to repeated frequency, the lesson attempts to increase the salience of the target forms in several ways. Firstly, learners are required to comprehend the new forms in the opening activity, before then having to produce them in discussion. Secondly, explicit attention is brought to the adverbial forms again by the teacher, but this time with a focus on the stress patterns attached to the phrases. This repeated and varied attention to the linguistic form of the lesson is designed to increase both saliency and frequency.

The teaching of these forms also takes a lexical approach, teaching phrases instead of lists of words. This lesson could have started by teaching the words *near, next, separate, away,* and so on. But instead, the prepositions are taught as collocational phrases. After all, the locational use of *next* always collocates with the particle *to*. So *next to* should be taught as a fixed phrase from the beginning. As an aside, it would be appropriate to follow the teaching of *next to* with the teaching of the temporal use of the word *next*, as in: *Next, I will read you a story*. This is based on research that shows learners are better able to learn abstract extensions of word meaning if they have been taught the literal, physical meaning first.[2] Importantly, the phrases are taught in context and in association. Because psycholinguistic research supports the view that lexical knowledge is stored in networks connected by association of meaning, all new vocabulary items should be taught in association with related items.

Also drawing from the cognitive view of knowledge is the way that the phrases in this lesson are taught. When teaching locational meaning, it is natural to illustrate location visually as we do in this lesson. From a cognitive point of view, doing so appeals to two modes of processing, the visual mode and the aural mode. This multi-modal approach may in and of itself lead to more successful learning. Whether it does or not, it certainly serves to increase the salience of the forms in question. Moreover, asking the students to manipulate the objects to reinforce the meanings of these phrases further is an application of the idea that there is a positive connection between kinetics, or physical movement, and learning.

Returning to our discussion of frequency, being limited to just one lesson gives us only a snapshot of teaching in this classroom. Yet the brief outline of the unit in which this lesson occurs, along with the sketch of all of the units preceding and following this one, shows continuous seeding and recycling that will be inherent to principled language teaching. Moreover, there is a full range of seeding and recycling to include reinforcement of language at the lexical level, at the grammatical level, for pronunciation, and for areas of language use as well.

Accounting for Interlanguage Development

Another general piece of the puzzle, as important for teaching as input, is the nature of second language development. Three of the observations by VanPatten and Williams (2007) address this specifically. First is the generalisation that language development is systematic. This is the basic insight underlying the fourth observation: *Learners' output (speech) often follows predictable paths with predictable stages in the acquisition of a given structure*. While this is not readily seen in our single lesson plan, the sketch of the syllabus shows language focus with increasing complexity as the course progresses. We can see this, for example, in the focus on pronunciation which starts at the level of individual sounds in Unit 1: single consonants and then consonant clusters, stress within a word and then stress at the level of the phrase, and so on. In terms of grammatical forms, the emphasis is on noun phrases and then more complex noun phrases. Then there is (recycled) emphasis on simple verb phrases, before the focus turns to adverbial phrases in our zoo lesson. Of course, none of these grammatical forms is likely to be completely new to all students. They will have encountered these in their natural input in past lessons and explicitly at more junior levels of instruction.

Yet predictable paths and stages can help us with decision-making for language teaching in different ways. If you are a syllabus designer, an understanding of these stages of development is crucial. Yet even the classroom teacher following a set syllabus would do well to be aware of paths of language development in order to make decisions about everyday questions including what to emphasise within the lesson, what to teach explicitly, what to recycle and what requires corrective feedback. This last point is the area over which teachers in any teaching context have the most control and that they should therefore think about carefully. It is a fact of life that there is a limit to what one can do in a single lesson on a single day. Teachers have constantly to make decisions about how to use the limited amount of time that they have with their students. It is with this in mind that our lesson plan includes the identification of areas in which the teacher will engage in corrective feedback.

Constant correction is both unrealistic for the teacher and demotivating for the student. The commitment to humanism inherent to communicative language teaching can lead some teachers to avoid correction at all, especially correction in verbal contexts. The approach taken here is that feedback should be restricted to those areas identified as achievable at the learners' current level of development. These areas include those that have been explicitly taught in the lesson, which in turn are presented at the correct stage in language development. In the case of our lesson, 'The zoo', they are the correct use of location adverbs, recently taught vocabulary, phrasal stress and appropriate register. This is supported by research on corrective feedback, which indicates increased usefulness if the learner is 'ready'. In other words, if learners are at the appropriate stage in the developmental path, then corrective feedback can have positive effects for learning.

Stage-wise development is also one reason why the new linguistic information in our lesson focuses on the fine-grained distinctions between adverbial phrases such as *near, next to* and *separate.* At this intermediate level, the learners should already have a basic store of adverbials. This lesson may add some completely new expressions, although there will be some individual variation as some learners will have larger or more robust lexical stores than others. Yet all learners will benefit from the recycled emphasis on adverbial phrases, especially as it builds on the verb phrases that came in the lesson the day before. As shown in Table 7.2, the previous lesson reinforced the distinction between habitual expressions using the simple present, and expressions for current activity using the present progressive. The idea of adverb phrases after verb phrases (and verb phrases after noun phrases) is endorsed by Pienemann's Processability Theory, which provides a clear order of language development in terms of complexity. Within this lesson we can also see growing complexity as learners first comprehend and then produce the forms, followed by production with correct phrasal stress.

Also true of second language development is the fifth observation: *Second language learning is variable in its outcome.* This is another reason why continuous recycling is needed. Some learners will acquire and/or learn some aspects of language before or quicker than others. This is the great mystery of second language development. While researchers continue to try to find answers to why this happens, we teachers would do well to accept it as reality and do our best to accommodate it in our teaching. What does seem to be emerging are some generalities about those areas of language which seem to develop and those that are more prone to fossilisation, a point relevant to the observation about difference in development across the linguistic system.

Returning to variability in general outcome, we might consider what this means for questions of assessment. From an SLA point of view, assessment may be useful for monitoring learners in order to determine what point they have reached along the path of development. Knowing that development is step-wise, it would be unfair to expect learners to reach a stage far beyond the stage in which the course began. Equally, it is unrealistic to expect all learners to achieve the same level in the same amount of time. Thus, it would not be reasonable to expect all learners to achieve the same level in assessment. Of course, there are legitimate factors involved in assessment, such as institutional pressures to report on progress in a formal and standard way such that individual learners can be ranked and measured. From the point of view of language development, this will document the variability that we have come to expect. Thinking of our discussion of input in the last section, perhaps formal assessment should also include a measure of how much input an individual learner has exposed themselves to outside of the class. An 'effort' mark such as this would reflect the learner's potential development while allowing for variation in terms of actual development in the time constraints of the course. Additionally, the washback effect might encourage learners to seek as much input as possible in order to receive the reward of higher marks, all of which will hopefully improve their language ability.

One alternative implication for assessment is that there is a principled reason to test precisely what was explicitly taught. If implicit acquisition is beyond the control of the teacher or learner, and if we are not entirely aware of what aspects of input become intake for the learner, then perhaps it is unfair to test anything connected with implicit acquisition. Explicit, metalinguistic knowledge, on the other hand, is by definition identifiable. If metalinguistic knowledge is knowledge that can be learned through deliberate attention and hard work, then the logical conclusion is that testing such knowledge is valid and fair. Of course, it must be recognised that such assessment can only provide a fraction of any learner's total language knowledge and ability. But one logical conclusion of the view we have presented is that there could be a place for using traditional testing practices.

Beyond variability in general outcome, we have seen that *Second language learning is variable across linguistic subsystems.* As already mentioned, some aspects of language seem to develop more readily than others. In general, those aspects of language connected with meaning seem to be acquirable, as are core properties of syntax. It is the area of functional morphology that seems particularly troublesome for acquisition. This is why returning to a relatively basic distinction between simple present and progressive present in the previous lesson is not unwarranted. Verbal morphology is one area which needs continuous practice and rehearsal before it can be mastered. Notice, by contrast, that there is no explicit teaching of word order within the adverbial and prepositional phrases in this lesson. Teaching the phrases in terms of their meaning and having the learners use them in appropriate contexts should be enough to allow for the relevant properties of word order to develop implicitly (unless the native language causes them to use an incorrect order, in which case explicit instruction is advised). Explicit emphasis in this and all of the lessons on aspects of pronunciation, by contrast, is needed because of the difficulty learners have in the acquisition of phonology. Intra-linguistic variability is also useful when thinking about corrective feedback. Those areas which seem open to explicit learning may benefit more from corrective feedback. Whether a teacher corrects in areas that have been found impervious to deliberate learning may depend on external language teaching pressures.

Deciding What to Teach (and What Not to Teach)

In addition to helping us think about how to teach, an understanding of research and theory can help us to determine what to teach. It may also inform us about what not to teach. One point which we have only touched on in this discussion so far is the issue of native language transfer. While we know that there are effects from native language transfer, for this lesson, we have not specified the native language of the learners. That we have specified a foreign language context allows us to assume the learners share a mother tongue. Regardless of the native language, any lesson can appeal to those aspects of commu-nication that are largely cross-linguistic. In this lesson, the emphasis on word stress in the phrase is, for the most part, one that holds across languages. So, you may ask, what is the value of teaching something that the learners are already likely to know? There are several reasons for this. Firstly, there is no reason to expect that the learners will know which aspects of communication are universal, and which are not. Secondly, by drawing on existing L1-based knowledge, learners should be able to transfer that knowledge explicitly for successful application in the second language. The way that this lesson is structured allows for renewed attention to the forms which are the linguistic aim of the lesson, but with a different emphasis, and one which is likely to be easily picked up on. All of this will help learners to feel good about what they are learning and thus remain more engaged.

Even though there is clear evidence of native language effects in second language development, we also know that *there are limits on the effect of a learner's first language.* This is because some of these effects can be overcome through implicit development and/or explicit learning. With the latter in mind, corrective feedback may be of particular use in overcoming native language transfer effects. In fact, research in this exact area has shown that explicit instruction helped French learners overcome the subset problem which occurs with adverb placement, since French includes the superset option of verbs before and after the main verb, while English allows only the subset pre-verb option. This is why the caveat was given in the above section urging the explicit teaching of word order in adverbial phrases if needed for reasons of L1 transfer. Of course, gains have only been shown to hold in the short term. Yet as this is an area of research that has very little data, it remains an empirical question whether and the degree to which explicit learning can result in long-term gains.

All of these points about second language development connect to the only observation we have yet to address, the ninth in our original list: *There are limits on the effects of instruction on SLA.* This may not be a notion that we like to think about as teachers. Yet it is a generalisation that any teacher would surely agree with, and one that is borne out in empirical research as well. This, again, has direct implications for deciding what to focus on with corrective feedback. While you can insist that your students include the agreement -*s* morpheme on every regular 3rd person singular verb, the robust result that this is an area that learners seldom master suggests that you might divert your energies into something more useful. This is further supported by the more functional observation that absence of agreement does not cause problems for understanding in spoken language. From a communicative language point of view, then, it may not be worth insisting on it.

CONCLUSION

In this chapter, we have explored one lesson plan in an attempt to illustrate how knowledge of abstract principles of linguistics and research in second language development manifests itself in the language classroom. There was no attempt to propose any new super-method. In this post-methods era, it is widely accepted that no such method exists. Instead we found ourselves with a mix of contemporary and traditional approaches to language teaching, trying to take a range of factors into account working within a degree of practical, real-life constraints as regards questions of theory and research. The main aim was to uncover some of the theoretical points which are foundational to sound language-teaching practices. While some teachers may do these things instinctively, well-qualified tea-chers will also be able to justify them in terms of theory and research.

Because we defined a 'generic' teaching context in this chapter, a number of important issues have not been discussed. In particular, differences in age of acquisition are irrelevant for this discussion of one single class of teenagers. Additionally, we have not addressed differences in levels of proficiency. Do all of these points still hold at beginner and advanced levels? These and other current questions in language development and language teaching form the basis of the next and final chapter of this book.

FOR DISCUSSION

1. Develop a lesson plan for the class directly before or after the 'Zoo' lesson presented in this chapter. Be ready to justify the different parts of your lesson in terms of what you know about language and/or second language development.
2. Develop a lesson plan and exchange it with a classmate. Identify the beliefs about language and second language development that you can see in your classmate's lesson plan.
3. Sketch a lesson plan that adheres to a strictly structural or form-based view of language. Then sketch one that is exclusively function-oriented. Discuss the merits and shortcomings of each.
4. Discuss the lesson plan given in this chapter in terms of cultural appropriateness. (Think about culture in terms of traditions in society as well as educational culture.)
5. Discuss how you would alter this lesson if the context of the class differed in terms of

    a. proficiency: beginners vs advanced
    b. age: young children vs adults
    c. class size: 50 vs 5 students.

6. Develop supplementary activities that you could do with this lesson if the class were twice as long or as activities to be done outside of class.
7. Discuss the extent to which the lesson presented in the chapter is appropriate for teaching languages other than English.

NOTES

1. As mentioned in Chapter 1, the majority of existing textbooks on language teaching take a more 'external' approach.
2. See Boers (2000) and (2001) for research on words and idioms, respectively. For papers that explicitly apply cognitive linguistic research to classroom teaching, see the (2008) edited volume by Frank Boers and Seth Lindstromberg.

8

PRACTICE AND PRACTICES – RESPONDING TO STUDENT NEEDS

∽

INTRODUCTION

The last chapter presented a lesson plan for deconstruction in terms of its underlying beliefs. The aim was to draw connections between linguistic theory and agreed generalisations coming out of research in SLA on the one hand, and the language classroom on the other. We did so, assuming the most widespread teaching context possible. In this chapter, we address questions of language development and language teaching which could not be discussed in the very general context defined in Chapter 7. We do so by broadly assuming the same syllabus and unit topics, but adapting them to suit different types of learners. You will notice that, while many (though not all) of our points are valid for the teaching of any language, we have again limited our discussion to English language teaching contexts. Firstly, we address questions relevant to adult language learning at low levels of language proficiency. We then go to the other end of the spectrum to discuss the teaching of language at very high levels of language competence. Because all of our discussions about teaching have assumed adult learners, we then address the question of age, exploring the lesson in a child second language development context. We end this chapter by exploring a current controversial topic which has arisen out of the unique position that English holds in the world when we consider our lesson from the point of view of the English as a Lingua Franca (ELF) agenda.

LOW-LEVEL ADULT ESL LEARNERS

Adults relocating to new countries are often faced with not only a new environment and culture, but also the difficulty of learning a new language. Thus, in this section we consider adults newly arrived in country, whether for work or accompanying a partner who has immigrated for work. We envision a range of professional backgrounds and ages as well as a mixture of male and female students. Additionally, we are assuming learners who are literate with a secondary level of education – though many of the points we will make could be relevant to secondary school learners as well.[1] The teaching context assumed is some kind of further education institute or 'night class'. We also assume an English-speaking country, and assume at least a rudimentary knowledge of English given the pervasive nature of English in the world today. Thus, in terms of level, these are not absolute beginners. Instead, we are defining these learners' 'low' proficiency as the lowest level in the CEFR proficiency scheme, the A1 category. As characterised there, A1-level learners:

> Can understand and use familiar everyday expressions and very basic phrases aimed at the satisfaction of needs of a concrete type. Can introduce him/herself and others and can ask and answer questions about personal details such as where he/she lives, people he/she knows and things he/she has. Can interact in a simple way provided the other person talks slowly and clearly and is prepared to help. (CEFR, p. 5)

While 'The zoo' may seem like a juvenile topic for adults, it does not have to be. With consideration, most topics can be modified so they are appropriate to the needs of the group in question. In order to illustrate, we will keep the topic, but modify it. As presented in Chapter 7, the lesson occurs within a unit about zoos as tourist attractions, with the day's lesson entitled: 'The zoo: a map'. The changes to the lesson plan are to teach (rather than recycle) basic vocabulary and for the main language focus to be asking for directions.

The first task remains essentially the same, asking learners to position animals in response to verbal input, creating a layout for a zoo. The difference is a much more basic set of vocabulary, including common animal names and simple prepositional phrases for location. Given the needs of this group, instead of asking learners to debate the merits of particular choices in positioning animals, Task 2 would ask them to use the map they have created to practise asking and giving directions. This task would come with a pre-task review of vocabulary and phrases for asking directions. For homework, it is still important for learners to expose themselves to as much input as possible, but instead of asking learners to read for 30 minutes, they would be asked to look for articles on-line or in print that have something to do with animals and to come to the next class having noted down as many headlines of articles to do with animals as they can find. This kind of task requires engagement with language without the burden of having to read and understand text fully, which may be too challenging at this level.

The most important point in teaching 'low-level' learners is the recognition that the label 'low' refers exclusively and only to language ability. Fundamental to teaching in this context is genuine respect for the learners, both in terms of their rich life experiences and their existing abilities in other areas, whether academic or not. There is no justification for equating difficulty in communicating in a second (or third) language with low levels of general intelligence or a lack of rich knowledge. Beyond level of formal education, which admittedly may vary, as adults these learners have a fully developed set of cognitive resources and deserve the dignity and respect that is accorded adults in any setting. Moreover, as these learners are likely to be taking your English class for very specific reasons, it is crucial for you as a teacher to identify their individual language-learning needs, and to try to address these as much as you can, while also keeping the needs of the whole class in mind.

What, then, can we take from linguistic research when we consider teaching in a low-level context? It seems that adult learners readily acquire core language structure such as the basic word order within sentences and most phrases.[2] Perhaps surprisingly, in time, adult learners can even acquire complex structural forms such as questions and relative clauses. Thus, given the limits that exist in any teaching context, it makes sense to provide as much natural input as possible to foster acquisition of core syntactic properties and to use precious class time for explicit instruction on other aspects of language. Specifically, at early stages, learners need to learn vocabulary explicitly to increase their range of resources for expression. In addition to amount, the type of vocabulary is important. Based on research in cognitive psychology, at this level it makes sense to teach generic instead of very specific vocabulary items. For example, in our lesson it is the most common animal names that should be taught, not obscure ones. Additionally, at this level you should teach a full set of basic location words like *next to*, *behind* and *in front of*, which capture the basic positional options instead of teaching multiple ways to express the same basic notion. In other words, avoid bombarding the learners unnecessarily with variants on *next to*, such as *beside*, *near* or *to the right/left of*, unless explicitly needed for communication.

Of course, the demands of a particular class or teaching situation may not allow for the luxury of providing rich authentic input to facilitate (the eventual) acquisition of syntactic forms. Thus, it may be that you explicitly teach some aspects of grammar, appealing to your adult learners' general intelligence to learn rules and patterns explicitly, in order to consciously apply them in their language production as a compensatory measure. This approach is certainly appropriate for grammatical points which include functional morphology, such as verbal agreement and plural forms. The somewhat depressing research showing that even very advanced learners can often continue to have difficulty with functional morphology in spontaneous production is tempered by the fact that learners can come to know the rules explicitly and can apply them if careful attention is given to production.

Another implication from research is that there is value in teaching formulaic expressions. As we saw in Chapter 6, research on very beginning-level learners shows that phrases that include grammar beyond a learner's level can be taught as fixed phrases, or unanalysed chunks. In a very first lesson, for example, the incomplete phrase *I'm a . . .* can be taught as a fixed opener in which to add nouns such as *student, man* or *nurse*. Only later will learners learn that this useful chunk comprises a 1st person singular pronoun, a 1st person singular form of the verb *to be* and, perhaps later still, an article. There is no reason why the use of formulaic chunks should not be extended for use in a lesson like ours to facilitate communication and interaction. For example, your lesson could include the teaching of a flexible general expression for asking for a specific location such as: *Could you tell me where the nearest* [noun] *is?* This might even be repeatedly practised in to order to achieve automatisation without concern for the particular linguistic features it contains. Looking ahead, when learners are ready to handle more complex language they may be able to make use of this stored chunk to develop the specific features of grammar and pronunciation that it entails. The exact properties of modals, for example, are beyond the A1 level of proficiency of these learners.

Another important point about these learners is that, as adults, they will have a fully developed, albeit implicit, knowledge of the semantic interpretation that underlies all of language by virtue of speaking whatever language(s) they already speak. Part of learning a language is learning how to map existing knowledge of meaning on to the specific forms in the new language. For this reason, in addition to the usual teaching of new language points, you should constantly rephrase what you say to learners in order to maximise their ability to make sense of the input. In addition, you could devote time in your teaching to developing their own ability to rephrase as a strategy for making themselves better understood. As there is likely to be frequent communication breakdown for these learners, emphasis on strategic competence is easily justified. In sum, when teaching adults with low levels of language proficiency, the advice here is to maximise their existing stores of knowledge, focus the explicit teaching on vocabulary as the building blocks of language, and carefully choose which aspects of grammar you teach explicitly.

ADVANCED-LEVEL ADULT EAP LEARNERS

Presenting a different set of challenges are learners at the other end of the proficiency spectrum. As with the previous section, the label 'advanced' refers to language ability; however, for the context assumed here the learners are relatively advanced in terms of educational level as well. For this discussion I will assume a typical context which calls for the teaching of advanced learners: the university. Many students who go abroad for a higher degree need language support before they begin their degree course. The context for our discussion, therefore, is an institute of higher education on a preparation course for students already accepted to do postgraduate level study in a particular discipline, but needing to improve their English. So prevalent is this area of teaching that it has developed as a distinct subfield known as **English for Academic Purposes**, or **EAP**.[3] While some EAP programmes are large and resourced enough to provide discipline-specific classes, most programmes teach a more general form of academic English and so we will assume a general EAP course for our learners. We can map our learners' ability on to the CEFR, putting them in the C1 category. Accordingly, a C1 learner:

> Can understand a wide range of demanding, longer texts, and recognise implicit meaning. Can express him/herself fluently and spontaneously without much obvious searching for expressions. Can use language flexibly and effectively for social, academic and professional purposes. Can produce clear, well-structured, detailed text on complex subjects, showing controlled use of organisational patterns, connectors and cohesive devices. (CEFR, p. 5)

Of course, the idea of asking these learners to make a map of a zoo is completely inappropriate. Instead, we will retain the animal theme, but instead discuss biodiversity and the effect of climate change on animal life, in preparation for the unit on animal rights to come. In terms of lesson plan, this class will start by making use of the homework that students will have done before class. For homework, each student will have been asked to find a primary source in the university's library relevant to the question of animals and climate change, to skim it and to be prepared to give the class a general idea of what it is about. Additionally, students will be asked to bring a copy of the reading to class. The lesson itself begins with a brief discussion of the reading that the students have done. The main language focus of this class, however, will be one central to EAP: language for argumentation. In class, students are asked to identify specific sentences/phrases in their chosen source which indicate development of an argument. This could range from common short phrases, such as *Author (date) claims that . . .* to more complex phrases, such as *While some insist that x, a more reasonable view is y.* The task is for each student to go through the source picking out phrases for argumentation to record in a list. The aim of the day's lesson will be to create a single class list of phrases for argumentation from the individual contributions of the learners.[4] Homework will then be for the learners to write a paragraph about animals and climate change which uses as many of the phrases from the list as possible.

At this level, learners have a well-developed knowledge of grammar rules and a wide range of dictionary knowledge. What they often lack is native-like grammatical accuracy and pronunciation, as well as the more subtle knowledge of how particular words or structures are used. Because these learners need to develop the language and conventions used within the academic community, it is natural that most EAP programmes rely heavily on a **Genre Analysis** approach to teaching.[5] In this context, a genre is a communicative event that is associated with a specific group who have a shared purpose. A text within a particular genre, whether written or spoken, can be identified by specific structure, linguistic features, terminology and register.[6] There are, in other words, features that clearly identify an essay as different from a newspaper article or an email. Because advanced learners already have a well-developed level of general English knowledge, situating their language learning directly in the genre of academic English provides a very useful way for improving not only their language level, but also the specific language knowledge they will need in order to succeed on their degree course. Our lesson exemplifies a Genre Analysis approach. The basis of the lesson is an example from the genre of academic writing which the learners have chosen, and the focus is on one distinctive feature of the genre: 'language for argumentation'.

Connecting this lesson back to the discussions of linguistics and SLA, the use of 'authentic' materials is a principled choice and can be justified when thinking of the research showing that learners are able to acquire some very subtle, so-called poverty of the stimulus phenomena. While explicit attention is being paid to the features of academic text in the lesson, learners are also receiving natural input which will allow for implicit acquisition as an added bonus. The use of authentic materials also allows for attention to subtle differences in the way language is actually used. The following verbs, for example, are broadly synonymous: *argue, claim, assert.* However, a sophisticated writer will know that *assert*, in contrast with *argue*, suggests the argument is not well supported. One useful tool for both teachers and learners at this level is the use of **concordancing**. One of the many benefits of the Internet is access to very large databases of language. There are free concordancing websites that allow anyone to search databases of text for examples of specific words or phrases. A careful analysis of examples of *assert* and *argue* from a concordancer could show the difference between the use of these two words.[7]

You will have noticed that this lesson requires quite a high level of analysis on the part of the learner. As with all teaching, the strengths of the particular learners should be recognised and utilised in the classroom. For this group, because they have been accepted for postgraduate study, it is safe to assume a high level of general intelligence and educational training. Moreover, when considering the needs of this group, it is appropriate to develop their analytical skills to equip them better for postgraduate study. Thus, it is not inappropriate to teach them to engage in some basic discourse analysis. With this kind of training they will be able to read not just for academic content, but to develop their own abilities to write as well.

As illustrated here, language teaching at this level and for this context is heavily skills-based, focusing on the academic skills of research, reading and writing. Yet this does not mean that the more traditional areas of language instruction are ignored. Again appealing to existing research, we know that very advanced speakers often fossilise in the areas of functional morphology such as verbal agreement and grammatical words such as articles – at least in terms of implicit, automised language production. Keeping in mind that much of the language production burden for this group will fall on their ability to write, emphasis should be given to editing skills so that these minor errors are caught and fixed as part of the writing process. For speaking, by contrast, the needs are different. In an academic setting it is the ideas that matter most in speaking, whether inside or outside the class. Thus, emphasis should be placed on areas of expression and interpretability. In the final section of this chapter, we will take this idea further when we explore one radical idea which clearly delimits which features of language are important for interpretability. For now, we will leave this discussion and move on to another context which highlights different points about language development.

YOUNG LEARNERS

Almost all of the discussion in this book has been about adult learners. In this section we will make use of our lesson to discuss briefly some of the issues relevant to child second language development. The first tricky question is what age constitutes child second language learning, as opposed to bilingualism on the one hand and 'adult' learning on the other. As mentioned in Chapter 1, if a child is exposed to two languages simultaneously from birth, this is generally understood to result in two native languages, or a bilingual child.[8] Following the practice that has become accepted in the field, we use the term **child L2** to refer to the situation in which a child already has a native language (or two) when they begin to develop an additional language. This is also sometimes referred to as successive child bilingualism. While an exact age for child L2 is not agreed, the age by which a child will have developed the core structure of their native language in terms of sentence structure and pronunciation is usually accepted to be 5 years.[9] For the upper boundary, the long tradition of viewing puberty as the dividing line between child and adult learning is broadly supported by empirical research. Setting aside the complications surrounding the critical period, therefore, we will define child L2 acquisition as second language development between the ages of 6 and 13.[10]

For this particular lesson, we will assume 9-year-old learners, an age in the middle of the child L2 range. The class size is 24 and the setting a primary school in one of the many countries which have introduced English at the primary level. In other words, we assume an EFL, not an ESL context.[11] In terms of the CEFR, these children are nearing the A1 level, having had three years of non-intensive English lessons as part of the weekly curriculum. A lesson about animals in a zoo is very accessible for children. For the young learners, we would include the same level of vocabulary as for the A1 adult learner: namely, basic animal names and single preposition/adverb phrases for location. Yet we would limit the number of animals to only five or six. We would, however, retain the original B2-level linguistic aim of phrasal stress, though, as we will see, the way of teaching it would be different.

For the lesson plan, we would replace the pre-task with explicit instruction on zoo animal names using pictures. The pre-task from the original lesson in which the learners place animals on their desk in response to instruction from the teacher would then become the main task. Instead of cards with the animal names written on them, however, both teacher and learners will have pictures of the animals. A second difference is that the teacher would model the placement for the children to follow as s/he gives instructions. Once the animals are laid out on each desk, the children will be asked to practise the animal names and phrases of location by repeating the same placement exercise with variations in placement, and without modelling from the teacher. The next modification to the 'game' is for the teacher to hand out each of the teacher's animal pictures to a different child to call out the placement instruction for the rest of the class to follow. As the children are doing this, the teacher will recast the children's phrases, paying particular attention to pronunciation and phrasal stress. While this game could be repeated as many times as time and interest allow, the next task is for the children to glue their animals on to a large piece of paper to make a map. The last step in the lesson is to begin teaching the spelling of each of the animal names. This might begin in this lesson but be completed in the next. Hopefully there will also be time for the children to draw cages, trees and flowers on their maps. Homework, if appropriate in the institutional context, would be to practise writing a couple of the new animal names taught in this lesson.

The lesson is designed to take into account the cognitive level of 9-year-old children in relation to type of task, expectations, response and engagement. In addition, the lesson recognises the child–adult relationship with clear instructions and ample modelling from the teacher, so that the children feel well supported as they learn new things. After doing the task with clear and structured support, it is appropriate to encourage children of this age to become more independent by asking them to do the task themselves with support readily available, and then involving them in the role of giving instructions. This lesson also recognises that the children will already have the concepts associated with the task; they will be familiar with zoos, zoo animals and the concept of location and relative placement. Practising the unfamiliar language associated with these known concepts is facilitated by reliance on the ability children have to be creative

– not only to engage their interest, but also to make up for linguistic deficiencies.

Notice that the lesson requires much more listening than speaking from the children. This is appropriate given the importance of input in language acquisition. The assumption here is that the teacher would be doing his/her best to speak exclusively in English throughout the lesson. It is not unreasonable to expect a silent period as part of early child second language development. While the children at this age and with a couple of years of classroom exposure should hopefully be beyond a silent period, the variability expected among learners means that some may not. An attentive teacher will choose those children who are ready and comfortable with the demands of speaking for the task that asks them to deliver instruction to the class. The emphasis on oral instead of visual input is also deliberate. There is an extent to which heavy dependence on literacy might adversely affect some aspects of language development. If new words or phrases are presented in writing first, child learners could make a connection between form and pronunciation which could be unhelpful, given that many words do not correspond exactly to their spelling. By using pictures and oral presentation first, the children will rely on the sounds of the words and phrases before learning to spell them.

From a linguistic point of view, the main difference between this lesson and the lesson for adults is the balance of implicit and explicit instruction. Because the ability for metalinguistic knowledge develops with age, certain types of explicit instruction would be particularly unhelpful. We mentioned that phrasal stress would remain an aim in this lesson. However, the lesson does not contain any explicit instruction on phrasal stress. Instead, when giving instructions, the teacher would be expected to model phrasal stress, perhaps in a somewhat exaggerated fashion.[12] Additionally, at every opportunity the teacher is to recast not only the pronunciation, but also the correct phrasal stress. This is because of both the cognitive limitations of children with regard to metalinguistic knowledge and the research which supports a potential among child learners for acquisition within the domain of phonology. Similarly, the explicit teaching of words is limited to animal names. The focus on location phrases is integrated into the placement task, but without explicit teaching before the task, nor with explicit practice in writing after. This is because of the child's ability to acquire grammatical structures. Vocabulary building, by contrast, benefits from explicit instruction, regardless of the age of the learner.

In sum, despite the research showing that that there is no specific age for a critical period for language acquisition, we know that for successful language development, younger is better. For both general cognitive and specific linguistic reasons, children should receive less explicit instruction and more natural unexplained engagement with language than their adult counterparts. Since research suggests that development of inflectional morphology and phonology seems to mirror the native language situation for young learners, it is especially important that these areas are 'taught' using lots of rich authentic input with ample time for comprehension before expecting accurate production from children. Yet production is important as well, so children should be given opportunities to use the language they are learning.[13] Finally, we know that some aspects of language rely on explicit instruction and experience, regardless of age. New words can be learned with the aid of instruction and opportunities for practice. And, considering the cognitive levels of child learners, repetition of activities and mimicry of the teacher are much more appropriate then for adults. Thus, while there are some similarities for teaching adults and children, there are also many differences.

THE GLOBAL CONTEXT: ENGLISH AS A LINGUA FRANCA

While most of this book has been concerned with issues that are relevant to the teaching of any language, these last two chapters have illustrated the main points based on specific English language teaching contexts. The reason to include a section on ELF is that any discussion of English language teaching needs to acknowledge the unique position that English holds as a global language. It is widely accepted that there are more non-native speakers of English than there are native speakers. Moreover, the most prevalent use of English among non-native users is with other non-native speakers, not with native speakers.[14] It is in this context that the term **English as a Lingua Franca**, or ELF, has come into being. The argument is that ELF should be seen as a legitimate form of English alongside the many other varieties that exist, from 'inner circle' dialects such as General American and Received Pronunciation to 'outer circle' varieties such as Singapore English or Indian English.[15]

While ELF is argued to be a legitimate form of English, it is not being promoted as yet another dialect of English, just as ESL and EFL are not varieties of English. The main point that distinguishes ELF from other contexts is its intended use. Both EFL and ESL view the ultimate aim of the learner to be native-like production of the language of a particular (usually inner circle) English-speaking group, whether Australian, American or British, for example. ELF, by contrast, views the ultimate aim as being able to communicate successfully with other speakers, whether native or, more probably, non-native. What matters most for ELF is successful interaction, not the degree to which features of English approximate any one particular dialect. That the majority of non-native interactions are with other non-native speakers is the reason why the label *lingua franca* has been applied.

This view of English as an international language is very much in concert with a view of language as dynamic and constantly changing. It is uncontroversial to say that language is always changing, often as a result of contact with other languages. What makes ELF different is the recognition that changes to the English used in international interaction are predominantly a product of non-native speaker influence, not native speaker innovations. The idea is that ELF speakers use a particular set of English features which are needed in order to communicate, whether they conform to 'standard' dialect features or are influenced by the speaker's native language. Central to the ELF research agenda is to describe what non-native speakers of English actually do when they speak, not to prescribe what they should do.

The methodology of ELF research is to record real interactions and to note which features of English seem to be required for interpretability and which lead to breakdown in communication. For example, in her work on English phonology, Jenkins (2000) shows that features of pronunciation often taught in English language classrooms, including word stress, connected speech, weak forms and stress-timed rhythm, are unnecessary at best and can be, at worst, unhelpful for intelligibility. Similarly, the ability for a learner to produce either the voiced /ð/ of *this* or the unvoiced /θ/ *thank* is not necessary for interpretability as these sounds can be replaced with /d/ and /t/ respectively, and interpretability is maintained.

If one truly accepts the idea of ELF, the logical conclusion to the language classroom can be rather radical. If the genuine aim for teaching is to lead to learners with the skills needed for successful communication, and if that communication is likely to be largely with other non-native speakers, then it is no longer the specific features of a specified or accepted dialect that need teaching, but instead the features of ELF. In this way, ELF challenges the native speaker norm which predominates in English language teaching. We begin our discussion of ELF in the classroom by asking in what context it might be appropriate to take an ELF perspective. In our discussions of

English language teaching so far we have considered four contexts. Both the original lesson plan and the child L2 lesson were devised with an EFL context in mind. The advanced and low-level learner contexts, by contrast, were defined as ESL contexts. Since ESL refers to teaching within a country in which English is a native language, successful communication with native English speakers is an appropriate aim and thus ELF would not be as appropriate as the main guiding principle – though it may be useful for learners to be aware of the features of ELF.

In an EFL classroom, it is more likely that learners who become users of English will primarily interact with other non-native speakers and thus ELF is more appropriate for an EFL context. Of our two EFL contexts, however, we will rule out the child L2 context as an appropriate context for applying ELF for several reasons. Firstly, language teaching at this level and age is foundational in nature, with attention to teaching core vocabulary and fostering as much natural acquisition as possible. The ability for children to acquire language naturally means that some of the difficult features of English, such as certain aspects of pronunciation and grammatical morphology, are candidates for native speaker levels of knowledge. Thus, we would support the more traditional EFL approach to teaching children in order to maximise the child's ability to acquire language, with any of the standard dialects as the appropriate stated aim.

The adult, secondary language teaching context, by contrast, may be a more appropriate place to consider ELF principles because those learners who, upon completing their studies, find that they need to use English are likely to use it with other non-native speakers. However, this idealistic position completely disregards the pragmatic reality that secondary schooling includes formal assessment and tends to be reliant on mass-produced mainstream textbooks. While it may be that the ELF agenda is so persuasive that one day it is accepted in EFL contexts, the current situation is far from this point. This causes me to hesitate to promote an ELF-based curriculum, but instead, to endorse ELF as a valuable part of teacher training courses so that teachers are aware of the concept and familiar with the linguistic features of ELF. This knowledge is likely to be very useful at higher levels of secondary schooling when deciding which features of language to insist that learners master, and which to overlook, especially when teaching speaking and when managing interaction in the classroom.

While an ELF-based syllabus does not seem entirely appropriate for the contexts discussed so far, there is a context in which ELF should inform the basic principles of teaching: any professional development context in which learners are developing their English for use in workplace interaction with other non-native speakers. Thus, the context we will consider here is one of adult workers in a multinational corporation or a not-for-profit organisation who will regularly come into contact with people from a range of linguistic backgrounds. We will place our learners at the same B2 level as our original lesson plan, but the overall aims of the course will be quite different. There is no formal assessment, nor any expectation that these learners might move to an English-speaking country. Instead, these learners know that they are going to need to use English in order to be effective at their job.

Retaining our zoo theme, we would alter the lesson to suit this group of learners. Recognising the need for conflict resolution that comes up at personal and institutional levels in most professional settings, we would present the learners with a scenario in which a zoo is in deficit and deciding how it might cope with the news that it must sell half of its land and get rid of half of its animals. After putting the class into groups and handing out cards outlining details of the scenario, the first task of this lesson would be to ask each group to come up with a five-year business plan for the zoo. The second task would be for each group to present their plan to the rest the class, who are evenly divided between zoo employees and zoo shareholders.

In this lesson, primary emphasis is placed on discussion and negotiation because this is the kind of language skill these learners are expected to need in their professional settings. The influence of ELF underpins the lesson, which revolves around verbal interaction. Taking the concept of ELF one step further, however, this lesson will also include, as a regular feature on this language programme, one 'language monitor' per group. Taking it in turns so that all students act at some point as 'language monitor', this role would rotate from person to person from lesson to lesson. Every time there is groupwork, then, one member of the group would be designated a 'language monitor'. The task of the language monitor is to observe the group interaction silently, making note of all instances in which there was any difficulty in understanding on the part of any member of the group. After the first group discussion task in our lesson, the monitors would present their notes to the class. Then, with the aid of the teacher, the class would analyse and discuss the causes of breakdown in communication. So as not to disrupt the main task too much, the teacher would plan to address the highlighted points more explicitly in a follow-up class. The monitors would be asked to continue their note-taking during the second whole-class discussion.

The rationale behind the regular use of language monitors is the idea that learners will be better users of language if they are aware of which features of their language tend to lead to breakdown of communication. With this awareness, they can work to develop these areas in their own speech, and to look to them in the speech of others if they find themselves on the receiving end of communication break-down. Notice that the application of ELF here is not to teach any specific features explicitly as correct or incorrect, but instead to apply the rationale of ELF for determining which features of English are worthy of concern. One reason for this is the fact that language is dynamic. Despite the regularities that are emerging in research on ELF, from situation to situation, the exact causes of communication breakdown are likely to alter. Moreover, this approach avoids any potentially patronising attitude whereby learners are made to feel as though they are being taught some simplified form of English on a 'good-enough' basis. In a sense, this approach is one which places strategic competence at its core, as learners are taught to hone in on potentially problematic areas of both their own language and the language of those they are likely to encounter when using English. Thus, like all of the approaches discussed in these last two chapters, this approach takes as a starting point for the specific needs of the particular set of learners in each given context, drawing on understanding of both conceptions of language and research in SLA to inform the particular parameters of the lesson.

CONCLUSION

We have covered much ground in this book, from questions of theoretical linguistics to the practice of teaching. We started by asking the very basic question of what language is, looking at a range of answers. We have ended this book by taking the question to a specific extreme by asking what the English language is. While many per-spectives and many answers have been given throughout, hopefully you will hesitate to assume that any one answer is wholly acceptable and applicable for all situations. In fact, in many ways this book raises more questions than it answers. One danger of this is that teachers may feel as though the lack of definitive, agreed answers among researchers means that no one has any answers. Yet hopefully you will instead have developed a deeper understanding of the complexity of your subject area: language. And you will now have a sense of some of the agreed generalisations which have emerged from SLA research coming out of a range of linguistic perspectives. In this way, the decisions that you make in your classroom can be informed not only by intuition, your experience and the pressures of your particular context, but by research and understanding of both language and how language develops.

FOR DISCUSSION

1. For each of the four contexts given here, map out the lesson plan as described, using the format for the lesson plan given in Chapter 7. Then compare and contrast the interaction patterns for each lesson. What connection is there between interaction patterns and the particular context?
2. Find a lesson plan designed for secondary school teaching. Modify it to suit low-level learners, advanced-level learners or child L2 learners.
3. Go back, once again, to the ten observations about second language development. To what extent are they equally relevant for the different contexts we have considered?
4. All of the lessons made use of task-based learning. Modify one to reflect a PPP structure. Then try modifying it to adhere to one of the 'designer' approaches presented in Chapter 6.
5. Discuss the merits and limitations of ELF. To what extent is the ELF concept useful for your English language teaching context? Is the ELF concept applicable to any other languages that you are familiar with other than English?
6. What do you consider the most important points made in this book? To what extent will they affect your views on teaching? What, specifically, could you plan to do differently as a teacher that you did not do before (as a language teacher or learner)?

NOTES

1. Research on illiterate adults learning a second language (or students with interrupted formal education) is a small but growing area of interest. See Kurvers, van de Craats and Young-Scholten (2006), and Tarone and Hansen (to appear). Details about a professional organisation dedicated to Low Education Second Language and Literacy Acquisition (LESLLA) can be found at http://www.leslla.org/.

2. While learners seem to have very little difficulty with word order within noun, verb and prepositional phrases, there can be difficulty of ordering of adjectives within noun phrases for many learners.

3. Not only is this an area of professional expertise, but one of academic interest as well. See the regularly issued *Journal of EAP,* published by Elsevier, for academic papers devoted to research in EAP.

4. John Morley at Manchester University has developed a very useful and extensive collection of phrases such as these, organised by different types, all relevant to academic English. His Academic Phrasebank can be found at: http://www.phrasebank.manchester.ac.uk/

5. John Swales is widely regarded for both academic and pedagogical contributions to the fields of genre analysis and EAP. See Swales (1990), and for a very useful pedagogical work, Swales and Feak (1994).

6. Genre analysis has developed out of systemic functionalist approaches to language. The earliest use of the term genre in English language teaching is attributed to Tarone et al. (1981). See Paltridge (2001) for a very clear discussion of genre and language teaching.

7. One particularly good concordancer is provided within the University of Quebec's Compleat Lexical Tutor site at: http://www.lextutor.ca/con-cordancers/concord_e.html. It has a wide range of database collections to search from, distinguishing between spoken and written collections of text. Additionally, at the time of writing, it includes databases in both French and German in addition to English.

8. For a review of research in simultaneous bilingualism, see Meisel (2004).

9. For discussion of the age at which children are said to have a fully developed grammar, see Guasti (2002).

10. See Philp, Oliver and Mackey (2008) and Snyder (2007) for discussions of age and other issues relevant to child language learning. For a collection of empirical studies on child L2 from a generative perspective, see Haznedar and Gavruseva (2008).

11. Interestingly, most of the child L2 research has been done in either immersion settings or naturalistic settings, in other words in the ESL context. Very little research has been done in the child EFL classroom.

12. Even in native language acquisition, intonation is known to develop at a relatively late age, certainly after the age of 5, but before our cut-off age of 13.

13. Recall from Chapter 5 that research in immersion classrooms shows that input alone is not sufficient.

14. While the exact figures behind these claims are hotly disputed, the general claim as put forward by Graddol (1997, 2006) is largely accepted.

15. Two leading proponents of ELF are Jennifer Jenkins and Barbara Seidlhofer. See Jenkins (2007) for an overview of ELF and for references to other proponents of the ELF agenda. The Inner vs Outer Circle concept is from Krachu (1985).

GLOSSARY

Access to UG The phrase used to describe the extent to which second language development is constrained by Universal Grammar. Because it suggests an active, deliberate process, it has mostly been abandoned in favour of the term *UG-constrained development* instead.

Accuracy Usually mentioned in contrast with fluency, this refers to the extent to which a language learner is able to produce (and comprehend) language without errors or mistakes.

Acquisition Implicit development which occurs without conscious or deliberate effort.

Acquisition by Processing Theory (APT) A theory proposed by John Truscott and Mike Sharwood Smith as part of MOGUL, in which learning occurs through the exposure to and reinforcement of input.

Acquisition-Learning Hypothesis The hypothesis proposed by Krashen to distinguish between implicit and explicit development of knowledge. For Krashen, these types of language knowledge remain distinct.

Activation level The extent to which a particular representation of knowledge in the mind is primed, or ready to be called on in response to some signal or input.

Active learning A basic tenet of communicative language teaching, this refers to the participation of learners in discovering knowledge and developing abilities themselves, instead of passively receiving input from the teacher or course materials.

Affective factors Personal factors that may affect linguistic development, such as motivation, personality, attitude and other emotional factors.

Affective Filter Hypothesis Within Krashen's Monitor Model, the Affective Filter refers to a psychological hindrance to language development that can result from a particular learner's levels of motivation, interest and other emotional factors.

Approach The underlying conceptual basis for making decisions. With regard to teaching, this may include conclusions based on empirical results, more intuitive-based inclinations or ideas that have developed based on personal experience.

Associative learning A view of learning held by cognitivists whereby learning involves making connections between new knowledge and existing knowledge.

Audiolingual Approach An approach to teaching language based on the ideas of Behaviourism, in which repeated input and rapid-fire drilling are core to developing language.

Authentic materials Resources used for language teaching which were not specifically designed for the classroom nor for language teaching. Typical examples include material found on the Internet, or printed in newspapers or magazines.

Automatisation The point at which knowledge no longer makes use of explicit attention but instead exists without explicit awareness.

Avoidance The tendency for language learners to refrain systematically from using a particular linguistic form in favour of an easier alternative form that expresses the same meaning.

Behaviourism This theory from psychology, which reached prominence in the 1950s, was based on experimental work with animals and posited a view of human behaviour which depended on experience and conditioning for the formation of habits.

Bilingual This term contrasts with child L2 development, referring to the situation in which a speaker has native-level knowledge and ability in two (or more) languages as a result of full exposure and development of the languages from infancy.

Bottleneck Hypothesis A hypothesis proposed by Slabakova (2008) which argues that some aspects of language, such as functional morphology, create a 'bottleneck', causing difficulty for language development.

Brain The physical organ encased in the skull; for humans it consists of two hemispheres and is made up of neurons, axons, etc.

Child L2 development This refers to the development of a second (or additional) language through exposure to that language after native language development, but before the so-called critical period has passed, approximately between the ages of six and thirteen.

Co-construction The idea that development is not uni-directional; for language teaching this refers to language knowledge developed by learners and the effect on those imparting that knowledge, as well as the properties of language itself.

Cognate Words in different languages that are related to each other etymologically and thus share a common root. For example, *luminous* in English and *luminoso* in Spanish are both derived from the Latin root *lumin-*, which means *light*.

Cognitive Linguistics A branch of linguistics that is closely associated with research in psychology in terms of theoretical orientation and methodology.

Colligation Phrases that are regularly used together to such an extent that they take on the feeling of a fixed phrase.

Collocation Words that are regularly used together to such an extent that they take on the feeling of a fixed phrase.

Communicative competence The notion proposed by Dell Hymes to counter

Chomsky's competence/performance distinction; it refers to the knowledge and abilities required for a speaker to be able to participate successfully in a speech community.

Communicative Language Teaching (CLT) A very broad term which encompasses any approach to language teaching which takes communication as its most fundamental aim.

Communities of practice Within Situated Learning Theory, identifiable groups whose members have shared aims and norms with specified functions.

Community Language Learning Drawing on ideas from counselling, Charles Curran's approach to language teaching emphasises collaboration and community development as a social process.

Competence The term proposed by Chomsky to refer to the core linguistic knowledge that all native speakers of a language develop, whether they have explicit knowledge of the properties of language or not. It contrasts with 'performance' and exists as an idealised version of language.

Complexity Theory As recently applied to language, a theory that sees language as in a perpetual state of change as a result of internal and external pressures.

Comprehensible input Part of Krashen's Input Hypothesis, this describes the optimal type of input for learners – that which is one step ahead of the learner's current language level, also referred to as $i + 1$.

Comprehension approaches This refers to any method of language teaching which considers comprehension as primary to learning and more important to the learning process than production.

Concordancing The use of a concordancer, which is a search engine connected to a large database of texts, in order to discover how specific words or phrases have been used in existing texts.

Connectionism In psychology, this view sees cognitive knowledge, including language, as one intricate system of connections, and not inventories of symbols and abstract rules.

Construction A mapping between form and meaning which follows an identifiable linguistic pattern and is associated with particular meaning.

Content-Based Instruction (CBI) An approach to language instruction in which a subject area, such as geography or science, is taught through the medium of the target language instead of the explicit teaching of language as a subject.

Contrastive Analysis An approach to second language development begun in the 1940s by Charles Fries, based on comparisons between linguistic structures in the target and native languages.

Cooperative language learning This refers to the practice of collaborative learning in groups as a way of improving individual learners' abilities.

Corpus Linguistics A branch of linguistics based on a methodology which searches databases of existing language in order to make claims about the nature of language and/or the use of language.

Creative Construction Hypothesis Also called the L2=L1 hypothesis, this hypothesis argued that second language development makes use of the same innate processes as native language development.

Critical period The window of time in which a biologically constrained ability such as language can develop.

Critical Theory As an approach to language and language learning, this theory recognises the importance of power relations within particular communities.

Cues The features of a signal that help to determine the most probable match between the signal and existing knowledge.

Deductive Learning by making sense of rules that explicitly state the properties of the phenomenon in question.

Descriptive grammar The grammar of a language as defined by the attested use of the speakers of that language.

Direct Method An approach supported by the Reform Movement in the early 1900s in which all language teaching was done exclusively through the medium of the target language.

Discourse competence The term used by Canale and Swain (1980) to refer to the features of language which determine how texts, whether written or spoken, are interconnected.

English as a Foreign Language (EFL) English taught in a context in which English is not the language widely spoken in the country in which it is being taught.

English as a Lingua Franca (ELF) A recently proposed variation of English which is made up of those features of the language which are necessary for successful communication, whether they conform to one of the accepted 'standard' dialects of English or not.

English as a Second Language (ESL) English taught in a context in which English is widely spoken, usually as the official language of the country in which it is being taught.

English for Academic Purposes (EAP) A type of ESP which teaches the English as needed specifically for use in academic settings.

English for Specific Purposes (ESP) An approach to teaching English in which the specific needs of the learners are determined in order to inform the content of the course. These needs are more commonly professional, such that there are ESP courses and textbooks with titles like *English for Nursing*, or *English for Bankers*, and so on.

Entrenchment The process by which knowledge becomes strengthened, such that it is more stable and more robust in the mind.

Error Non-targetlike use of language which reflects a consistent rule or linguistic constraint.

Error Analysis The methodology used to analyse second language learner production in terms of effects from the native language.

Exemplar-driven learning This captures the notion that language development occurs through repeated exposure to examples of the new language point in question.

Explicit input Information about or explanation of language, such as rules, definitions or norms of use.

False friends Words that are similar in two different languages, usually because of a shared etymological root, but which have evolved to have divergent meanings. They are false friends as they may in fact mislead the speaker into assuming they know the meaning of the word.

Field In Systemic Functional Grammar, this refers to the nature of the activity which forms the context for a particular text.

Fluency The ability to produce (and comprehend) language without pauses or errors which may lead to a breakdown in communication.

Focus on Form An approach to teaching language which attends to meaning first, addressing difficult forms that cause problems for learners as they arise.

Focus on FormS An approach to teaching language which attends exclusively to the forms or structures of language. In its extreme form, it includes the repeated drilling of decontextualised language patterns.

Focus on Meaning An approach to teaching language which attends exclusively to the meaning of language without any explicit instruction on the form of language.

Foreigner-talk The modification of language production by a speaker to adapt to the language ability of the listener. This might involve the use of simple structures or even non-standard forms.

Formulaic language Set phrases or clauses which are frequently used in language production without modification.

Fossilise, Fossilisation These terms characterise the stage in which a learner's knowledge is no longer developing. While they are often applied generally, it is usually more accurate to refer to the fossilisation of specific language features for any particular speaker.

Frequency An important requirement for learning within associative learning processes, as repeated examples of input are needed for cognitive development.

Full Transfer A theoretical stance in SLA in which the starting point of second language development is assumed to be the grammar of the existing first language in its totality.

Functional Linguistics A branch of linguistics that approaches language in terms of its function or use, and bases its analysis on the meaning of language in context.

Fundamental Difference Hypothesis Proposed by Robert Bley-Vroman (1990), this hypothesis assumes a qualitative difference between child first and adult second language development.

Fuzziness Associated with Prototype Theory, this refers to the indistinct nature of categories, especially at the boundaries.

General knowledge/cognition The encyclopedic knowledge that a person develops from experience over time. This ranges from knowledge of specific facts to knowledge underlying skills such as driving a car.

Generative Linguistics A branch of linguistics that views language as the product of a universal set of constraints which, once acquired, allow for creative generation of language within those constraints.

Genre Analysis As an approach to teaching, exemplary texts associated with a particular speech community are used to teach the specific properties of that text type as well as practices of the speech community in question.

Grammar Translation The approach to language teaching which grew out of the way that Classical languages like Latin and Ancient Greek were taught. In this approach literary texts are translated with a focus on grammar, as well as on the cultural values embedded in the text.

Grammatical/Linguistic competence The term used by Canale and Swain (1980) to characterise grammatical knowledge as one type of knowledge required for communicative competence.

Grammatical Metaphor This term, as used by Halliday, refers to the way in which particular grammatical structures are extended in order to serve a particular communicative function.

Head Parameter A universal parameter which regulates whether the main word in a phrase precedes or follows the dependent words within the phrase.

Humanism An approach to teaching that comes out of the Progressive movement in education whereby the needs of learners as individuals and as people are seen as primary.

Immersion approaches An approach to foreign or second language instruction in which all classes are taught in the target language and not through the medium of the language of the wider community.

Implicit input The target language input to which a language learner is exposed. This means that explicit input is also implicit if it is delivered exclusively using the language.

Inductive Learning by making sense of examples that give rise to regularities that illustrate the properties of the phenomenon in question.

Inflectional morphology The functional elements in language required for grammaticality, but which may or may not hold much semantic meaning. Examples from English include 3rd person singular -*s*, progressive -*ing* and articles *a(n)/the*.

Information gap A frequently used technique in communicative language teaching, this refers to any task which requires learners to gather information, whether from classmates or other sources. Such a task is assumed to be motivating, as it requires the learner to discover new information actively.

Input Enhancement Promoted by Sharwood Smith (1993), this refers to the practice of drawing attention to particular language forms in attempt to increase the salience of the forms in question.

Input Hypothesis Krashen's hypothesis which says that the most effective input for the learner is that which is one step ahead of the learner's current interlanguage.

Input Processing An approach proposed by VanPatten whereby language development occurs when the learner's processing abilities initially lead to a misinterpretation because of limitations at particular stages of learning.

Integrated skills This refers to the idea that language should be taught in such a way as to make use of speaking, listening, reading and writing together, instead of teaching them as separate skills.

Interaction Hypothesis Proposed by Long (1981, 1983), this hypothesis holds that language development requires learners to make sense of and make sense in the target language.

Interlanguage (IL) A term coined by Larry Selinker (1972) to describe the grammar of the learner acquiring another language. This grammar is understood to be systematic, rule-based and dynamic.

Inter-linguistic variation Differences that exist between different languages.

Internalisation The development of psychological functions as a result of interaction between the individual and the social environment.

Intra-linguistic variation Differences that exist within a single language system.

L1/language transfer The influence that the existing language(s) has when learning or using a second, or additional, language.

Language Acquisition Device (LAD) Coined by early generativists to refer to the part of the mind implicated in native language development, this term has been largely abandoned because of the mechanistic image it suggests.

Languaging Coined by Swain (2006), this term refers to the process required of learners to do the hard work of making meaning through interaction in order for language development to occur.

Langue A term used by Ferdinand de Saussure to refer to the properties of the language system itself, in contrast with *parole*.

The Learnables This teaching method, developed by Harris Winitz, centres on pictures and spoken input, graded in such a way as to lead to effective language development.

Learner autonomy The idea that language learners should take responsibility for their language development instead of relying heavily on the teacher and/or the classroom materials.

Learner diary A technique for facilitating language teaching whereby learners are asked to record their learning experiences on a regular basis, usually in the form of a journal entry or a blog.

Learning Explicit development which occurs through conscious or deliberate effort.

Lexical Approach Associated with Michael Lewis, this approach teaches words and word combinations, as language is viewed solely as words and not a system of rules based on structural principles.

Lexical Metaphor The extension of a word or phrase to a meaning beyond the literal.

Linguistic Determinism This strong version of the Sapir–Whorf Hypothesis holds that language determines the way people think.

Linguistic general knowledge Explicit knowledge of the properties of language, also known as metalinguistic knowledge.

Linguistic knowledge Implicit knowledge of language made use of in language processing and production without explicit awareness or understanding.

Linguistic Relativism This weaker version of the Sapir–Whorf Hypothesis holds that language has an effect on the way people think.

Literacy The ability to make sense of the written representation of a language, usually in the form of a writing system, such as an alphabet.

Markedness This refers to the extent to which some linguistic form is more common, usual or simple in comparison with other forms. A subject relative clause, such as *the girl who ran away*, for example, is considered less marked than a possessive relative clause, such as *the girl whose puppy ran away*.

Mediation Within a sociocultural approach, the function that language serves to connect an individual and the social environment.

Metalinguistic knowledge Explicit knowledge of language which allows for thoughts about and discussion of language in terms of rules, patterns and generalisations.

Method The way in which lessons are structured and delivered. This is usually based on one's approach to language in addition to more practical constraints such as type of learners or institutional setting, as well as questions of general pedagogy.

Mind The cognitive functions and representations of cognitive functions associated with the brain.

Minimalist Theory The most recent version of Chomsky's theory, this maintains the essential concepts of generativism, but reduces the mechanisms involved in the theory to a minimum.

Mistake A one-off blunder which can be attributed to factors outside the core grammatical system, such as fatigue, anxiety or distraction.

Mode In Systemic Functional Grammar, this refers to the medium through which a particular text is delivered.

Modular, Modularity of Mind A view of how language is represented in the mind proposed by Fodor (1983) which posits language as a distinct type of knowledge akin to the senses and unlike general knowledge.

Modular Linguistic Knowledge Core knowledge of language, such as syntax and phonology, which all native speakers have despite not being explicitly aware of that knowledge.

Modular On-line Growth and Use of Language (MOGUL) A framework developed by John Truscott and Mike Sharwood Smith which draws from a range of linguistic approaches to make sense of the complex process of language development.

Monitor Hypothesis Proposed by Krashen, this hypothesis captures the ability that cognitively mature adults have to gauge and alter their language output explicitly.

Monitor Model The label given to Krashen's ideas about how adult second language development happens. It includes five hypotheses: Acquisition-Learning Hypothesis, Affective Filter Hypothesis, Input Hypothesis, Monitor Hypothesis, and Natural Order Hypothesis.

Monolingual Having a fully developed linguistic system for only one language which has developed as a result of exposure from infancy.

Multiple sensitive periods This term captures the idea that different aspects of development of a complex system such as language are likely to have different time periods in which natural, full development is possible.

Nativism The theory that language is a biological property with which humans are endowed, which includes a predisposition for language development. Special nativism further posits language as a distinct or privileged type of cognitive ability, distinct from other types of cognition.

Natural Approach An approach to language promoted by Krashen and Terrell (1983), which took a native language approach to second language teaching.

Natural Order Hypothesis The hypothesis proposed by Krashen based on research on the development of English functional morphemes; it claims that second language development follows a 'natural' path, regardless of other factors such as native language, age, type of input and so on.

Needs analysis The practice of formally assessing the needs of the learners in order to deliver language classes effectively. This may take the form of a formal battery of questions to design a whole course or of a more day-to-day monitoring of students' needs in order to deliver lessons that are as relevant to the students as possible.

Negative evidence Explanations about what is unacceptable, ungrammatical or not possible in the grammar of a language.

Negotiation of meaning Within the Interaction Hypothesis, this is the process by which learners develop language ability as they work through challenges in their ability to communicate.

Neo-Vygotskyan The term is used to refer to sociocultural ideas that have recently developed from the ideas proposed by L. S. Vygotsky in the early 1900s.

Nominalisation An example of grammatical metaphor, this refers to a process in which an event whose basic grammatical form is verbal is presented in a nominal form instead.

Noticing Having wide intuitive appeal but little theoretical underpinning, this concept was proposed by Schmidt (1990, 1993) to refer to the idea that input has to be taken up by learners in order for learning to take place.

Notional Syllabus The term used by David Wilkins to describe a language syllabus which takes notions and functions as its basic organising principle, in contrast with a more structural or grammatical syllabus.

Null Subject Parameter A universal parameter which regulates whether a language allows sentences without overt subjects or not. Spanish is an example of a grammatically based null subject language while Japanese is a discourse-based null subject language. English, by contrast, requires overt subjects.

Object Regulation The first stage of development as understood by Vygotsky, in which learners rely on objects to make sense of what they are learning.

Oral Approach An approach to teaching proposed in the early 1900s in England, which advocated the teaching of language in increasingly complex sequences, with a focus on speaking. It came to be associated with the Situational Approach.

Other Regulation In this early stage of development, as understood by Vygotsky, learners rely on others for assistance and direction as they learn.

Output Hypothesis Proposed by Swain (1985), this hypothesis challenged Krashen's Input Hypothesis, arguing that language production is also necessary for language development.

Parole A term used by Ferdinand de Saussure to refer to the properties of language as evidenced through the use of language, in contrast with *langue*.

Performance The term proposed by Chomsky to characterise the language that is produced by a speaker, which may or may not mirror the underlying competence of the speaker, as it is prone to deficiencies due to distraction or other production pressures.

Plato's Problem This refers to a general learning problem articulated by Plato which asks how a person can come to know so much more than the limited set of data to which he/she is exposed. Generativists have applied this question to language to support a nativist stance.

Post-Methods Era This is the term that has been used to describe the current era in language teaching, as there is general agreement that there is no one foolproof method which is effective for all language learners in all language-learning contexts.

Poverty of the stimulus The observation that the input, or stimulus, to which any child is exposed is impoverished in relation to the complexity of knowledge that the child comes to know as a native speaker of a language.

PPP: Present, Practise, Produce This is a well-known structure for lesson planning, widely adopted since the 1970s for language teaching.

Prescriptive grammar The grammar of a language as set out by those who want to specify the rules of a language in terms of correct forms. This grammar may or may not completely correspond to what is attested among speakers of the language.

Priming The process whereby the mind has been prepared for a particular signal by activating some associated concept first, thereby leading to quicker activation in response to the signal.

Principles and Parameters The name given to the generative theory of the 1980s which captured the properties of language into universal principles with parameters accounting for cross-linguistic differences.

Private speech From a Vygotskyan approach, inner speech directed to oneself to mediate between thinking and behaviour.

Proceduralisation The process whereby a skill becomes automatic, allowing for action without any conscious thought or attention to that action.

Process vs product In the context of language teaching, this opposition refers to the ability to do some language-related activity, process, as opposed to the actual language output, product.

Progressivism A movement in mainstream education in the twentieth century which emphasises and values the needs of individuals, especially in terms of how they might take responsibility for their own learning by becoming more active learners.

Property Theory In second language acquisition, this describes a theory which offers an explanation for the particular properties of any particular stage of learner development at a moment in time.

Prototype Theory A theory which says that the ability to classify concepts into categories is basic to human cognition. Prototypes are best examples of a category, as they have a large number of core attributes of the category in question.

Rassias Named after its founder, John Rassias, this teaching method sees language as a cultural artefact which must be learned from within its social context.

Realia Artefacts used in class that reflect the culture or practices of the target language community, including leaflets, pictures, radio broadcasts, televised programmes, and so on.

Reflective learning The idea that learning will be more effective if learners are aware of and able to reflect on their learning experience.

Reform Movement In response to Grammar Translation in the 1880s, this approach to language teaching advocated teaching in terms of the four skills.

Resting level The level of a particular representation of knowledge when it is not active.

Rheme A term proposed by the Prague School to contrast with theme, rheme refers to idea that the speaker moves to, or the new information in a sentence or utterance.

Salience The extent to which something is clear, prominent or noticeable. In language learning it often refers to more prominent features of language, such a stressed syllables, in contrast with weak forms such as unstressed syllables.

Sapir–Whorf Hypothesis This refers to the controversial claim that language affects or even determines thought, named after Edward Sapir and Benjamin Whorf.

Scaffolding Proposed by educational psychologist Jerome Bruner, this metaphor refers to the support provided by teachers in order for learners to develop knowledge and skills.

Schema A framework or blueprint for a concept developed in an individual's mind, based on both personal experience and human processes of cognition.

Selective error correction The practice of choosing which learner errors to correct, based on a principled reasoning and knowledge of interlanguage in addition to the more pedagogically motivated considerations of motivation and learner needs, for example.

Self-regulation A developmental stage beyond other regulation in which a learner is able to rely on themselves for particular knowledge and skills.

Semiotics The study of the relationship between signs and meaning, semiotics has had a large influence on the development of functional approaches to language.

Sensitive Period A more accurate way to characterise the time period for development of a biologically constrained property such a language. While development may still occur outside the 'sensitive period', it is not likely to develop naturally and fully.

Silent period A time period associated with native first language acquisition in which the child understands language that they are not yet able to produce. It has been suggested that adult language learners may also have a silent period.

Silent Way Devised by Caleb Gattengo, this teaching method de-emphasises input and forefronts the active learner instead. Teachers are to remain as silent as possible so as to allow learners to work out properties of the language for themselves.

Situated Learning Theory A theory which views learning as inextricably tied to context and culture, and to the authentic activities within particular communities.

Situational Approach An approach to teaching that developed in the early 1900s in Australia, which emphasised the teaching of language in context.

Sociocultural theory An approach which sees language as a product of society instead of a biological feature of being human.

Sociolinguistic/Pragmatic competence The term used by Canale and Swain (1980) to characterise knowledge required for appropriate use of a language in terms of the norms and conventions of the speakers of the language.

Speech Act Theory Proposed by John Searle, this theory captures the meaning of linguistic expressions by analysing the locutionary, illocutionary and perlocutionary acts within an utterance.

Standard Theory, Extended Standard Theory and **Revised Extended Standard Theory** The subsequent names given to early revisions of generative theory proposed by Noam Chomsky in the 1950s, 1960s and 1970s.

Strategic competence The term used by Canale and Swain (1980) to refer to knowledge needed to repair breakdown in communication.

Structuralism This mainstream approach to linguistics in the late nineteenth century analysed language in terms of its structures, with particular emphasis at the level of phoneme and morpheme.

Structure dependency/preservation This refers to the universal property of all languages whereby language rules or constraints respect the structure of the language and not, for example, linear rules, even if such rules seem more 'logical'.

Subset Principle A principle that helps to explain how complex knowledge such as language is acquired. By this principle, a learner will have a predisposition for a subset of knowledge and only adopt the larger relevant superset based on evidence in the input.

Suggestopedia Developed by Georgi Lozanov, this approach to teaching combines 'psycho-relaxation' techniques with a firm authority figure to promote language development.

Systemic Functional Grammar (SFG) The functionalist theory proposed by Michael Halliday which posits language as communication; this approach is especially known for its analysis of discourse.

Target language The language that the learner is trying to acquire.

Task A language learning activity with a goal that is not specifically linguistic, but which is designed to require the use of particular linguistic features, forms, knowledge and/or ability.

Task-based learning A communicative approach to language teaching which centres on carefully constructed tasks.

Teacher-talk The modification of language by a teacher in order to adapt to the language proficiency of the learners, usually by using simple structures and well-known vocabulary.

Techniques The specific way of carrying out teaching within a teaching method and adhering to approach: for example, the actual lesson plan template or the way in which a teacher checks for understanding.

Tenor In Systemic Functional Grammar, this refers to the relationships between the producer and receiver(s) of a particular text.

Text Either written or spoken, a text is a sample of discourse produced within a specific context for a particular function.

Theme A term proposed by the Prague School to contrast with rheme, theme refers to the starting point or already known information in a sentence or utterance.

Total Physical Response (TPR) Developed by James Asher, this approach to teaching places much stock in kinetics and the extent to which learning is seen as a product of stimulus and response.

Transformations and Transformational Generative Grammar The basis of early generative theory, this refers to the relationship between grammatical constructions. For example, an interrogative sentence in English is a transformation of declarative sentence that involves the movement of a *wh-* word to the beginning of the sentence.

Transition theory In second language acquisition, this describes a theory which offers an explanation for how a learner moves from one stage of development to another.

UG-constrained development The more current term used to refer to the extent to which second language development is constrained by principles of Universal Grammar.

Unanalysed chunk A phrase which is taught and learned as one single unit corresponding to a specific meaning and/or functional intent without attention given to the meaning of the smaller units which make up the phrase, nor their grammatical properties.

Universal Grammar (UG) The set of universal constraints by which all natural languages abide.

Usage-based Usage-based approaches to language emphasise the role that using language plays in the development of language.

Vernacular The local form of a language which is widely used by a community of speakers; this form may or may not correspond to the standard, and thus usually more prestigious, form of the same language.

Zone of proximal development (ZPD) As defined by Vygotsky, the potential range of development for any given learner, as determined in relation to the learner's current abilities.

REFERENCES

ॐ

Aarts, B. (2007), *Syntactic Gradience: The Nature of Grammatical Indeterminacy*, Oxford: Oxford University Press.

Adger, D. (2003), *Core Syntax: A Minimalist Approach*, Oxford: Oxford University Press.

Aitchison, J. (1998), *The Articulate Mammal: An Introduction to Psycholinguistics*, 4th edn, London: Routledge.

Ammar, A. and P. Lightbown (2003), 'Teaching marked linguistic structures – more about the acquisition of relative clauses by Arab learners of English', in A. Housen and M. Pierrard (eds), *Investigations in Instructed Second Language Learning*, Berlin: Mouton de Gruyter, pp. 167–98.

Anthony, E. (1963), 'Approach, method and technique', *English Language Teaching*, 17: 63–7.

Asher, J. (1966), 'The learning strategy of the total physical response: A review', *Modern Language Journal*, 50: 79–84.

Asher, J. (1977), *Learning Another Language through Actions: The Complete Teacher's Guide Book*, Los Gatos, CA: Sky Oaks.

Atkinson, D. (2002), 'Toward a sociocognitive approach to second language acquisition', *Modern Language Learning*, 86: 525–45.

Austin, J. L. (1962), *How to do Things with Words*, Oxford: Oxford University Press.

Bailey, N., C. Madden and S. Krashen (1974), 'Is there a "natural sequence" in adult second language learning?', *Language Learning*, 24: 235–43.

Benson, P. (2001), *Teaching and Researching Autonomy in Language Learning*, Harlow: Pearson Education.

Beretta, A. (1990), 'Implementation of the Bangalore Project', *Applied Linguistics*, 11: 321–37.

Bialystok, E. and K. Hakuta (1994), *In Other Words: The Science and Psychology of Second-Language Acquisition*, New York: Basic.

Biber, D., S. Conrad and R. Reppen (1998), *Corpus Linguistics: Investigating Language Structure and Use*, Cambridge: Cambridge University Press.

Birdsong, D. (1992), 'Ultimate attainment in second language acquisition', *Language*, 68: 706–55.

Birdsong, D. (ed.) (1999), *Second Language Acquisition and the Critical Period Hypothesis*, Mahwah, NJ: Lawrence Erlbaum.

Bley-Vroman, R. (1990), 'The logical problem of foreign language learning', *Linguistic Analysis*, 20: 3–49.

Block, D. (2007), *Second Language Identities,* London: Continuum.

Bloomfield, L. (1933), *Language,* New York, NY: Holdt.

Boers, F. (2000), 'Metaphor awareness and vocabulary retention', *Applied Linguistics,* 21: 553–71.

Boers, F. (2001), 'Remembering figurative idioms by hypothesising about their origin', *Prospect,* 16: 35–43.

Boers, F. and S. Lindstromberg (eds) (2008), *Cognitive Linguistic Approaches to Teaching Vocabulary and Phraseology,* Berlin: Mouton de Gruyter.

Bongaerts, T. (1999), 'Ultimate attainment in foreign language pronunciation: The case of very advanced foreign language learners', in D. Birdsong (ed.), *Second Language Acquisition and the Critical Period Hypothesis,* Mahwah, NJ: Lawrence Erlbaum, pp. 133–59.

Bongaerts, T., B. Planken and E. Schils (1995), 'Can late learners attain a native accent in a foreign language? A test of the Critical Period Hypothesis', in D. Singleton and Z. Lengyel (eds), *The Age Factor in Second Language Acquisition,* Clevedon: Multilingual Matters, pp. 30–50.

Brown, R. (1973), *A First Language: The Early Stages,* London: George Allen & Unwin.

Bruner, J. (1961), 'The act of discovery', *Harvard Educational Review,* 31: 21–32.

Bruner, J. (1967), *On Knowing: Essays for the Left Hand,* Cambridge, MA: Harvard University Press.

Butler, C. (2003), *Structure and Function: A Guide to Three Major Structural-Functional Theories. Part 1, Approaches to the Simplex Clause,* Amsterdam: John Benjamins.

Canale, M. and M. Swain (1980), 'Theoretical bases of communicative approaches to second language teaching and testing', *Applied Linguistics,* 1: 1–47.

Carroll, S. (2001), *Input and Evidence: The Raw Material of Second Language Acquisition,* Amsterdam: John Benjamins.

Carter, R. (1998/2000), *Mapping the Mind,* London: Phoenix.

Chomsky, N. (1965), *Aspects of the Theory of Syntax,* Cambridge, MA: MIT Press.

Chomsky, N. (1970), 'Linguistic theory', in M. Lester (ed.), *Readings in Applied Transformational Grammar,* New York, NY: Holt, Reinhart & Winston.

Chomsky, N. (1981), *Lectures on Government and Binding: The Pisa Lectures,* Dordrecht: Foris.

Chomsky, N. (1986), *Barriers,* Cambridge, MA: MIT Press.

Chomsky, N. (1995), *The Minimalist Program,* Cambridge, MA: MIT Press.

Clahsen, H. and U. Hong (1995), 'Agreement and null subjects in German L2 development: New evidence from reaction-time experiments', *Second Language Research,* 11: 57–87.

Corder, P. (1967), 'The significance of learners' errors', *International Review of Applied Linguistics*, 5: 161–9.

Corder, P. (1971), 'Idiosyncratic errors and error analysis', *International Review of Applied Linguistics*, 9: 147–59.

Corder, P. (1981), *Error Analysis and Interlanguage*, Oxford: Oxford University Press.

Coulmas, F. (1989), *The Writing Systems of the World*, Oxford: Blackwell.

Council of Europe [accessed November 2009], *The Common European Framework of Reference for Languages*, http://www.coe.int/t/dg4/linguistic/CADRE_EN.asp.

Cowie, A. P. (ed.) (1998), *Phraseology, Theory Analysis and Applications*, Oxford: Oxford University Press.

Croft, W. (2001), *Radical Construction Grammar*, Oxford: Oxford University Press.

Croft, W. and A. Cruise (2004), *Cognitive Linguistics*, Cambridge: Cambridge University Press.

Curran, C. (1976), *Counseling-Learning in Second Languages*, Apple River, IL: Apple River.

Dam, L. (1995), *Autonomy from Theory to Classroom Practice*, Dublin: Authentik.

Danesi, M. (1995), 'Learning and teaching languages: The role of "conceptual fluency"', *International Journal of Applied Linguistics*, 5: 3–20.

Daniels, P. and W. Bright (eds) (1996), *The World's Writing Systems*, Oxford: Oxford University Press.

de Bot, K., W. Lowie and M. Vespoor (2007), 'A dynamic systems theory approach to second language acquisition', *Bilingualism: Language and Cognition*, 10: 7–21 and 51–5.

Dekydtspotter, L. (2001), 'The Universal Parser and interlanguage: domain-specific mental organization in the comprehension of combien interrogatives in English–French interlanguage', *Second Language Research*, 17: 91–143.

Dekydtspotter, L. and J. Hathorn (2005), 'Quelque chose (. . .) de remarquable in English–French acquisition: Mandatory, informationally encapsulated computations in second language interpretation', *Second Language Research*, 21: 291–323.

Dekydtspotter, L., R. A. Sprouse and B. Anderson (1997), 'The interpretive interface in L2 acquisition: The process–result distinction in English–French interlanguage grammar', *Language Acquisition*, 6: 297–332.

Dekydtspotter, L., R. A. Sprouse, K. Swanson and R. Thyre (1999), 'Semantics, pragmatics and second language acquisition: A case of combien extractions', in A. Greenhill, H. Littlefield and C. Tano (eds), *Proceedings of the 23rd Annual Boston University Conference on Language Development, Volume 1*, Somerville, MA: Cascadilla, pp. 162–71.

Dekydtspotter, L., R. A. Sprouse and R. Thyre (1998), 'Evidence for Full UG

Access in L2 acquisition from the interpretive interface: Quantification at a distance in English–French interlanguage', in A. Greenhill, M. Hughes, H. Littlefield and H. Walsh (eds), *Proceedings of the 21st Annual Boston University Conference on Child Development, Volume 1*, Somerville, MA: Cascadilla, pp. 141–52.

Dewey, J. (1938), *Experience and Education*, New York, NY: Kappa Delta Pi.

Dewey, J. (1944), *Democracy and Education*, New York, NY: Free Press.

Dik, S. C. (1978), *Functional Grammar*, Amsterdam: North Holland.

Diller, K. (1971), *The Language Teaching Controversy*, Rowley, MA: Newbury House.

Doughty, C. and J. Williams (1998), *Focus on Form in Classroom Second Language Acquisition*, Cambridge: Cambridge University Press.

Dulay, H. and M. Burt (1973), 'Should we teach children syntax?', *Language Learning*, 23: 245–58.

Dulay, H. and M. Burt (1974), 'Natural sequences in child second language acquisition', *Language Learning*, 24: 37–53.

Dulay, H. and M. Burt (1975), 'Creative construction in second language learning and teaching', in M. Burt and H. Dulay (eds), *On TESOL '75: New Directions in Second Language Learning, Teaching and Bilingual Education*, Washington, DC: TESOL, pp. 21–32.

Eckman, F. (1977), 'Markedness and the Contrastive Analysis Hypothesis', *Language Learning*, 27: 315–30.

Ellis, N. (2003), 'Constructions, chunking and connectionism: The emergence of second language structure', in C. Doughty and M. Long (eds), *Handbook of Second Language Acquisition*, Oxford: Blackwell, pp. 63–103.

Ellis, N. (2007), 'The associative-cognitive CREED', in B. VanPatten and J. Williams (eds), *Theories in Second Language Acquisition: An Introduction*, Mahwah, NJ: Lawrence Erlbaum, pp. 77–95.

Ellis, R. (1994), 'A theory of instructed second language acquisition', in N. Ellis (ed.), *Implicit and Explicit Learning of Languages*, London: Academic, pp. 79–114.

Ellis, R. (1997), 'SLA and language pedagogy: An educational perspective', *Studies in Second Language Acquisition*, 20: 69–92.

Ellis, R. (2003), *Task-based Language Learning and Teaching*, Oxford: Oxford University Press.

Evans, V. and M. Green (2006), *Cognitive Linguistics: An Introduction*, Edinburgh: Edinburgh University Press.

Fawcett, R. P. (2000), *A Theory of Syntax for Systemic Functional Linguistics*, Amsterdam: John Benjamins.

Fillmore, C. (1988), 'The mechanisms of "Construction Grammar"', *Proceedings of the Fourteenth Annual Meeting of the Berkeley Linguistics Society*, 14: 35–55.

Finer, D. (1991), 'Binding parameters in second language acquisition', in L. Eubank (ed.), *Point Counterpoint: Universal Grammar in the Second Language*, Amsterdam: John Benjamins, pp. 351–74.

Finer, D. and E. Broselow (1986), 'Second language acquisition of reflexive-binding', in S. Berman, J.-W. Choe and J. McDonough (eds), *Proceedings of NELS 16*, University of Massachusetts at Amherst: Graduate Linguistics Students Association, pp. 154–68.

Firth, A. and J. Wagner (1997), 'On discourse, communication, and (some) fundamental concepts in SLA research', *Modern Language Journal*, 81: 285–300.

Flege, J. E. (1999), 'Age of learning and second language speech', in D. Birdsong (ed.), *Second Language Acquisition and the Critical Period Hypothesis*, Mahwah, NJ: Lawrence Erlbaum, pp. 101–31.

Flege, J. E. (2009), 'Give input a chance!', in T. Piske and M. Young-Scholten (eds), *Input Matters in SLA*, Bristol: Multilingual Matters, pp. 175–90.

Fodor, J. (1983), *Modularity of Mind: An Essay on Faculty Psychology*, Cambridge, MA: MIT Press.

Fries, C. (1952), *The Structure of English: An Introduction to the Structure of English Sentences*, New York, NY: Harcourt, Brace.

Gass, S. (1982), 'From theory to practice', in M. Hines and W. Rutherford (eds), *On TESOL '81*, Washington, DC: Teachers of English to Speakers of Other Languages, pp. 129–39.

Gass, S. and L. Selinker (2008), *Second Language Acquisition: An Introductory Course*, 3rd edn, London: Routledge.

Gattegno, C. (1972), *Teaching Foreign Languages in Schools: The Silent Way*, 2nd edn, New York, NY: Educational Solutions.

Gattegno, C. (1976), *The Common Sense of Teaching Foreign Languages*, New York, NY: Educational Solutions.

Goldberg, A. (2006), *Constructions at Work: The Nature of Generalization in Language*, Oxford: Oxford University Press.

Goldschneider, J. M. and R. DeKeyser (2001), 'Explaining the "natural order of L2 morpheme acquisition" in English: A meta-analysis of multiple determinants', *Language Learning*, 51: 1–50.

Graddol, D. (1997), *The Future of English?* London: British Council.

Graddol, D. (2006), *English Next. Why Global English May Mean the End of 'English as a Foreign Language'*, London: British Council.

Greenberg, J. (1963), 'Some universals of grammar with particular reference to the order of meaningful elements', in J. Greenberg (ed.), *Universals of Language*, Cambridge, MA: MIT Press, pp. 73–113.

Guasti, M. T. (2002), *The Growth of Grammar*, Cambridge, MA: MIT Press.

Halliday, M. A. K. (1985), *An Introduction to Functional Grammar*, London: Edward Arnold.

Halliday, M. A. K. (2004), *An Introduction to Functional Grammar*, 3rd edn, London: Edward Arnold.

Harley, B. and W. Wang (1997), 'The critical period hypothesis: where are we now?', in A. de Groot and J. Kroll (eds), *Tutorials in Bilingualism, Psycholinguistic Perspectives*, Mahwah, NJ: Lawrence Erlbaum, pp. 19–51.

Haspelmath, M. (2006), 'Against markedness (and what to replace it with)', *Journal of Linguistics*, 42: 25–70.

Hayes, W. (2006), *The Progressive Education Movement: Is it Still a Factor in Today's Schools?*, New York, NY: Rowman & Littlefield.

Haznedar, B. (2001), 'The acquisition of the IP system in child L2 English', *Studies in Second Language Acquisition*, 23: 1–39.

Haznedar, B. and E. Gavruseva (eds) (2008), *Current Trends in Child Second Language Acquisition: A Generative Perspective*, Philadelphia, PA: John Benjamins.

Hensch, T. K. (2004), 'Critical period regulation', *Annual Review of Neuroscience*, 27: 549–79.

Hilles, S. (1986), 'Interlanguage in the pro-drop parameter', *Second Language Research*, 2: 33–52.

Holme, R. (2004), *Literacy: An Introduction*, Edinburgh: Edinburgh University Press.

Howatt, A. P. R. and H. G. Widdowson (2004), *A History of English Language Teaching*, 2nd edn, Oxford: Oxford University Press.

Hutchinson, T. and A. Waters (1987), *ESP: A Learner Centred Approach*, Cambridge: Cambridge University Press.

Hyltenstam, K. (1977), 'Implicational patterns in interlanguage syntax variation', *Language Learning*, 27: 383–411.

Hymes, D. (1972), 'On Communicative Competence', in J. B. Pride and J. Holmes (eds), *Sociolinguistics: Selected Readings*, Harmondsworth: Penguin, pp. 269–93.

Ingram, D. (1989), *First Language Acquisition: Method, Description and Explanation*, Cambridge: Cambridge University Press.

Ingram, J. (2007), *Neurolinguistics: An Introduction to Spoken Language Processing and Disorders*, Cambridge: Cambridge University Press.

Ioup, G., M. Boustagui, M. El Tigi and M. Moselle (1994), 'Re-examining the critical period hypothesis: A case study of successful adult SLA in a naturalistic environment', *Studies in Second Language Acquisition*, 16: 73–98.

Jenkins, J. (2000), *The Phonology of English as an International Language*, Oxford: Oxford University Press.

Jenkins, J. (2007), *English as a Lingua Franca: Attitude and Identity*, Oxford: Oxford University Press.

Johnson, J. and E. Newport (1989), 'Critical period effects in second language learning: The influence of maturational state on the acquisition of English as a second language', *Cognitive Psychology*, 21: 60–99.

Kanno, K. (1997), 'The acquisition of null and overt pronominals in Japanese by English speakers', *Second Language Research*, 13: 265–87.

Kanno, K. (1998), 'The stability of UG principles in second-language acquisition: Evidence from Japanese', *Linguistics*, 36: 1125–46.

Keck, C., G. Iberri-Shea, N. Tracy-Ventura and S. Wa-Mbaleka (2006), 'Investigating the empirical link between task-based interaction and acquisition: A meta-analysis', in J. Norris and L. Ortega (eds), *Synthesising Research on Language Learning and Teaching*, Amsterdam: John Benjamins, pp. 91–132.

Keenan, E. and B. Comrie (1977), 'Noun phrase accessibility and Universal Grammar', *Linguistic Inquiry*, 8: 83–9.

Kementerian Pelajaran Malaysia [Malaysian Ministry of Education] (1975), *English Language Syllabus in Malaysian Schools Tingatan* [Level] 4–5, Kuala Lumpur: Kementerian Pelajaran.

Klein, W. and Perdue, C. (1997), 'The basic variety (or: Couldn't natural languages be much simpler?)', *Second Language Research*, 13: 301–47.

Krachu, B. (1985), 'Standards, codification and sociolinguistic realism: the English language in the outer circle', in R. Quirk and H. G. Widdowson (eds), *English in the World: Teaching and Learning the Language and Literature*, Cambridge: Cambridge University Press.

Kramsch, C. (2003), 'Second language acquisition, applied linguistics and the teaching of foreign languages', *Language Learning Journal*, 28: 66–73.

Krashen, S. (1977), 'Some issues relating to the Monitor Model', in H. Brown, C. Yorio and R. Crymes, *On TESOL '77*, Washington, DC: TESOL.

Krashen, S. (1981), *Second Language Acquisition and Second Language Learning*, Oxford: Pergamon.

Krashen, S. (1982), *Principles and Practice in Second Language Acquisition*, Oxford: Pergamon.

Krashen, S. (1985), *The Input Hypothesis: Issues and Implications*, London: Longman.

Krashen, S. D. (2004), *The Power of Reading: Insights from the Research*, Portsmouth, NH: Heinemann.

Krashen, S. D. and T. D. Terrell (1983), *The Natural Approach: Language Acquisition in the Classroom*, New York, NY: Pergamon.

Kurvers, J., I. van de Craats and M. Young-Scholten (2006), 'Research on low-educated second language and literacy acquisition', in J. Kurvers, I. van de Craats and M. Young-Scholten (eds), *Low Educated Adult Second Language and Literacy Acquisition*, Utrecht: LOT.

Labov, W. (1973), 'The boundaries of words and their meaning', in C.-J. N. Bailey and R. Shuy (eds), *New Ways of Analyzing Variation in English*, Washington, DC: Georgetown University Press, pp. 340–73.

Lado, R. (1957), *Linguistics Across Cultures*, Ann Arbor, MI: University of Michigan Press.

Lakoff, G. (1987), *Women, Fire and Dangerous Things: What Categories Reveal about the Mind*, Chicago: University of Chicago Press.

Langacker, R. (1987), *Foundations of Cognitive Grammar, Volume I, Theoretical Prerequisites*, Stanford, CA: Stanford University Press.

Lantolf, J. (ed.) (2000), *Sociocultural Theory and Second Language Learning*, Oxford: Oxford University Press.

Lantolf, J. and S. L. Thorne (2006), *Sociocultural Theory and the Genesis of Second Language Development*, Oxford: Oxford University Press.

Lardiere, D. (1998), 'Dissociating syntax from morphology in a divergent L2 end-state grammar', *Second Language Research*, 14: 359–75.

Larsen-Freeman, D. and L. Cameron (2008), *Complex Systems and Applied Linguistics*, Oxford: Oxford University Press.

Laufer, B. and S. Eliasson (1993), 'What causes avoidance in L2 learning: L1–L2 difference, L1–L2 similarity, or L2 complexity?', *Studies in Second Language Acquisition*, 15: 33–48.

Lave, J. and E. Wenger (1991), *Situated Learning: Legitimate Peripheral Participation*, Cambridge: Cambridge University Press.

Lenneberg, E. (1967), *Biological Foundations of Language*, New York, NY: Wiley.

Lewis, M. (1993), *The Lexical Approach*, London: Language Teaching.

Lewis, M. (2000), 'Language in the lexical approach', in M. Lewis (ed.), *Teaching Collocation: Further Developments in the Lexical Approach*, Hove: Language Teaching, pp. 126–54.

Lightbown, P. (1985), 'Great expectations: Second language acquisition research and classroom teaching', *Applied Linguistics*, 6: 173–89.

Lightbown, P. (2000), 'Anniversary Article: Classroom SLA Research and Second Language Teaching', *Applied Linguistics*, 21: 431–62.

Lightbown, P. (2003), 'SLA research in the classroom/SLA research for the classroom', *Language Learning Journal*, 28: 4–13.

Lightbown, P. and N. Spada (2006), *How Languages are Learned*, 3rd edn, Oxford: Oxford University Press.

Little, D., J. Ridley and E. Ushioda (eds) (2003), *Learner Autonomy in the Foreign Language Classroom: Teacher, Learner, Curriculum and Assessment*, Dublin: Authentik.

Long, M. (1981), 'Input, interaction, and second-language acquisition', in H. Winitz (ed.), *Native Language and Foreign Language Acquisition*, Annals of the New York Academy of Science, Vol. 379, pp. 259–78.

Long, M. (1983), 'Native speaker/non-native speaker conversation and the negotiation of comprehensible input', *Applied Linguistics*, 4: 126–41.

Long, M. (1991), 'Focus on form: a design feature in language teaching methodology', in K. de Bot, R. B. Ginsberg and C. Kramsch (eds), *Foreign Language Research in Cross-Cultural Perspective*, Amsterdam: John Benjamins.

Long, M. (1996), 'The role of the linguistic environment in second language acquisition', in W. Ritchie and T. Bhatia (eds), *Handbook of Second Language Acquisition*, San Diego, CA: Academic Press, pp. 413–68.

Long, M. and G. Crookes (1992), 'Three approaches to task-based syllabus design', *TESOL Quarterly*, 26: 27–55.

Long, M. and C. Sato (1984), 'Methodological issues in interlanguage studies: an interactionist perspective', in A. Davies, C. Criber and A. Howatt (eds), *Interlanguage*, Edinburgh: Edinburgh University Press, pp. 253–79.

Lozanov, G. (1978), *Suggestology and Outlines of Suggestopedy*, New York, NY: Gordon & Breach.

Lust, B. and C. Foley (eds) (2004), *First Language Acquisition: The Essential Readings*, Oxford: Blackwell.

MacLaughlin, D. (1998), 'The acquisition of the morphosyntax of English reflexives by non-native speakers', in M. L. Beck (ed.), *Morphology and its Interfaces in Second Language Knowledge*, Amsterdam: John Benjamins, pp. 195–226.

MacWhinney, B. (ed.) (1999), *The Emergence of Language*, Mahwah, NJ: Lawrence Erlbaum.

Marsden, H. (2005), 'L2 poverty of the stimulus at the syntax–semantics interface: Quantifier scope in non-native Japanese', in Y. Otsu (ed.), *Proceedings of the Sixth Tokyo Conference on Psycholinguistics*, Tokyo: Hituzi Syobo, pp. 217–41.

Marsden, H. (2008), 'Pair-list readings in Korean–Japanese, Chinese–Japanese, and English–Japanese interlanguage', *Second Language Research*, 24: 189–226.

Marsden, H. (2009), 'Distributive quantifier scope in English–Japanese and Korean–Japanese interlanguage', *Language Acquisition*, 16: 135–77.

Meisel, J. M. (2004), 'The bilingual child', in T. K. Bhatia and W. C. Ritchie (eds), *The Handbook of Bilingualism*, Oxford: Blackwell, pp. 91–113.

Meisel, J. M., H. Clahsen and M. Pienemann (1981), 'On determining developmental stages in natural second language acquisition', *Studies in Second Language Acquisition*, 3: 109–35.

Mueller, J. (2005), 'Electrophysiological correlates of second language processing', *Second Language Research*, 21: 152–74.

Musumeci, D. (1997), *Breaking Tradition: An Exploration of the Historical Relationship between Theory and Practice in Second Language Teaching*, Boston: McGraw Hill.

Myles, F., J. Hooper and R. Mitchell (1998), 'Rote or rule? Exploring the roles of formulaic language in classroom foreign language learning', *Language Learning*, 48: 323–63.

Nation, I. S. P. (2001), *Learning Vocabulary in Another Language*, Cambridge: Cambridge University Press.

Nattinger, J. R. and J. S. DeCarrico (1992), *Lexical Phrases and Language Teaching*, Oxford: Oxford University Press.

Newmeyer, F. (1998), *Language Form and Language Function*, Cambridge, MA: MIT Press.

Norton, B. (2000), *Identity and Language Learning: Gender, Ethnicity, and Educational Change*, Harlow: Longman/Pearson.

Norton, B. and K. Toohey (eds) (2004), *Critical Pedagogies and Language Learning*, Cambridge: Cambridge University Press.

Nunan, D. (2004), *Task-Based Language Teaching*, Cambridge: Cambridge University Press.

O'Grady, W. (1999), 'Toward a new nativism', *Studies in Second Language Acquisition*, 21: 621–33.

O'Grady, W. (2003), 'The radical middle: Nativism without universal grammar', in C. J. Doughty and M. H. Long (eds), *The Handbook of Second Language Acquisition*, Oxford: Blackwell, pp. 43–62.

Paltridge, B. (2001), *Genre and the Language Learning Classroom*, Ann Arbor, MI: University of Michigan Press.

Paradis, M. (2004), *A Neurolinguistic Theory of Bilingualism*, Amsterdam: John Benjamins.

Philp, J., R. Oliver and A. Mackey (2008), *Second Language Acquisition and the Younger Learner*, Amsterdam: John Benjamins.

Pienemann, M. (1998), *Language Processing and Second Language Development: Processability Theory*, Amsterdam: John Benjamins.

Pienemann, M. (ed.) (2005), *Cross-linguistics Aspects of Processability Theory*, Amsterdam: John Benjamins.

Pinker, S. (1994), *The Language Instinct: How the Mind Creates Language*, New York, NY: Harper Collins.

Piske, T. and M. Young-Scholten (2009), *Input Matters in SLA*, Bristol: Multilingual Matters.

Prabhu, N. S. (1987), *Second Language Pedagogy*, Oxford: Oxford University Press.

Radford, A. (1997) *Syntax: A Minimalist Introduction*, Cambridge: Cambridge University Press.

Richards, J. and T. Rodgers (2001), *Approaches and Methods in Language Teaching*, Cambridge: Cambridge University Press.

Robinson, P. (1995), 'Attention, memory and the "noticing" hypothesis', *Language Learning*, 45: 283–31.

Robinson, P. and N. Ellis (2008), *Handbook of Cognitive Linguistics and Second Language Acquisition*, Mahwah, NJ: Lawrence Erlbaum.

Rosch, E. (1973), 'Natural categories', *Cognitive Psychology*, 4: 328–50.

Rosch, E. (1975), 'Cognitive Reference Points', *Cognitive Psychology*, 7: 532–47.

Rothman, J. and M. Iverson (2007), 'On L2 Clustering and Resetting the Null Subject Parameter in L2 Spanish: Implications and Observations', *Hispania*, 90: 329–42.

Russell, J. and N. Spada (2006), 'The effectiveness of corrective feedback for the acquisition of L2 grammar: A meta-analysis of the research', in J. Norris and L. Ortega (eds), *Synthesising Research on Language Learning and Teaching*, Amsterdam: John Benjamins, pp. 133–64.

Rutherford W. (1968), *Modern English: A Textbook for Foreign Students*, New York, NY: Harcourt, Brace & World.

Rutherford, W. (1987), *Second Language Grammar: Learning and Teaching*, London: Longman.

Schachter, J. (1974), 'An error in error analysis', *Language Learning*, 24: 205–14.

Schmidt, R. W. (1990), 'The role of consciousness in second language learning', *Applied Linguistics*, 11: 129–58.

Schmidt, R. W. (1993), 'Awareness and second language acquisition', *Annual Review of Applied Linguistics*, 13: 206–26.

Schumann, J. (1979), 'The acquisition of English negation by speakers of Spanish: a review of the literature', in R. Anderson (ed.), *The Acquisition and Use of Spanish and English as First and Second Languages*, Washington, DC: TESOL, pp. 3–32.

Schwartz, B. D. (1993), 'On explicit and negative data effecting and affecting competence and linguistic behavior', *Studies in Second Language Acquisition*, 15: 147–63.

Schwartz, B. D. and M. Gubala-Ryzak (1992), 'Learnability and grammar reorganization in L2A: Against negative evidence causing unlearning of verb movement', *Second Language Research*, 8: 1–38.

Schwartz, B. D. and R. A. Sprouse (1994), 'Word order and nominative case in non-native language acquisition: a longitudinal study of (L1 Turkish) German interlanguage', in T. Hoekstra and B. D. Schwartz (eds), *Language Acquisition Studies in Generative Grammar*, Amsterdam: John Benjamins, pp. 317–68.

Schwartz, B. D. and R. A. Sprouse (1996), 'L2 cognitive states and the full transfer/full access model', *Second Language Research*, 12: 40–72.

Scovel, T. (1979), 'Review of Suggestology and Outlines of Suggestopedy', *TESOL Quarterly*, 13: 255–66.

Searle, J. R. (1969), *Speech Acts. An Essay in the Philosophy of Language*, Cambridge: Cambridge University Press.

Sebeok, T. A. (1966), *Portraits of Linguists: A Biographical Source Book for the History of Western Linguistics 1746–1964*, Bloomington, IN: Indiana University Press.

Selinker, L. (1972), 'Interlanguage', *International Review of Applied Linguistics*, 10: 209–30.

Sfard, A. (1998), 'On two metaphors for learning and the dangers of choosing just one', *Educational Researcher*, 27: 4–13.

Sharwood Smith, M. (1993), 'Input enhancement in instructed SLA: Theoretical bases', *Studies in Second Language Acquisition*, 15: 165–79.

Sharwood Smith, M. (1994), *Second Language Learning: Theoretical Foundations*, London: Longman.

Sharwood Smith, M. (2004), 'In two minds about grammar: On the interaction of linguistic and metalinguistic knowledge in performance', *Transactions of the Philological Society*, 102(2): 255–80.

Singleton, D. and L. Ryan (2004), *Language Acquisition: The Age Factor*, 2nd edn, Clevedon: Multilingual Matters.

Slabakova, R. (2008), *Meaning in the Second Language,* Berlin: Mouton de Gruyter.

Snow, C. and M. Hoefnagel-Höhle (1978), 'The critical period for language acquisition: evidence from second language learning', *Child Development*, 49: 1114–28.

Snyder, W. (2007), *Child Language: The Parametric Approach*, New York, NY: Oxford University Press.

Steinberg, D. and N. Sciarini (2006), *An Introduction to Psycholinguistics*, 2nd edn, Harlow: Pearson/Longman.

Stevick, E. (1990), *Humanism in Language Teaching*, New York, NY: Oxford University Press.

Swain, M. (1985), 'Communicative competence: Some roles of comprehensible input and comprehensible output in its development', in S. Gass and C. Madden (eds), *Input and Second Language Acquisition*, Rowley, MA: Newbury House, pp. 235–52.

Swain, M. (2005), 'The output hypothesis: Theory and research', in E. Hinkel (ed.), *Handbook on Research in Second Language Teaching and Learning*, Mahwah, NJ: Lawrence Erlbaum, pp. 471–84.

Swain, M. (2006), 'Languaging, agency and collaboration in advanced second language proficiency', in H. Byrnes (ed.), *Advanced Language Learning: the Contribution of Halliday and Vygotsky*, London: Continuum, pp. 95–108.

Swales, J. (1990), *Genre Analysis: English in Academic and Research Settings*, Cambridge: Cambridge University Press.

Swales, J. and C. Feak (1994), *Academic Writing for Graduate Students*: A *Course for Nonnative Speakers of English*, Ann Arbor, MI: University of Michigan Press.

Tarone, E., S. Dwyer, S. Gillette and V. Icke (1981), 'On the use of the passive in two astrophysics journal papers', *ESP Journal*, 1: 123–40.

Tarone, E. and K. Hansen (to appear), 'Alphabetic literacy and second language acquisition by older learners', in J. Herschensohn and M. Young-Scholten (eds), *The Handbook of Second Language Acquisition*, Cambridge: Cambridge University Press.

Taylor, J. R. (1995), *Linguistic Categorization: Prototypes in Linguistic Theory*, 2nd edn, Oxford: Clarendon.

Thomas O. (1965), *Transformational Grammar and the Teacher of English*, New York, NY: Holt, Reinhart, & Winston.

Tomasello, M. (2003), *Constructing a Language*, Boston, MA: Harvard University Press.

Traxler, M. J. and M. A. Gernsbacher (eds) (2006), *Handbook of Psycholinguistics*, 2nd edn, Amsterdam: Academic.

Truscott, J. (1998), 'Noticing in second language acquisition: a critical review', *Second Language Research*, 14: 103–35.

Truscott, J. and M. Sharwood Smith (2004a), 'Acquisition by processing: A modular perspective on language development', *Bilingualism: Language and Cognition*, 7: 1–20.

Truscott, J. and M. Sharwood Smith (2004b), 'How APT is your theory: present status and future prospects', *Bilingualism: Language and Cognition*, 7: 43–7.

Vainikka, A. (1993/94), 'Case in the development of English syntax', *Language Acquisition*, 3: 257–325.

Van den Branden, K. (ed.) (2006), *Task-Based Language Education: From Theory to Practice*, Cambridge: Cambridge University Press.

VanPatten, B. (1996), *Input Processing and Grammar Instruction: Theory and Research*, Norwood, NJ: Ablex.

VanPatten, B. (2004), 'Input processing in SLA', in B. VanPatten (ed.), *Processing Instruction: Theory, Research and Commentary*, Mahwah, NJ: Lawrence Erlbaum, pp. 1–31.

VanPatten, B. (2009), 'Processing matters in input enhancement', in T. Piske and M. Young-Scholten (eds), *Input Matters in SLA*, Bristol: Multilingual Matters, pp. 47–61.

VanPatten, B. and J. Williams (2007), *Theories in Second Language Acquisition*, Mahwah, NJ: Lawrence Erlbaum.

Van Valin, R. D. and W. A. Foley (1980), 'Role and reference grammar', in E. Moravcsik and J. R. Wirth (eds), *Current Approaches to Syntax*, New York, NY: Academic, pp. 329–52.

Vygotsky, L. S. (1979), 'Consciousness as a problem in the psychology of behaviour', *Soviet Psychology*, 17: 3–35.

Vygotsky, L. S. (1986), *Thought and Language*, translated by A. Kozulin, Cambridge, MA: MIT Press.

Webster, J. (ed.) (2007), *Collected Works of M. A. K. Halliday*, London: Continuum.

Weinert, R. (1995), 'The role of formulaic language in second language acquisition: A review', *Applied Linguistics*, 16(2): 180–205.

Wenger, E. (1998), *Communities of Practice: Learning, Meaning and Identity*, Cambridge: Cambridge University Press.

White, L. (1989), 'The principle of subjacency in second language acquisition: do L2 learners observe the subset principle?', in S. Gass and J. Schachter (eds), *Linguistic Perspectives on Second Language Acquisition*, Cambridge: Cambridge University Press.

White, L. (1992), 'Long and short verb movement in second language acquisition', *Canadian Journal of Linguistics*, 37: 273–86.

White, L. (2003a), 'Fossilization in steady state L2 grammars: Persistent problems with inflectional morphology', *Bilingualism: Language and Cognition*, 6: 129–41.

White, L. (2003b), *Second Language Acquisition and Universal Grammar*, Cambridge: Cambridge University Press.

White, L. and F. Genesee (1996), 'How native is near-native? The issue of ultimate attainment in adult second language acquisition', *Second Language Research*, 11: 233–65.

Wilkins, D. A. (1976), *Notional Syllabuses*, Oxford: Oxford University Press.

Willis, J. and D. Willis (eds) (1996), *Challenge and Change in Language Teaching*, Oxford: Heinemann.

Willis, D. and J. Willis (2007), *Doing Task-Based Teaching*, Oxford: Oxford University Press.

Winitz, H. (ed.) (1981), *The Comprehension Approach to Foreign Language Instruction*, Rowley, MA: Newbury House.

Wode, H. (1977), 'On the systematicity of L1 transfer in L2 acquisition', *Proceedings from 1977 Second Language Research Forum (SLRF)*, Los Angeles, CA: University of California Press, pp. 160–9.

Wode, H. (1978), 'Developmental sequences in naturalistic L2 acquisition', in E. Hatch (ed.), *Readings in Second Language Acquisition*, Rowley, MA: Newbury House.

Wood, D., J. Bruner and G. Ross (1976), The role of tutoring in problem solving, *Journal of Child Psychology and Psychiatry*, 17: 89–100.

Wray, A. (2002), *Formulaic Language and the Lexicon*, Cambridge: Cambridge University Press.

Yoken, M. (ed.) (2007), *Breakthrough: Essays and Vignettes in Honour of John A. Rassias*, New York, NY: Peter Lang.

Yuan, B. (2001), 'The status of thematic verbs in the second language acquisition of Chinese', *Second Language Research*, 17: 248–72.

Zobl, H. (1980), 'The formal and developmental selectivity of L1 influence on L2 acquisition', *Language Learning*, 30: 43–57.

Zuengler, J. and E. Miller (2006), 'Cognitive and sociocultural perspectives: Two parallel SLA worlds?', *TESOL Quarterly*, 40: 35–58.

INDEX

❧